*Bicycling Chickamauga Battlefield:
The Cyclist's Civil War Travel Guide*

BICYCLING CHICKAMAUGA BATTLEFIELD

The Cyclist's Civil War Travel Guide

Sue Thibodeau

*The <u>one and only</u> book
that you need to bicycle Chickamauga!*

Bicycling Chickamauga Battlefield:
The Cyclist's Civil War Travel Guide

Copyright © 2021 Sue Thibodeau

All Rights Reserved. No part of this publication may be reproduced, stored in an archival or retrieval system, distributed, or transmitted, in any form or by any means, including electronic or mechanical means, except in the case of brief quotations embodied in critical reviews and certain other non-commercial uses permitted by copyright law, without the prior written permission of the author.

Map Rendering Copyright © 2021 Sue Thibodeau
Map Data Copyright © OpenStreetMap contributors
www.openstreetmap.org/copyright
Liberation Sans Font Family, SIL Open Font License (OFL) 1.1

Published by Civil War Cycling
Digital (PDF) companion maps are sold separately by
www.civilwarcycling.com and www.suethibodeau.com
(E-mail) inquiries@civilwarcycling.com
154 Cobblestone Court Drive #110
Victor, New York 14564

No Warranty. This book is distributed in the hope that it will be useful, but without any warranty; without even the implied warranty of merchantability or fitness for a particular purpose.

Consult your doctor before any form of exercise, including bicycling. The bicycling directions provided in this book and all companion maps are for planning purposes only. Actual conditions (road, traffic, weather, or other events) may require you to adjust your route or actions, especially as required to obey all laws, signs, alerts, and notices. If there are mistakes in this book, or if the park road network or policies have changed since this writing, it remains your responsibility always to act in ways that are safe, healthy, and legal. The author and publisher disclaim any and all liability. Please visit http://www.nps.gov/chch for official and up-to-date information about park roads, amenities, and policies.

ISBN 978-1-7326038-2-0 (pbk)

20211211-L6-1.5
Second Printing

About the Author

Chickamauga Battlefield (Fort Oglethorpe, GA)
79th Pennsylvania Infantry Monument

Sue Thibodeau is a bicycling enthusiast, computer scientist, and former teacher. She creates guidebooks and maps for learning American Civil War history outdoors, on a bike. Her prior books include *Bicycling Gettysburg National Military Park* (2019); *Maps to Bike Gettysburg* mini-book series (2021); and *Bicycling Antietam National Battlefield* (2020). Sue also publishes digital touring maps through Civil War Cycling, www.civilwarcycling.com.

Battlefield touring on a bicycle?

Every U.S. Civil War battlefield that you visit will evoke different feelings. Gettysburg summons stories about Abraham Lincoln and Robert E. Lee. Antietam stirs thoughts about the common soldier fighting in a cornfield near a remote country church. And then there's Chickamauga. This heavily wooded, blue-green battlefield nestled along Chickamauga Creek, Georgia, is hauntingly beautiful and geographically disorienting. The site calls up images of a defeated Federal army desperately fighting to hold a hill.

Chickamauga's red asphalt roads wind through mature trees and grassy fields that intersect to form looped pathways. A bicyclist can appreciate how confusing it must have been for two armies to coordinate their actions with a sky full of foliage blocking their view. This guidebook will take you beyond the official National Park Service auto tour for a mostly chronological retelling of the story of the Battle of Chickamauga (September 18–20, 1863). Unlike the NPS tour, we cover more than the last day of battle. However, because the battle was so chaotic, it is not possible to ride along a strictly linear timeline.

Bicycling Chickamauga Battlefield will help you to gain a high-level understanding of the battle—one that is informed by geography and local farming families. The book's 18 color maps direct your navigation through the park, and bicycle cues suggest places to stop on your 12.6-mile ride. For a smooth riding experience, this book does not identify all of Chickamauga's 600+ monuments, but instead, preselects a sampling and categorizes them by theme. There are 77 color photos that will help you to find monuments and farms.

You will learn the most if you read this book before your tour. Then on your ride, follow the book's navigational cues to find and visit historic sites, or ride wherever your curiosity directs you.

Please visit civilwarcycling.com to purchase (optional) digital companion maps for bicycling the Chickamauga battlefield in Fort Oglethorpe, GA (part of Chickamauga and Chattanooga National Military Park).

Dedication

I dedicate this book to my two adult children, Barbara Emily and Matthew August, and their father, my husband of thirty-five years, Timothy Matthew Thibodeau. I am grateful for their love and support over the years as I schemed to find every excuse possible to travel south from New York to bike a battlefield park in Pennsylvania, Maryland, Tennessee, Georgia, and (hopefully soon) Mississippi. Although my children currently have only a passing interest in American history, they remind me that storytelling matters—including Tim's and my stories about exhilarating rides over meaningful, historic landscapes.

CONTENTS

Take a Ride Back in Time	11
PART I: INTRODUCTION	**29**
1. Chickamauga on a Bicycle	31
2. The Battle of Chickamauga	71
PART II: PLANNING YOUR TRIP	**85**
3. Gathering Your Gear	87
4. Transportation and Lodging	93
PART III: ENJOY YOUR RIDE!	**97**
5. How to Read Bicycle Cues	99
6. Route 1 Loop (12.6 Miles)	101
7. Route 2 Loop (12.9 Miles)	117
8. Route 3 Loop (8.8 Miles)	121
PART IV: MONUMENTS AND STRUCTURES	**125**
9. State Monuments	127
10. The States at Chickamauga	139
11. Memorial Shell Monuments	179
PART V: RESOURCES	**191**
Glossary	193
Bibliography	198
Notes	201
Index	224

MAPS

Map 1. Chickamauga and Chattanooga Battlefield Area 23
Map 2. Chickamauga Battlefield Park 26
Map 3. Battle Highlights, September 19–20, 1863 27
Map 4. Symbols, Terms and Abbreviations 28
Map 5. Chickamauga Roads and Main Horse/Hiking Trails 35
Map 6. Key Landmarks at Chickamauga Battlefield 49
Map 7. Chickamauga Family Farms 53
Map 8. September 18—Crossing Chickamauga Creek 76
Map 9. September 19—The Fight East of LaFayette Road 77
Map 10. September 20—Longstreet's Breakthrough 78
Map 11. September 20—Stand-Off at Snodgrass Hill 79
Map 12. Route 1 "Half Day Loop" (12.6 Miles) 101
Map 13. Segment A Map (to Alexander's Bridge) 104
Map 14. Segment B Map (to Snodgrass Hill) 109
Map 15. Segment C Map (return to Visitor Center) 114
Map 16. Route 2 "Fields of Chickamauga Loop" (12.9 Miles) 117
Map 17. Route 3 "Eastern Woods Loop" (8.8 Miles) 121
Map 18. State Monuments at Chickamauga 131
Map 19. Memorial Shell Monuments at Chickamauga 180

TABLES

Table 1. Chickamauga Bicycle Routes 46
Table 2. State Affiliations for Each Army 67
Table 3. USA Abbreviated Order of Battle 68
Table 4. CSA Abbreviated Order of Battle 69
Table 5. Chickamauga Casualties 80
Table 6. Bicycle Cue Key 99
Table 7. Segment A Cue Sheet (to Alexander's Bridge) 105
Table 8. Segment B Cue Sheet (to Snodgrass Hill) 110
Table 9. Segment C Cue Sheet (return to Visitor Center) 115
Table 10. USA Military Units at the Battle of Chickamauga 140
Table 11. CSA Military Units at the Battle of Chickamauga 141

x

Take a Ride Back in Time

Riding Southwest on Battleline Road (6th Indiana Infantry Monument)

Bicycling Chickamauga Battlefield

In September 1863, the Battle of Chickamauga was a Confederate victory that forced the Army of the Cumberland, under William S. Rosecrans, to retreat to Chattanooga and submit to a siege. But that was not the end of it. When Ulysses S. Grant assumed command of all armies in the western theater, he replaced Rosecrans with George H. Thomas, who broke the siege. Then in 1864, Grant's subordinate, William T. Sherman, targeted the Deep South as part of his Atlanta Campaign. The U.S. Civil War battles in Tennessee and Georgia thus heavily influenced the war's outcome. Once the Union army permanently held Chattanooga and its railroads, river ports, and roads, the Confederacy was vulnerable to collapse and extinction, which came only one year later.

Dedicated in 1895, Chickamauga and Chattanooga National Military Park was the first national military park in the United States. The National Park Service currently preserves and protects its more than 9,000 acres of historic land spread over six different sites in northern Georgia and south-central Tennessee. All together, these sites belong to Chickamauga and Chattanooga National Military Park. In the fall of 1863, more than 100,000 Civil War soldiers fought several battles across this mountainous swath of land that was critical to the defense of the southern confederacy.

The Chickamauga battlefield was the site of the September 18–20, 1863, brutal clash of two armies on the west side of Chickamauga Creek, near modern-day Fort Oglethorpe, Georgia. Here, Confederate Gen. Braxton Bragg's 65,000 soldiers of the Army of Tennessee defeated Union Maj. Gen. William Starke Rosecrans' 60,000 soldiers of the Army of the Cumberland. In total, about 34,624 men were killed, wounded, missing, or captured. Although this battle was the largest Confederate victory in the west, Bragg did not pursue the retreating Rosecrans to the river city of Chattanooga. This "gateway to the Confederacy" became forever closed to Confederate control.[1]

For bicyclists, the Chickamauga battlefield offers a unique opportunity to study the Battle of Chickamauga, while riding on flat roads and through more than 5,500 acres of densely wooded forest. You will stop to study battlefield monuments placed by Civil War veterans and consider the stories that they wanted to preserve.[2] Notably, two of them—Henry Van Ness Boynton and Ferdinand Van Derveer—led the federal effort that began in 1890 to establish Chickamauga and Chattanooga National Military Park. Their vision was to commemorate the battlefield actions of both armies through the erection of mostly regimental interpretative and commemorative structures. In the 1890s, veterans marked battle positions with about 457 cast iron tablets and 191 cannons. In all, they erected more than 680 markers, cannons, and monuments, according to the *Chickamauga Battlefield Cultural Landscape Report* (2004).[3]

Writing twenty-six years after the Battle of Chickamauga, Boynton described the significance of the commemorative project in words that resonated with thousands of veterans who wanted their stories told:

> ... the thunders of the deadliest battle of modern times were rolling over the low lands and re-echoing from the mountains which look down upon Chickamauga. Many great battles shook our continent and attracted the attention of the world as our war went on; but the splendid facts of the bitter, stubborn, and desperate contest along the unknown stream, in the thick forests which lined it, and on the ridges which dominated them, were, for years, almost completely hidden from the public as were the armies which operated over this obscure and tangled field.[4]

Take a Ride Back in Time

However, the Chickamauga battlefield is more than a nineteenth century military scene; the landscape points to the devastating impact on Georgia farming families whose lives were totally upended by the battle's carnage and destruction. For example, Eliza Glenn's house burned to the ground, but not before Rosecrans claimed it as his army headquarters. (Today, only a simple cast iron sign marks the Glenn site). Forced out of her home, Mrs. Glenn sought refuge in the one-room cabin of her close neighbor, Hiram Vittetoe, a "staunch Rebel sympathizer" of French descent. For two days, the Vittetoe family huddled in a dark hole covered by boards within their cabin; that is, until Mr. Vittetoe announced excitedly that "the Rebels have the field!" and his wife and three daughters ran out to greet Tennessee soldiers in Brig. Gen. Bushrod R. Johnson's division.[5]

The Vittetoe family endured the sights and sounds of the fighting at Snodgrass Hill on September 20 without having to vacate their home. However, the battle forced other Chickamauga families quickly to abandon their properties. Historian Peter Cozzens described one evacuation this way:

> George Snodgrass was a stubborn old man, but he was no fool. He had refused to leave when the first Yankee foragers showed up at his doorstep on 18 September, but when bullets began to drop around his house and through the ceiling the next afternoon, Snodgrass packed up his family and retreated to a ravine deep in the woods northwest of the farm.[6]

George and Elizabeth Snodgrass' log cabin was bloodstained and uninhabitable after its repurposing as a Union field hospital. (The cabin was rebuilt sometime after 1890, and the current structure likely contains some of the original wood). According to the Walker County, Georgia historian, writing in 1932 but quoting a September 1923 article in the *Chattanooga Times*, "the Snodgrass family did not return to their home till the close of the war. They suffered the destitution common to the people of the south."[7]

While riding north on Glenn-Kelly Road, you will climb up the 100-foot rise to Snodgrass Hill and visit the Snodgrass cabin and a large eastern red cedar tree that casts welcome shade. The log cabin stands on the hotly contested ridge on which Maj. Gen. George H. Thomas earned the nickname, "the Rock of Chickamauga," for his service in the final hours of the battle that saved the Army of the Cumberland from annihilation.[8] A Virginia native, Thomas' family had disowned him for remaining in the Union army when his immediate superiors, Robert E. Lee and Albert Sidney Johnston, had both resigned their commissions at the start of the war. During the U.S. Civil War, family conflicts and differences of allegiance extended to the highest ranks of political society. This is perhaps no more evident than by the death of Kentucky native and Confederate officer, Brig. Gen. Benjamin H. Helm (1831–1863). The thirty-two-year-old officer and former lawyer died at Chickamauga on the Kelly Farm. Helm's half-brother-in-law, President Abraham Lincoln, mourned his death.[9]

While riding south on Alexander's Bridge Road, you will see white-on-brown NPS signs that point the way to Helm's memorial monument. More broadly, with so many physical and natural landscape cues, a bicyclist can literally "take a ride back in time" and appreciate that this battle was as much about citizens as soldiers. The narrative unfolds as two raging armies clash in the woods and fields of Chickamauga's farming families. We cannot tell the full story without reference to the farms and the people who lived there. The high-stakes conflict swept up soldiers and citizens in a tempest that would decide both the future of a nation and that of this rural community.

As was common for this era, Chickamauga families—Brock, Brotherton, Dyer, Ingraham, Kelly, McDonald, Poe, and Snodgrass—put forward fathers and sons to fight for the Confederacy, especially as soldiers in the Army of Tennessee. During the battle, these and other families escaped to a wooded ravine northwest of Snodgrass Hill. For eight days, they were "utterly without shelter, and practically without food" when "dust hung over the valley like a pall, and many of the springs and wells were dry."[10] While George and Mary Brotherton camped in the ravine, their two oldest sons—Thomas and James—fought for the Confederate army. As noted by James Sartain in his *History of Walker County, Georgia*, the brothers were "much of the time in sight" of their family farm, especially the Brotherton cabin on LaFayette Road. Other Chickamauga men also fought here as Confederate soldiers, namely: John Brock's sons, William and John; Robert and Carrie Dyer's sons, Spill and John; and John and Pricilla McDonald's son, William; George Snodgrass' son, Charles; Elisha Kelly's son; and the young father, Larkin Poe.[11] Friends buried a local man, Pvt. John Ingraham, near where he died along Alexander's Bridge Road. His 1959 gravestone bears this inscription: "In Memory of John Ingraham / Private Co. K / 1st Confederate Regt. / GA Vols / Killed / Sept. 19, 1863."

Take a Ride Back in Time

As a bicyclist rides through the Chickamauga battlefield, it is easy to appreciate its natural amenities. Grassy meadows, prickly grass, and dark woody vegetation that obscures the horizon, all offer unparalleled beauty. You will see pine, oak, cedar, and hickory trees. Sometimes, toads, garter snakes, and eastern box turtles will cross your path. Among the park's fifty documented mammal species, you may see white-tailed deer and gray squirrels. And of its 175 species of birds, the northern cardinal, Carolina wren, red-eyed vireo, and tufted titmouse are among the most common.[12] In the spring, blue butterflies flitter about, and in the fall, monarch butterflies may swarm quickly across your path as they migrate south through the Tennessee Valley and on to Mexico. If you ride to Alexander's Bridge or hike to one of the difficult to access fords along Chickamauga Creek, you will hear softly trickling water and buzzing insects.

Although your ride will undoubtedly offer you a rich outdoor experience, it also presents a challenge: Your focus will oscillate between an experience of the natural landscape and the 1863 story of soldiers and civilians. On your ride, you will notice a somber silence that replaces what would have been a terrible cacophony in September 1863. While riding along the east side of Dyer Field (where it can be hot even in early spring), you can turn your thoughts from the day's pounding heat to the 1863 battlefield story. This is where Confederate infantry regrouped to launch repeated attacks on Snodgrass Hill. And pedaling more, you can relish gliding into the shady woodlot at the Poe House Site, where Union artillery batteries posted their guns on LaFayette Road.

The physical experience of bicycling naturally prompts us to ask historical questions about the weather, geography, biology, and more. For example, you may wonder like I did whether it was hot when soldiers fought on the Dyer, Snodgrass, and Poe properties. According to historian Kenneth W. Noe, U.S. Weather Bureau records indicate that "hot and dry" weather turned suddenly cool on September 19. Historian William Glenn Robertson notes that the temperature "dropped precipitously into the 30s during the night." In his official battle report, Col. George H. Nixon, 48th Tennessee Infantry, CSA, reported that the evening was cold.[13]

Why I Wrote This Book

Each time I design a bicycle tour of a U.S. Civil War battlefield, I learn something new about planning that prompts me to write yet another guidebook. That might seem like a strange statement, since one would expect the basic process to be the same—study park maps, learn about the battle, and research your lodging options. Of course, building a high-level understanding of the battle *before* your ride will help you to learn *during* the ride. But unlike Gettysburg and Antietam, it is much more challenging for the first-time Chickamauga visitor to find and read "that one" short, concise, visual, and easily understandable summary of the September 18–20, 1863, battle. This book attempts to bridge that gap for bicyclists who want to know a little something before they start pedaling. It is for bicyclists who want to arrive on the battlefield pre-oriented to Chickamauga's natural and physical landmarks.

If your goal is to tour a battlefield in a way that is not only efficient but also safe and educational, it can take a few trips to "get it right;" that is, unless you have a guidebook. I wrote *Bicycling Chickamauga Battlefield* to help "bicycling historians" get it right the first time. This is particularly important for bicyclists who must travel great distances and at great expense to tour a battlefield park.

Planning a bicycle tour of the Chickamauga battlefield is more complicated than for Antietam National Battlefield, for example. Whereas the official NPS Antietam auto tour follows the high-level chronology of the one-day battle, the Battle of Chickamauga defies a simple chronological narrative that maps easily to a battlefield route. This is because the battle involved innumerable uncoordinated and unanticipated military actions, and only with careful route planning can a bicyclist avoid the annoyance of constant backtracking. For Chickamauga, if your goal is to learn the battle story while riding, you will want a route that is not as confusing as the story itself. (To that point, it is interesting to note that the official NPS Chickamauga auto tour covers only the final day of the nearly three-day battle, largely side stepping our route planning challenge).

Further, the NPS Chickamauga auto tour covers only the west half of the battlefield park, and therefore omits other accessible and historically important sites, including Jay's Mill, Winfrey Field, and West Chickamauga Creek at Alexander's Bridge. And yet with respect to bicycling enjoyment, it is the *east* half of the park that offers five loops of roadway. This is a bonus for bicyclists who want to repeat loops for different purposes—for learning, reflection, meditation, or exercise. The first-time visitor to Chickamauga may not know from looking at the NPS map that the roads east of LaFayette Road are among the best roads in the park, both for learning and enjoyment. (On the other hand, monuments on the east half of the park mostly stand deep in the woods and well off the roadway. That means that your focus shifts from commemorative history to geography).

As one would expect, specific safety considerations are also unique to each national military park. This is mostly due to differing integrations between park and public roadways. For example, whereas it is relatively easy to avoid the east-west commercial road through Antietam (Maryland Route 34), at Chickamauga, the NPS auto tour includes a 3.3-mile stretch on a heavily trafficked commuter road that bisects the park (LaFayette Road).[14] With a guidebook—or some pre-knowledge about the Chickamauga road network—you can avoid much of LaFayette Road by connecting via Brotherton and Viniard-Alexander Roads on the east side. More broadly, most bicyclists want to have a general sense of the character and safety of the roads before planning a tour; for that reason, this book includes photos of roads that tell that story.

Beyond planning, each battlefield park is also different with respect to how easy it may be to learn history while following a particular bicycle route. For example, Gettysburg National Military Park installed wayside exhibits that one can read not more than a couple of steps from the roadway. However, at Chickamauga, the wayside exhibits are sparse, and historically informative inscriptions are on monuments and markers tucked away along hiking trails that are inaccessible to cars and bikes. One popular example is the John B. Hood Marker that stands on the west side of Glenn-Kelly Road. The marker is a simple, white-painted cast iron sign with this red-lettered inscription: "John B. Hood / Maj. Gen. C.S.A. / Wounded / Sept. 20, 1863." The sign faces Dyer Field and Snodgrass Hill, which was the main Confederate target after Lt. Gen. James Longstreet (and Hood's Corps) broke through the Union line at the Brotherton and Viniard farms in what people call, "Longstreet's Breakthrough."[15]

Is This Book for You?

Bicycling Chickamauga Battlefield is for people who want to learn more about the Battle of Chickamauga during a visit to the national military park at Fort Oglethorpe, Georgia. It will appeal to self-directed, adventurous learners who want the freedom to explore without needing the assistance of a park ranger. (The rangers possess a wealth of knowledge and can be entertaining storytellers, so when you are not bicycling, please consider a ranger-led tour). Although bicyclists will appreciate this book's custom touring tips, any interested reader can benefit from its condensed summaries of the complicated battlefield story.

Learning is easiest when you start with basic concepts and actively filter out unnecessary complexities. That is one aim of this book, and it requires pre-trip reading. For that reason, I recommend that at a minimum, you read the battle maps and summaries in Chapter 2 before starting your tour. For the extra preparation of reading Chapters 1 and 2 (in that order), you will be able to anticipate and understand your battlefield location while bicycling. Even with pre-reading, you will need this guidebook when confronted with Chickamauga's uniquely confusing and confounding geography (and the notable brevity of the official NPS park map). Chickamauga has densely wooded, winding roads that make it hard to see beyond the next bend, and even harder to envision the battle narrative. The good news is that these challenges become fun adventures with the help of a guidebook.

Learning Approach

Imagine that you have never been to Chickamauga and know little about the battlefield or battle. How would you approach the challenge to learn "just enough" to support a successful educational ride? This book describes and applies an effective learning technique for experiential learners on bikes. It provides the tools and materials that a bicyclist would need to learn about the Battle of Chickamauga and provides guidance on how to use the book's content. Before your ride, I encourage you to read Parts I and II so that you can arrive on the battlefield feeling oriented. Carry this guidebook with you, because the bicycling directions in Part III point to maps and historical summaries throughout this book. Even if you never plan a bicycle tour, Parts I and IV structures and sequences historical material in a way that supports incremental learning and retention.

You will look at maps and photos that spark curiosity about the names of physical and natural landmarks. You will wonder what stories lie behind the names and images; and how those stories played out over the land on which you ride. From one stop to the next, one story will connect to another. Where no connection is evident, you will remember and enjoy each story as an independent "building block" for the larger narrative that you are creating in your head. In this way, maps and photos encourage two learning activities: building knowledge and strengthening one's memory. This is because you will associate each image with a story or historical situation or event. Seeing the scenes or sights yourself, you strengthen the associations.

This guidebook describes and implements a visual and experiential learning *process* that begins with images and short histories about the area's natural and physical landmarks. Next, we introduce the Battle of Chickamauga through military maps and day-by-day summaries of battlefield actions. These two components—the battlefield and the battle—form the foundation on which a bicyclist will learn history. Continuing with this dual, thematic emphasis, the book tells the story of Chickamauga through a series of short histories about roads, fields, families, monuments, and official military and newspaper reports.

This technique leads to deliberate but varied repetition in the narrative's telling, which enables the reader to make connections that build knowledge and understanding. You will also develop a vocabulary for engaging primary source material that this book frequently quotes. The glossary on p. 193 provides a basic introduction to U.S. Civil War military terminology and concepts. For a battle "who's who," see the abbreviated listing on pp. 68–69.

Chapter Organization

Part I consists of two chapters and will appeal to both bicyclists and non-bicyclists. The first chapter describes and summarizes the historical significance of the Chickamauga landmarks that you will see on your ride. It covers Chickamauga's road network and bicycle route options; the Visitor Center; West Chickamauga Creek; and the fields and hills of 1863 farming families, including Winfrey, Brock, Brotherton, Poe, Viniard, Kelly, Dyer, Snodgrass, and McDonald.

Chapter two draws from the lessons of the prior chapter to construct a concise chronological military story using color maps that align with summary text. By the time you get to chapter two, you will have seen photos and maps that remind you of our story's "who and what," and you are now prepared to think more about "where and when." Although this guidebook does not explicitly consider "why," chapter two includes casualty statistics and cemetery photos that may help you to reflect on your own personal answer to the meaning of the Battle of Chickamauga.

Chapters three and four (Part II) briefly cover bicycle trip planning, including gear selection, transportation, and lodging. The text offers tips for recreational bicyclists who may be new to planning a day ride outside of their hometown. Please note that this book provides only general suggestions about where to look for dining, lodging, and bike rental or repair services near Chickamauga battlefield. As of this writing, there are excellent businesses near the battlefield, but this guidebook does not attempt to keep up with the inevitable ebb and flow of service options that will be available for you on your biking adventure.

Chapters five and six (Part III) provide detailed touring maps and turn-by-turn directions (called "cues") for three routes through the Chickamauga battlefield park. To keep this section tight, route cue sheets provide cross-references to photos and micro-histories in Part IV: "Monuments and Structures."

And finally, chapters nine, ten, and eleven (Part IV) identify and provide short histories for Chickamauga's six state monuments, eight memorial shell monuments, and a sampling of other monuments (primarily regimental structures). Most readers will consult Part IV as reference material and not read it straight through. That is because it is easier to understand Part IV's focus on military history when one is looking for more information on a specific topic.

Further Reading

For further reading, refer to the bibliography on p. 198. Advanced students and history buffs will want to read this book's endnotes for additional details, and for ideas finding primary source material. For up-to-date information about park alerts, visit the NPS website before your ride: https://www.nps.gov/chch/planyourvisit/conditions.htm.

Historical Approach

For context and depth, this book quotes primary sources, including government records, monument inscriptions, speeches, and nineteenth-century public histories and newspapers. Since our aims are modest, here is a description of what this book is *not*:

First, like all Civil War Cycling publications, this book does not identify or comment on opinions or controversies that tend to spark debate among historians. Instead, most sections include quotations from Chickamauga soldiers or citizens, and endnotes document both primary and secondary sources. When it is possible to reduce battlefield actions to factual statements, the book summarizes a commonly accepted narrative and presents a high-level description of the battle. For example, this book mentions fighting at Reed's Bridge and Alexander's Bridge on September 18 but does not analyze whether the battle was a three-day (September 18–20) or two-day (September 19–20) event. Historical questions such as this are beyond our scope.

As for larger questions—like whether or to what extent Bragg's complicated relationships with his subordinate generals contributed to missed battlefield opportunities—this book takes a pass. For example, the text does not analyze why Lt. Gen. Polk attacked later in the morning of September 20 than Bragg had ordered. Nor does it analyze how or why Rosecrans' order to Brig. Gen. Wood opened a gap in the Union line that, if not for Maj. Gens. Thomas and Granger, would have destroyed the Union army. More broadly, this book does not "second guess" military actions nor entertain "what if" speculations, like whether Bragg's army could have pursued and crushed the Union army before it completed an orderly retreat to Chattanooga. For simplicity, all military maps present only actual events, without commentary as to whether those events aligned to the armies' plans.

Second, the purpose of this book's military maps is to help bicyclists memorize very high-level tactical movements. To that end, the battle maps are deliberately impressionistic and military positions are not to scale. Not surprisingly, and mostly due to geography, a detailed depiction of the Battle of Chickamauga requires a work the size of a military atlas. That is because armies fought the battle—not by corps or divisions—but by brigades and even isolated regiments.

To promote and enable safe, historical tourism on a bike, this guidebook focuses exclusively on the Chickamauga battlefield park with little mention of other significant historic sites associated with the Chickamauga and Chattanooga Campaigns of 1863. For time and safety, the author encourages tourists to visit by car the following nearby sites: Missionary Ridge, Lookout Mountain, Orchard Knob, Chattanooga National Cemetery, and the Confederate cemetery established in 1920 in downtown Chattanooga. For a more expansive tour of Civil War Georgia, one might note that, according to an NPS report, Georgia has twenty-seven civil war battlefields that cover more than 231,500 acres, about 72,200 of which "retain sufficient significance and integrity to make them worthy of preservation."[16]

In summary, as a military travel guide for the Chickamauga battlefield, this book does not try to break new scholarly ground or make any political point. It does not address the causes of the war or comment on the complicated politics of (dis)union and (anti)slavery. Although in the South you will find tourist literature about the "War Between the States" or the "War of Northern Aggression"—and in the North, nineteenth-century records about the "War of Rebellion"—this book adopts the language of the National Park Service, the "United States Civil War."

Bicycling Chickamauga Battlefield invites you to learn American history by immersing yourself in the battlefield landscape in a physically active way. I hope that the guidebook inspires you to learn more about this landmark battle and the nineteenth-century farming families of northwest Georgia.

How to Use This Guidebook and Maps

You will learn the most about the Battle of Chickamauga if you refer to this guidebook while bicycling the park. Once again, Civil War Cycling's Chickamauga touring maps cover the battlefield in a way that helps you learn about the battle through the repetition of smaller stories that gradually form into a complete, chronological narrative. The complex and confusing character of the Battle of Chickamauga necessitates this approach. After all, bicyclists have no choice but to ride linearly, even though the battle's order of events is anything but linear. With that in mind, this book's maps intend to be helpful references for battlefield newcomers.

Take a Ride Back in Time

Before your ride, study each map. While riding, consult the bicycle cues to confirm your location and to refer to historical summaries associated with each battlefield site. Consider photocopying maps for personal (non-commercial) use for the convenience of having easy access to extra maps that can withstand a little drizzle. You will not regret stuffing paper maps into plastic sleeves or baggies, and then tucking them into your pocket or bag, or clipping them to your handlebars. Another option is to read directions from your PDF-enabled mobile device during a stop.[17] These digital maps are available for online purchase from Civil War Cycling at www.civilwarcycling.com. (The digital maps are *companions* to this paperback guidebook; the book itself is not available in digital format).

Getting Oriented

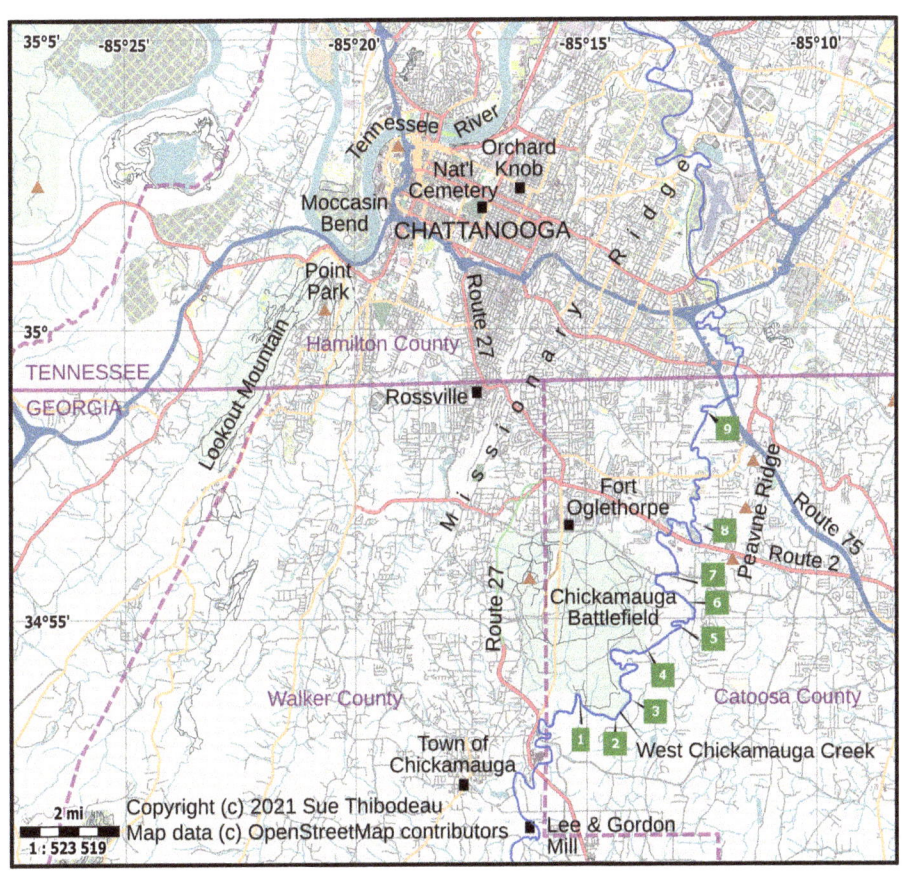

Map 1. Chickamauga and Chattanooga Battlefield Area

Bicycling Chickamauga Battlefield

The National Park Service manages six historic sites that cover 9,000 acres of park land in northwest Georgia and south-central Tennessee. Geographically disconnected from each other, these sites were part of two large military campaigns during the U.S. Civil War.

First, the Chickamauga Campaign (August–September 1863) began in mid-August when Rosecrans' Army of the Cumberland made its move southeast out of middle Tennessee toward Chattanooga. It ended when Bragg's Confederate Army of Tennessee routed the Federals at the Battle of Chickamauga (September 18–20, 1863).

Second, the Chattanooga Campaign (September–November 1863) began after the Battle of Chickamauga, when the Union army lived under siege in Chattanooga. Gen. Grant reorganized the Federal army, broke the siege, and fought several battles in the western theater. The rise of Grant and his military victories in Chattanooga mark a significant turning point in the war. Grant secured Chattanooga's railways, roads, and rivers for the Union and thus set the stage for Sherman's Atlanta Campaign in 1864.

The area map on p. 23 and the site list below identify the six geographical areas of Chickamauga and Chattanooga National Military Park. The green map labels identify fords along West Chickamauga Creek (p. 25). Knowing these names and locations provides a helpful context for understanding battle details.

National Military Park Historic Site Locations

1. Chickamauga Battlefield at Fort Oglethorpe, Georgia.
   Battle of Chickamauga, September 18–20, 1863.
2. Lookout Mountain in Tennessee and Georgia.
   The "Battle Above the Clouds," November 24, 1863.
3. Missionary Ridge in Tennessee and Georgia.
   The Battle of Missionary Ridge, November 25, 1863.
4. Moccasin Bend on the Tennessee River.
   A Union artillery site during the Siege of Chattanooga, September–November 1863.
5. Point Park, also called Signal Point, in Tennessee.
   An overlook between Signal and Raccoon Mountains during the Siege of Chattanooga, September–November 1863.
6. Orchard Knob in Chattanooga, Tennessee.
   Battles of Chattanooga, November 23, 1863.

Take a Ride Back in Time

Fords on West Chickamauga Creek

In preparation for what would become the Battle of Chickamauga, the Confederate army crossed West Chickamauga Creek from the east. On foot, horseback, and by wagon train, they crossed at fords along the creek's wooded and slippery banks. Here is a list of fords and bridges near the Chickamauga battlefield (see map on p. 23):

1. Hall's Ford
2. Dalton Ford
3. Thedford Ford
4. Alexander's Bridge
5. Lambert's Ford
6. Fowler's Ford
7. Reed's Bridge
8. Dyer's Bridge
9. Ringgold Bridge

Chickamauga Battlefield Park

It is surprisingly challenging for a bicyclist to find detailed but "simple" maps of Chickamauga. The official NPS map is good, but it is not ideal for bicyclists who need more visual navigation cues and historical context. Also, the NPS auto tour on its map neglects the eastern half of the battlefield and includes a long stretch of LaFayette Road, a double-yellow-lined commuter roadway that lacks shoulders. For hikers, the NPS publishes a paper map that has the title, "Chickamauga Battlefield Trail Map" (2005). This map is helpful for hikers and tourists on horseback but does not add any additional cycling-related detail to the NPS park brochure. Battlefield America publishes a waterproof and tear-resistant topographic map of the Chickamauga battlefield that includes the locations of all monuments, markers, and tablets; but this static view of the battlefield does not, by design, help with dynamic route planning.

To bridge the gap between a bicyclist's needs and what is available for bicycle tour planning, this guidebook has eighteen maps that each focus on a clear, specific theme. We trade completeness for conceptual clarity. The goal is to make one loop through the Chickamauga battlefield and feel good about having understood high-level themes and concepts. For more detailed knowledge, a bicyclist will typically ride another loop through the battlefield.

The next map focuses specifically on park roads and bicycling amenities. Most interior roads have a rural character, and except for a general lack of bicycle racks, parking is not an issue for bicyclists.

Bicycling Chickamauga Battlefield

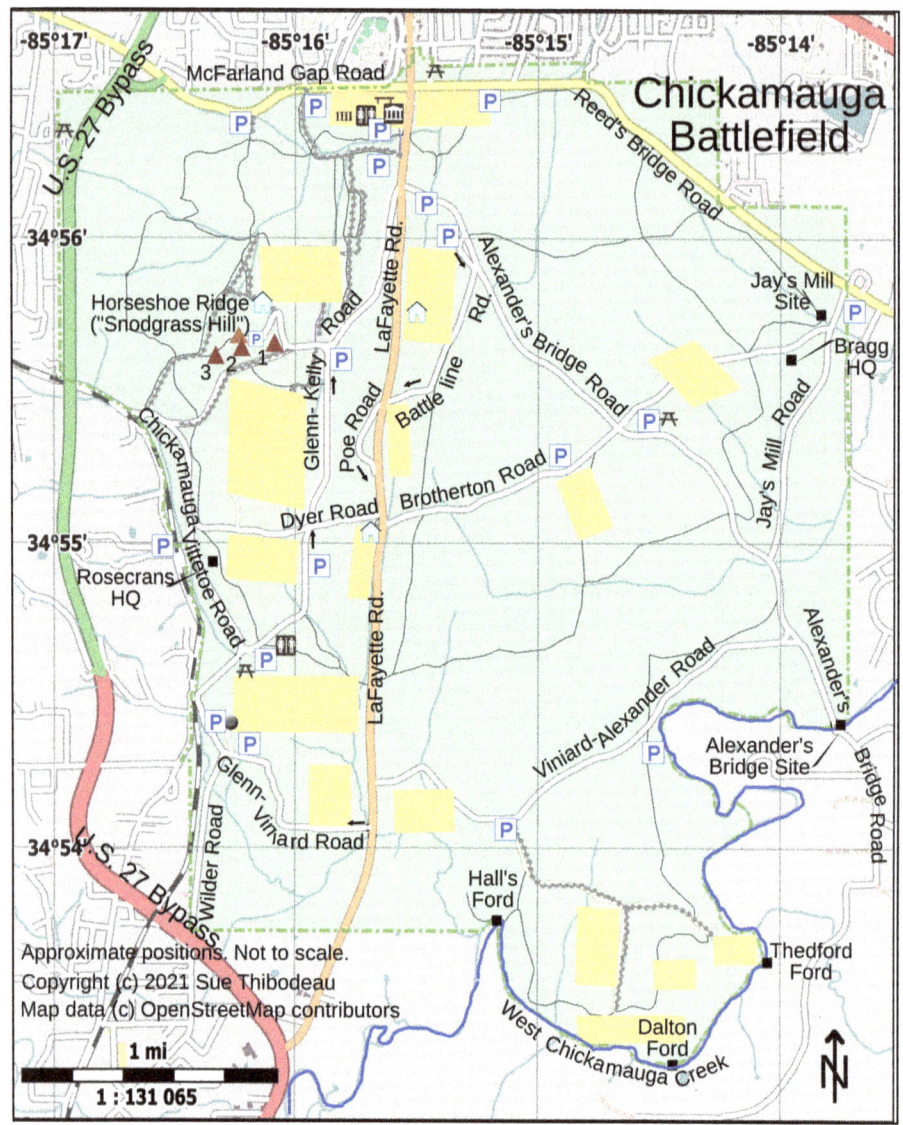

Map 2. Chickamauga Battlefield Park

The largest parking lots are located at the Visitor Center, the Wilder Brigade Monument (Glenn-Viniard Road), and the recreation field (Glenn-Kelly Road). The smaller parking lots are pull-out areas that will accommodate about four to six cars. Beyond the Visitor Center, park personnel will sometimes lock restroom facilities without notice. In the author's opinion, Chickamauga's picnic areas are more suited to tourists who arrive by car with coolers and cooking gear.

Take a Ride Back in Time

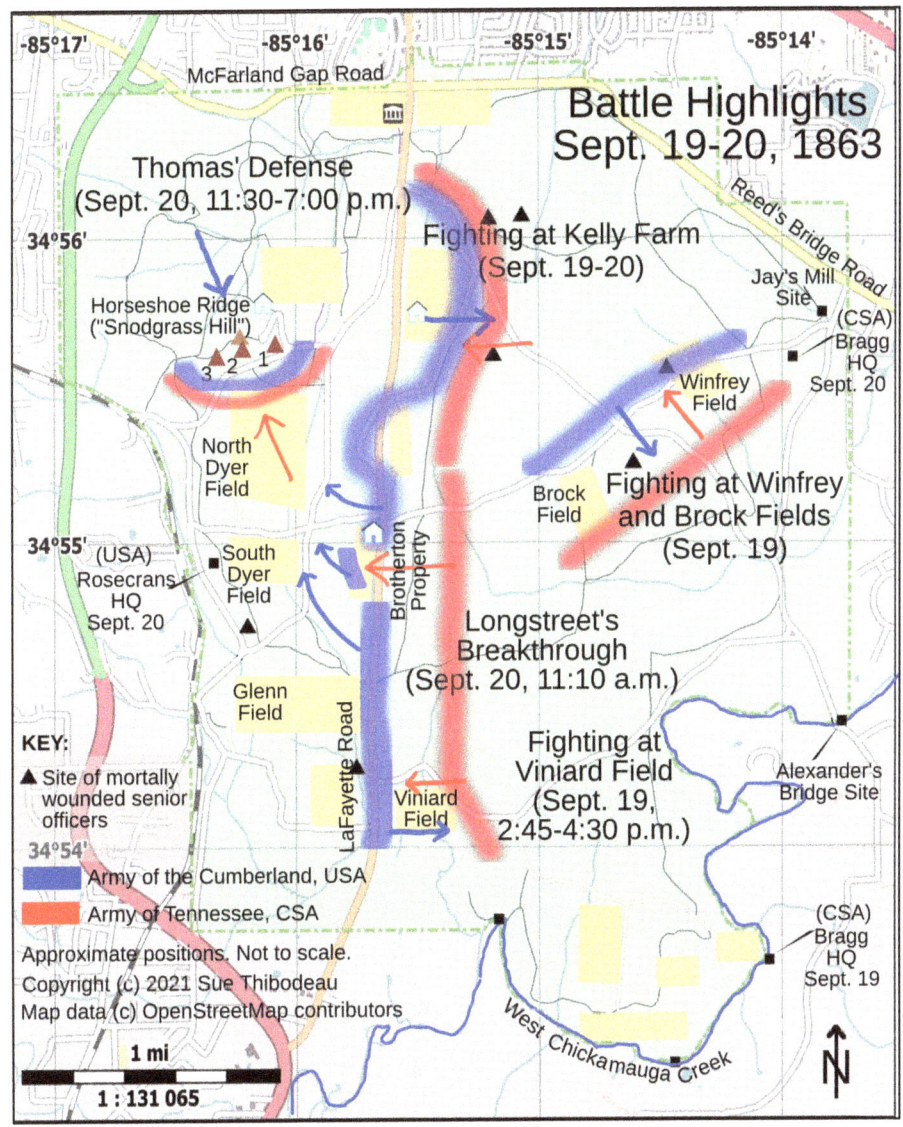

Map 3. Battle Highlights, September 19–20, 1863

Touring Tip: On the day of your bicycle tour, study the map above for help getting oriented on the battlefield. Next, study the military overview maps on pp. 76–79, which describe the Battle of Chickamauga in four chronological phases. Refer to this book's maps during your tour, because they will help you to connect your current location to what happened there in 1863.

Bicycling Chickamauga Battlefield

Map Key

🏛	Visitor Center
🚻	Restrooms
⛱	Picnic area
⊤⊤	Bench
IIII	Bicycle parking
P	Car parking
▲	Peak (Hills 1,2,3)
- - -	National park boundary
▇	Park or wooded area. Darker greens are more wooded.
▇	(Rosecrans) Army of the Cumberland, USA
▇	(Bragg) Army of Tennessee, CSA
🏠	Reconstructed cabin
■	Historic site
▪	Monument or marker
1	Numbered monument or historic site
▲	Memorial shell monument
HQ	Headquarters
●	Wilder observation tower
★	Starting point
▬	Cycling pathway
➡	Cycling path direction
➡	One-way traffic flow
⋯	Unpaved road (hike)
—	Pedestrian pathway
⋯	Horse and hiking trail
✳	Horse loading site

Military troop positions are approximate and not to scale.

All maps have North at the top.

Map 4. Symbols, Terms and Abbreviations

PART I: INTRODUCTION

1. Chickamauga on a Bicycle

> *No one seemed to know where our position was. All was doubt and uncertainty. The ground was wooded, broken with low, transverse hills and irregular knolls. The woods were open, but grown here and there with baffling stretches of dense underbrush. There were a very few small fields and indistinct roads.*[18]
> ~ Lt. Albion W. Tourgée, 105th Ohio Volunteer Infantry, USA

In his Ohio regimental history, *The Story of a Thousand*, Lt. Albion W. Tourgée described how Chickamauga's terrain, vegetation, and farm roads confused military commanders and significantly thwarted effective or even sensible military action. Chickamauga's geography impacted both armies—the Union Army of the Cumberland under Maj. Gen. William Starke Rosecrans, and the Confederate Army of Tennessee under Gen. Braxton Bragg. On September 19, 1863, Rosecrans wrote to General-in-Chief Henry Halleck in Washington, D.C. that "the battle-ground was densely wooded and its surface irregular and difficult. We could make little use of our artillery."[19] Confederate Brig. Gen. George Maney reported that his line "had become considerably disordered by its rapid movement through thick woods and undergrowth."[20]

The Chickamauga battlefield lies in a valley between Missionary Ridge on the west and Peavine Ridge on the east. It is located near the south end of the Appalachian Mountains, in northwest Georgia. On a non-biking day, you will want to visit nearby Missionary Ridge, Lookout Mountain, and Orchard Knob in Chattanooga. These battle sites were part of Gen. Ulysses S. Grant's broader campaign to permanently wrest Chattanooga from the Confederacy and open the Deep South to Federal conquest.

Mostly flat, the Chickamauga valley offers an easy venue for bicycling and hiking tours. Although the ride up Snodgrass Hill is an exception in terms of difficulty, the experience helps one to appreciate the Confederate struggle to seize the hill and win the battle. Notably, the park has more than fifty miles of hiking trails that are off-limits to bicyclists. One trail is steep but short, and that is the trail to the South Carolina State Monument south of Snodgrass Hill. To experience Chickamauga's quiet and rustic touring amenities, you will give up pedaled access to some historic sites. You can, however, chain and lock together your bikes for a walk down a pedestrian path.

Snodgrass Family Cabin and Eastern Red Cedar Tree

Pedestrian Path to South Carolina State Monument

Chickamauga on a Bicycle

Chickamauga Creek shapes part of the eastern boundary of the battlefield. It snakes north to the Tennessee River, near the water and railway hub of Chattanooga. Except for Alexander's Bridge in the southeast corner, the creek is not accessible to bicyclists from within park boundaries. If you want to explore the fords of Chickamauga Creek—where Confederate soldiers crossed from the east side prior to the first full day of battle on September 19—your best option is to contact a local sports store for kayak or canoe rentals and tips for using the launch point at Lee and Gordon's Mills (about 0.5 miles from the intersection of LaFayette Road and U.S. Route 27).

Chickamauga's forests and fields are its most memorable natural amenities, especially for bicyclists. Park roads wind through historic forests and groomed fields of variably tall grass. The touring experience is significant, because the NPS works to preserve and restore the battlefield to its 1863 state. This helps tourists more easily understand the Battle of Chickamauga.[21] In 1863, the Chickamauga forests included a patchwork of cedar glades, especially on the east side of LaFayette Road. The glades' open understory allowed for the effective use of firearms, but other woodlots, such as those near Kelly Farm, were densely thicketed. Visibility was also relatively good near open fields where September corn had been harvested. According to the *Cultural Landscape Report* prepared for the National Park Service, Chickamauga consisted of twenty-four farms in 1863. It had sixty-eight buildings and structures, including a church, tanyard, and log schoolhouse.[22] The NPS has reconstructed three of those buildings, including the previously mentioned Snodgrass House.

These geographic and structural considerations frame the bicyclist's predominant experience of the battlefield. We immediately notice that trees obstruct our view, thus making it hard to anticipate finding a particular hill, field, or roadway. The battlefield park can feel like a knotty jumble of woods and roads over which it is challenging to overlay an 1863 battle narrative. A bicyclist's disorienting, first experience of Chickamauga geography reminds one of the confusion that soldiers also experienced, and later described, with respect to the battle's terrain. Historian Steven E. Woodworth described the impact of the Chickamauga landscape on military actions in this way:

> In these woods no officer above brigadier could see all his command at once, and even the brigadiers often could see nobody's troops but their own and perhaps the enemy's.[23]

A Geography-Based, Thematic Approach

The following sections describe Chickamauga's roads and natural landmarks through the lens of farming families. This approach allows us to centralize and simplify the presentation of each of three bicycle routes. It also allows for a more coherent introduction to the Chickamauga story for people who may never plan a bicycle tour, or who want a thematic introduction to the Chickamauga battlefield.

Reading Tip: If you would rather jump immediately to a chronological summary of the battle, which includes four maps, please turn to Chapter 2, pp. 75–81.

The Roads at Chickamauga Battlefield

The Chickamauga battlefield park has twenty-two miles of paved roads (with about seventy pull-offs) and five miles of gravel or earthen roads.[24] This chapter provides photos and a short commentary on eight significant park roads, ordered mostly by what they have in common or how the roads connect. It does not provide an all-inclusive inventory of the park road network, but rather, an introduction to what you can expect while touring Chickamauga, whether by bike or car. This chapter also offers learning tips for connecting road names and shapes to the people and events of September 1863.

Most people intuitively understand the value of glancing over a road map before taking a tour. In addition, this book recommends viewing photos of different park roads and then associating each road with a Chickamauga family or battlefield event. When you do this before your ride, you can more easily associate your current location with the history that you are trying to learn. Because the roads are part of the battlefield story, they can help you build a mental framework for remembering what happened here in 1863. Tourists rarely think about the naming of the roads in U.S. military parks, but the names contain helpful clues about battlefield history. At Gettysburg, most park roads are named for Union generals, and a road's shape follows that general's battle line. But at Chickamauga, most roads bear the names of local farmers, and when hyphenated indicate which two farms the road connects.

First though, we offer a brief note about Chickamauga's hiking trails. For an extended tour of the battlefield, a bicyclist may want to

Chickamauga on a Bicycle

consider planning a hike, especially along Horseshoe Ridge, where monuments and markers are "hidden" in woodlots. The brown path in the map below shows a horse trail that is also popular with hikers. Trail conditions vary with park maintenance schedules to clear underbrush, trim trees, and mow fields. Rain and creek flooding also affect the usability of Chickamauga's complex trail network. Please note that bicyclists may ride only on paved roadways and gravel trails.

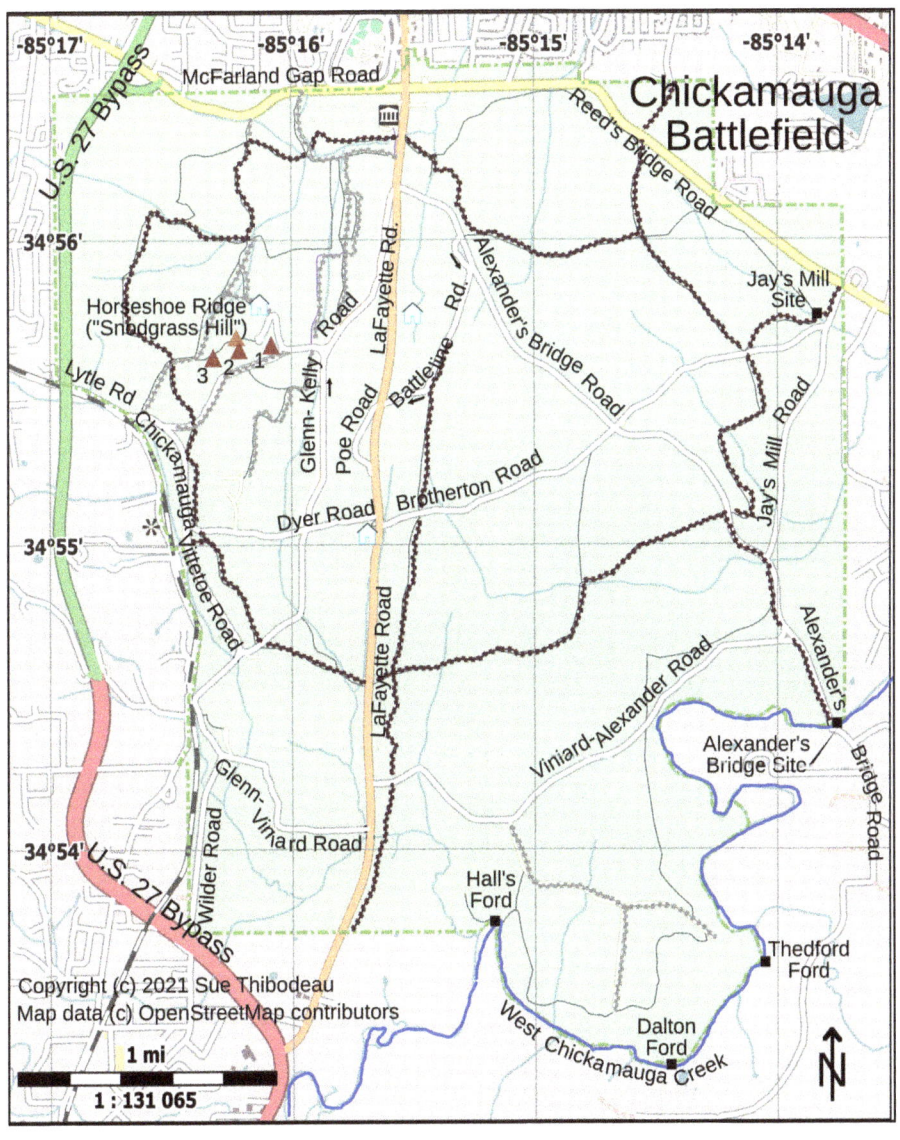

Map 5. Chickamauga Roads and Main Horse/Hiking Trails

Battleline Road (0.8 miles)

Let us first consider an exception to the naming of Chickamauga's park roads—and that is Battleline Road. We will briefly discuss two points. First, this modern road follows the 1863 shape of the Union battle line on and around the Kelly Farm. Second, the wooded terrain impaired visibility for effective artillery and small arms fire, while also making it possible for the Federals to build breastworks along this strong defensive position.

The Union Side of the Road

Built after the battle (during the "commemorative era"), this one-way road begins on the left flank of the Union Army of the Cumberland. The army's 14th Corps under Maj. Gen. George H. Thomas occupied the line. Rosecrans and Thomas agreed that the line must hold firm to safeguard the army's ability to return to Chattanooga. But Bragg wanted to turn the Union left flank to drive the army south and block its return north to the bustling transportation hub of Chattanooga.

Battleline Road Approach to 38th Indiana Monument

If you look south on Battleline Road (as in the above photo), Union monuments stand on the right side of the road. They mark the battlefield positions of Thomas' Corps. For example, the 38th Indiana Infantry Monument shown in the photo marks the regiment's position on September 20, until leaving the field at 5:30 p.m., after a full day of attacks and counterattacks. (For more about Indiana at Chickamauga, see p. 149). Conversely, Confederate monuments stand on the left side of the road. Bragg anchored his army's right flank about 75–250 yards into the woods and faced Thomas' defensive line on modern-day Battleline Road.[25]

A second example of how a monument's placement contributes to the historical record is the 21st Wisconsin Infantry Monument, which is on the right side of the road as you continue your ride south. (See the photo below). Like the 38th Indiana Infantry, this is where the Wisconsin regiment fought to hold Thomas' line on September 20.

Battleline Road Approach to 21st Wisconsin Monument

Chaotic Fighting in Dense Woods

Having discussed the rationale for the shape of Battleline Road and the placement of monuments, we next consider the dense woods through which the road passes. The following excerpt from a 21st Wisconsin Infantry record describes the difficulties that Chickamauga's wooded terrain imposed on the battle. Destroyed trees, broken and chaotic military communications, and captured flags and officers were all part of the story (see also, p. 176):

> On the morning of the 20th, the regiment with its brigade, was early placed in line of battle... At about 9 o'clock, a.m., the rebel forces commenced a series of terrible charges, which

were repeated until the close of that eventful day. ... [T]he trees on the line were nearly all cut down by the fire of the enemy's batteries. Near sundown, General Thomas ordered a retreat, the right wing having been flanked by the enemy. The Twenty-first did not receive the order, and held their line fighting until they saw the other regiments suddenly moving to the rear. Lieutenant Colonel Hobart then ordered the regiment to fall back to the second line of works, where, still fighting, they remained until nearly surrounded by the enemy. The regiment then attempted to cut its way to the rear, in which attempt Lieutenant Colonel Hobart, with about seventy officers and men, were captured. The flag of the Twenty-first, the last of the Fourteenth Corps, and its gallant Sergeant, remained in front until captured by the enemy.[26]

The Confederate Side of the Road

What about Confederate monuments on the left side of Battleline Road? Continuing your ride south, one notable example is the Texas State Monument. This red granite structure is identical in shape and style to the Texas state monuments erected on ten other Civil War battlefields, including Gettysburg and Antietam.

Battleline Road Approach to Texas State Monument

The monument's simple yet elegant design honors all soldiers equally, independent of the battlefield and the battle result. Inscribed in stone are these words: "Texas remembers the valor and devotion of her sons." At Chickamauga, soldiers from the Lone Star State fought in most sections of the battlefield, including early skirmishes at West Chickamauga Creek and on through the brutal attacks and counterattacks at Snodgrass Hill. Notably, as many as 4,400 Texans belonging to thirteen regiments fought on the Dyer, Kelly, Poe, and Viniard farms, and about one-quarter of them were mortally wounded.[27] For more details, please see pp. 137 and 172.

Glenn–Kelly & Glenn–Viniard Roads (2.1 & 1.1 miles)

Like Battleline Road, Glenn–Kelly Road is flat and smoothly paved in keeping with the overall character of the Chickamauga battlefield park. This and the fact that Chickamauga motor vehicle traffic is usually light make it an easy bike ride. (LaFayette Road is one notable exception).

Riding North on Glenn–Kelly Road (Longstreet's Corps HQ)

Glenn–Kelly and Glenn–Viniard Roads bear the name of a twenty-three-year-old widow, Eliza Camp Glenn, whose husband John died the previous spring after he was drafted into Confederate service. Rosecrans claimed the Glenn House for his Union headquarters during the Battle of Chickamauga, and it burned to the ground during the battle. Glenn–Kelly Road is also named for brothers Elijah (property owner) and Elisha Kelly (renter). Elisha and his wife lived in the Kelly House with their children, one of whom was a soldier in the 1st Georgia Infantry (CSA). The Kelly House (now reconstructed) was a field hospital during the battle.[28] As for the Glenn–Viniard Road, we discuss the Viniard family on p. 42.

In our overview of Battleline Road, we mentioned that the placement of monuments was based on regimental battlefield positions. Another tip for learning history while bicycling the battlefield is to remember that a pyramid-shaped monument with three sides identifies the mortal wounding of a brigade commander. A four-sided pyramid-shaped monument marks the location of a military headquarters during the Battle of Chickamauga.[29]

The previous photo shows a headquarters monument that is on the east side of Glenn–Kelly Road, just north of Dyer Road. The pyramid is a stack of eight-inch naval shells. The monument marks the September 20 (noon) headquarters of Maj. Gen. John B. Hood, part of Longstreet's Corps. If you follow the short pedestrian path on the bike's left, you will find a simple cast iron marker that identifies the location of Hood's wounding on that day.[30]

Glenn–Kelly Road Looking North (Dyer Field)

Chickamauga on a Bicycle

The previous photo shows Glenn–Kelly Road while facing north. Dyer Field is on the left and the South Carolina State Monument is on a rise to Snodgrass Hill.

Dyer Road (0.8 miles)

Dyer Road cuts east-west through Dyer Field, over Glenn–Kelly Road, and then ends near the Brotherton Cabin on LaFayette Road. Be careful at this intersection because it is not a four-way stop. Although you have the right of way while cycling north, cars coming from LaFayette Road on your right side may not notice you.

The Dyer family purchased the farm in 1847. (The 1863 house and farm buildings no longer exist). Spill B. Dyer was a Tennessee native who moved to Georgia with his father, R.H. Dyer, and settled in Chickamauga with his wife, Ellen Parker. The younger Dyer was thirty-three years old when he served as a courier for Gen. Bragg.[31]

Dyer Road Looking West (Mark Thrash Wayside Exhibit)

The wayside exhibit in the above photo honors Mr. Mark Thrash (c. 1820–1943), an enslaved man, who at the time of the Battle of Chickamauga lived in a two-room cabin on Dyer Field. (On September 20, 1863, Confederate Lt. Gen. Longstreet set up his left wing headquarters in this field). According to the NPS, Thrash claimed to have been a servant to a Confederate soldier (and to Robert E. Lee and Ulysses S. Grant). By 1900, he worked for the U.S. government as a laborer at Chickamauga and Chattanooga National Military Park, where he was employed for nearly fifty years.[32]

Viniard–Alexander Road (2.1 miles)

The Viniard-Alexander Road connects the Viniard farm near LaFayette Road to the Alexander farm on the east. Like the Brotherton Road farther north, this scenic and isolated roadway is not on the official NPS auto tour. Viniard-Alexander Road is densely wooded, narrow, and has few monuments but many commemorative tablets. Confederate tablets are red-on-white painted cast iron structures, and Union tablets are white-on-blue. The tablet in the next photo describes the September 19 battlefield action of Brig. Gen. Evander M. Law's brigade, in the woods about 0.8 miles east of LaFayette Road.

Viniard–Alexander Road

John P. Alexander owned 120 acres that spanned both sides of Chickamauga Creek. The dilapidated wooden bridge on Alexander's property was the site where Union Col. John T. Wilder's men from Indiana and Illinois blocked the crossing of Confederates from Mississippi and Arkansas on September 18. Tabler and Anna Viniard and their family of eight grew corn on the land over which thousands of soldiers fought on September 19. Wilder's Lightning Brigade slaughtered Confederate men in what was later called the "Ditch of Death" on the Viniard Farm. A son, James Viniard fought in the Confederate army but not at Chickamauga. Later, in 1864, Tabler Viniard enlisted in the 1st Georgia Infantry USA. His grave is in Chattanooga National Cemetery.[33]

Alexander's Bridge Road (2.9 miles)

Georgia State Road 149 becomes Alexander's Bridge Road at the Alexander's Bridge site, a southeast entrance to the Chickamauga battlefield park. This heavily wooded battle-era road has double-yellow-lines but provides several pull-offs. Vegetation on both sides of the road does not allow for emergency stops, but the sparsity of commemorative structures supports a pleasant ride. In 1863, this area was more open and provided visibility to area fields.

Alexander's Bridge Road Looking Northwest

Alexander's Bridge Road provides the only direct road access to Chickamauga Creek within the battlefield park's boundaries. However, from a parking lot about 0.1 miles southwest of the Law tablet (above), you will find access to a gravel road that forks to Dalton and Thedford Fords. According to the 2005 NPS "Chickamauga Battlefield

Trail Map," you may ride a bicycle on gravel roads (but the author has not followed the 1.0-mile path to the fords, where another 0.1 hike will get you to the creek).

Jay's Mill Road (1.1 miles)

Jay's Mill Road is named for local businessman William Jay, who operated a steam-powered sawmill on the south side of Reed's Bridge Road. At 710' elevation, the mill stands 10' higher than nearby West Chickamauga Creek.[34] A fresh-water spring both fed the boiler and attracted thirsty soldiers from Union Col. Daniel McCook's division (Gordon Granger's Reserve Corps).

According to Park Ranger Lee White, the 1st Georgia Cavalry (CSA) spotted the soldiers' fires on the morning of September 19, and a fight ensued. Army commander Rosecrans would thus learn that Confederate soldiers had crossed to the west side of the creek and were threatening the Union left.[35] Fortunately for the Union army, that prior night Rosecrans and Thomas had been moving troops north to anchor the army's left flank at the Kelly farmstead. (This is the line that follows the shape of modern-day Battleline Road).

Riding southwest on Jay's Mill Road

Although the National Park Service restores and preserves the 1863 landscape, their work is an ongoing effort that often involves undoing post-war development (like the removal of observation towers). In the photo above, the thick vegetation is not indicative of the 1863 battle scene, and so work is underway to clear the underbrush to open the battlefield view in this area. However, it is still generally true that a bicyclist's disorientation riding through densely wooded areas remains indicative of the confusion experienced by soldiers who fought at the Battle of Chickamauga.

Brotherton Road (2.0 miles)

Much like Jay's Mill Road, the ride down Brotherton Road is similarly wooded but opens in Winfrey and Brock Fields. The road extends southwest from Jay's Mill, crosses Alexander's Bridge Road, and then continues to LaFayette Road at the Brotherton Cabin and Brotherton Field. Monuments and tablets stand along Brotherton Road, sometimes near pull-off areas. Although more wooded today than in 1863, the approach to LaFayette Road was "a dense thicket and tangle of vines."[36] On this road you will ride through a cedar (limestone) glade, west of Brock Field.

The road bears the family name of local farmers George and Mary Brotherton, who had eight children, three of whom had enlisted in the Confederate army. On returning to her home after the battle, their daughter, Adaline, found that their milk cows had survived but nine Union soldiers in the Brotherton yard required burial.[37]

**Brotherton Road
(Near LaFayette Road)**

The author snapped this photo from the north side of Brotherton Road. In 1977, the Sons of Confederate Veterans, and the United Daughters of the Confederacy, dedicated the monument to "the men of Gen. Johnson's command who fought and died here." A nearby marker describes the actions of Confederate Brig. Gen. Bushrod R. Johnson's division on September 20 when a gap in the Union line enabled the left wing of the Army of Tennessee to break into Dyer Field. By 2 p.m., they had lined up to attack Snodgrass Hill.[38]

Chickamauga Bicycle Routes

Having summarized the character and history of Chickamauga's park roads (all smoothly paved), we turn to the topic of bicycle routes, specifically the three routes listed in the following table:

#	Route Name	Miles	Est. Hours	Page
1	Half Day Loop	12.6	3–4	101
2	Fields of Chickamauga	12.9	3–4	117
3	Eastern Woods Loop	8.8	1–2	121

Table 1. Chickamauga Bicycle Routes

Route 1—Half Day Loop, 12.6 miles

This guidebook provides detailed maps and touring directions for a 12.6-mile looped ride through the Chickamauga battlefield. Route 1 is Civil War Cycling's simplest "complete" loop through the Chickamauga battlefield. It provides maximum coverage of the park while strictly minimizing exposure to commuter traffic on LaFayette Road.

You will visit famous locations, including Snodgrass Hill; the Kelly and Brotherton Farms; Jay's Mill; and Alexander's Bridge. (See Chapter 1) On paved park roads, you will ride through historical fields and woodlots. You will also visit Chickamauga's six state monuments; pass by hundreds of regimental monuments; and may find eleven memorial shell monuments, some of which require a short hike. (See Chapters 9–11).

Assuming frequent stops to read NPS wayside exhibits and to study monument inscriptions, Route 1 ("Half Day Loop") is likely to take about 3–4 hours. However, if you are less serious about touring to understand the battle, most bicyclists can complete Route 1 in about 1–1.5 hours.

If you feel torn between an urge to keep riding and a conflicting desire to stop to study the battlefield, then you should consider this touring idea:

Touring Tip: Ride Route 1 twice. On your first ride, let your goal be to ride mostly non-stop through the battlefield so that you can enjoy the landscape, get familiar with the road network, and feel good about getting exercise. Then take a short break to hydrate and eat a small meal in preparation for your second ride. Your goal the second time around is to stop frequently, while using this guidebook to help you to learn about Chickamauga.

Routes 2 and 3

Routes 2 and 3 are examples of how easy it is to complete looped rides of varying lengths through the battlefield. At Chickamauga, eight park roads combine to connect to an outer "circle" of roads. Specifically, Dyer and Brotherton Roads join the western and eastern halves of the park; LaFayette Road (with Battleline and Poe Roads) connects north to south; and Alexander's Bridge, Jay's Mill, and Glenn-Kelly Roads connect diagonally. These interior roads carve the battlefield into nearly one dozen sections that you can circle around.

Whereas Route 1 will introduce you to the battlefield road network and provide access to natural and physical landmarks for learning about Chickamauga, Routes 2 and 3 have a different purpose. They are simply examples of battlefield loops. If you are touring the park and not wanting to stop, your best bet is to explore Chickamauga's scenic landscape by chaining together loops of roadway. Since the whole point of adopting this riding style is to explore freely and without planning constraints, this guidebook does not provide bicycle cues for Routes 2 and 3. If you have previously ridden Route 1, a simple map that traces a looped route will be more than sufficient.

Also, to keep this volume a manageable size (and portable), the book does not include detailed maps and touring directions for Routes 2 and 3. Instead, the text includes a route map without segment markings since the overlaps with Route 1 are obvious. The bicycle cues, amenities, monument locations, and historical commentary will be the same.

Landmarks at Chickamauga Battlefield

A bicyclist will want to understand Chickamauga's park road network to have a successful ride. We regard Chickamauga's roads as teaching tools for learning about the area's nineteenth century farming families. Not only do the roads connect farms on which soldiers fought a battle, but the road names also provide explicit clues as to who lived here in 1863. Even the official battle reports for both armies use Chickamauga family names to identify the roads, fields, hills, cabins, and woodlots that hosted the battle. The stories behind these natural and physical landmarks help us to expand the battle narrative to include the people of Chickamauga.

This introductory chapter on bicycling Chickamauga includes a section on the battlefield's most significant geographical landmarks. Although the material helps with bicycling orientation and navigation, it also frames the battle story in broader human terms to include the voices of both soldiers and farming families. In the following pages, we describe the Chickamauga landscape from the perspective of these families. After a brief introduction, Map 7 on p. 53 marks the locations of ten farmsteads:

	Page
Chickamauga Battlefield Park Visitor Center	50
Chickamauga Creek	51
Chickamauga Farmsteads	52
Winfrey Field	54
Brock Field	55
Viniard Field	56
Brotherton Field	57
Poe Field	59
Glenn Field	60
Dyer Field	61
Snodgrass Hill	62
Kelly Field	64
McDonald Field	65

Chickamauga on a Bicycle

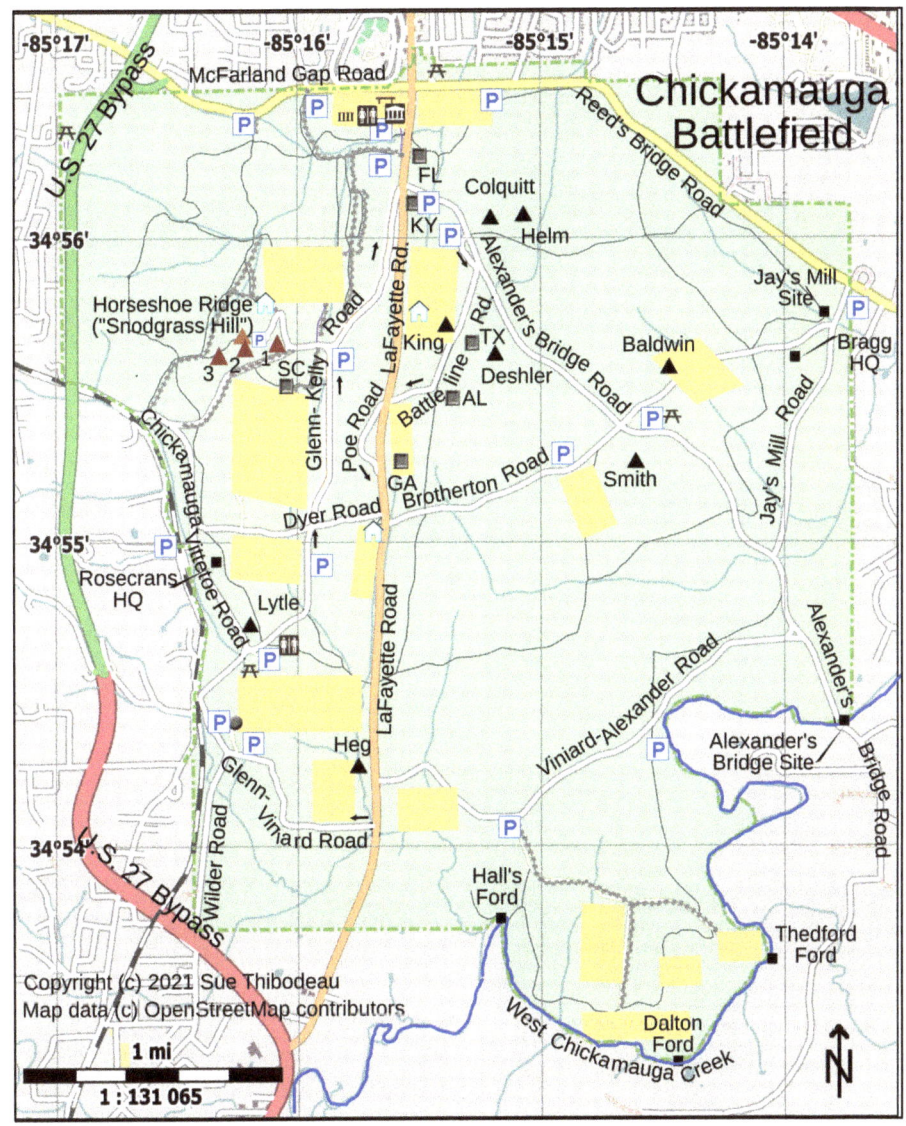

Map 6. Key Landmarks at Chickamauga Battlefield

In the decades after the battle, veterans erected monuments whose placement help tourists learn about the battle and bicyclists navigate the park. Chapters 9 and 11 include photos and micro-histories for every state and mortuary monument at Chickamauga. Since these are significant physical landmarks that you will want to visit, the map above (plus maps on pp. 131 and 180) identifies their location on the battlefield.

Chickamauga Battlefield Park Visitor Center

The Visitor Center for the Chickamauga battlefield is at 3370 LaFayette Road, Fort Oglethorpe, Georgia, about ten miles southeast of Chattanooga. For current information about park operating hours and alerts, see https://www.nps.gov/chch/planyourvisit/basicinfo.htm.

Six Civil War cannons ("guns") flank the Visitor Center entrance. Left to right in the photo: 6-pounder smoothbore; 12-pounder Howitzer; and 3-inch ordnance rifle. Inside the building you can browse the Fuller Gun Collection, which has shoulder arms that span nearly 400 years of American military history.[39]

Every thirty minutes, park visitors can enjoy a high-quality orientation film (currently free with a free park admission). The Visitor Center has a small gift shop and bookstore. While there, be sure to pick up a park map so that you can read about other historic sites in the 1863 Chickamauga Campaign.

It is easy for a first-time visitor to miss the shaded and comfortable seating area on the north side of the Visitor Center building (see photo). This peaceful, normally uncrowded spot in McDonald Field is near Confederate cannons and historic tablets.

Chickamauga Creek

> *The Chickamauga is not, as many suppose, a dark and sluggish stream, but a clear, sparkling creek over hung with willows, with green mossy banks where the pale lilies and watercress dip their beautiful heads in the passing wave.*[40]
> ~ Pvt. Van R. Willard, 3rd Wisconsin Volunteer Infantry, USA

View from South Side of Chickamauga Creek

If the waters of Chickamauga Creek were as clear as Pvt. Willard described, then it would seem to be a beautiful venue for baptizing sixteen soldiers in the Army of Tennessee, as happened in 1863. Historian William Glenn Robertson briefly described the baptisms in a book whose title, *River of Death*, alludes to the creek's darker history. The creek flows downstream to the Tennessee River at Chattanooga, where a water-born epidemic of Yellow Fever killed 366 citizens in 1878. Contrary to Pvt. Willard's written recollection, modern historians describe the creek as being brown and slow moving.[41]

Union Brig. Gen. John B. Turchin (1822–1901)—a Russian-born Imperial Army colonel who immigrated to the U.S. in 1856—described West Chickamauga Creek as having "innumerable crooks or bends." The creek flows northeast from McLemore's Cove, where Lookout Mountain and Pigeon Mountain meet. According to Turchin, the Chickamauga's banks "are in many places high and precipitous," and the valley on the west side of the creek is "a table-land, but slightly rolling, gradually rising" and "covered with scattered timber, principally oak, the woods in places being filled with thick underbrush."[42]

Chickamauga Farmsteads

> *The battle hadn't been going long when one of my brothers was brought to the house wounded. A few hours later another brother who had been hurt in the fight was brought there. ... The next morning we had the neighbors come and make a coffin and put the body into it. ... Some of the neighbors sang at the grave, and there we buried my brother while the battle was still goin' on.*[43]
> ~ Anonymous twelve-year-old boy at home, Chickamauga

Chickamauga's history pre-dates the battle that destroyed farming families in 1863. Before European-Americans claimed the bottomlands of the Chickamauga, a band of Cherokee migrated south through the Tennessee Valley to escape America's revolutionary war with the British. They settled in an area that included Chickamauga Creek, and so Caucasian frontiersmen called them "Chickamauga Cherokee." They established towns on the banks of the creek—land that Steven E. Woodworth described as "blackjack oak thicket" that "rolled upward in forest-covered hills."[44]

Not sixty years later, during the Trail of Tears (1836–39), the U.S. government forcibly removed and relocated the Cherokee to what is now Oklahoma. By 1863, Americans of English descent had built twenty-four farms in the area currently bounded by the national military park at Chickamauga battlefield. The September conflict destroyed most homes here. The NPS rebuilt the Brotherton, Kelly, and Snodgrass cabins to approximate their 1863 appearance. In addition to houses and farm buildings, Chickamauga citizens set aside land for at least four family cemeteries (for the Dyer, Hunt, Patrick, and Snodgrass families). Park signs identify only Hunt Cemetery, which is in the southeast corner of the battlefield, near the creek.

A woody forest dominates the Chickamauga landscape. Oak, white pine, and red cedar are among the most pervasive species. In 1863, agricultural fields and meadows comprised only about 20 percent of the battlefield area, whereas today 10 percent of the park is field or mowed grass. Farmers lived in simple log cabins; raised hogs; and planted corn, hay, and fruit orchards. Hop clover, meadow fescue, mouse-ear chickweed, and other weedy plants are common.[45]

Chickamauga on a Bicycle

The next sections describe 1863 battle events on Chickamauga's farms. The battle's impact on local families is an important part of Civil War history, and farmsteads were important landmarks for the execution of tactical maneuvers. According to the NPS, "The few scattered farmhouses and fields, such as the Kelly, Brock, Brotherton, Snodgrass, and Viniard places, were the only landmarks for assembling and rallying units as the battle ebbed and flowed."[46]

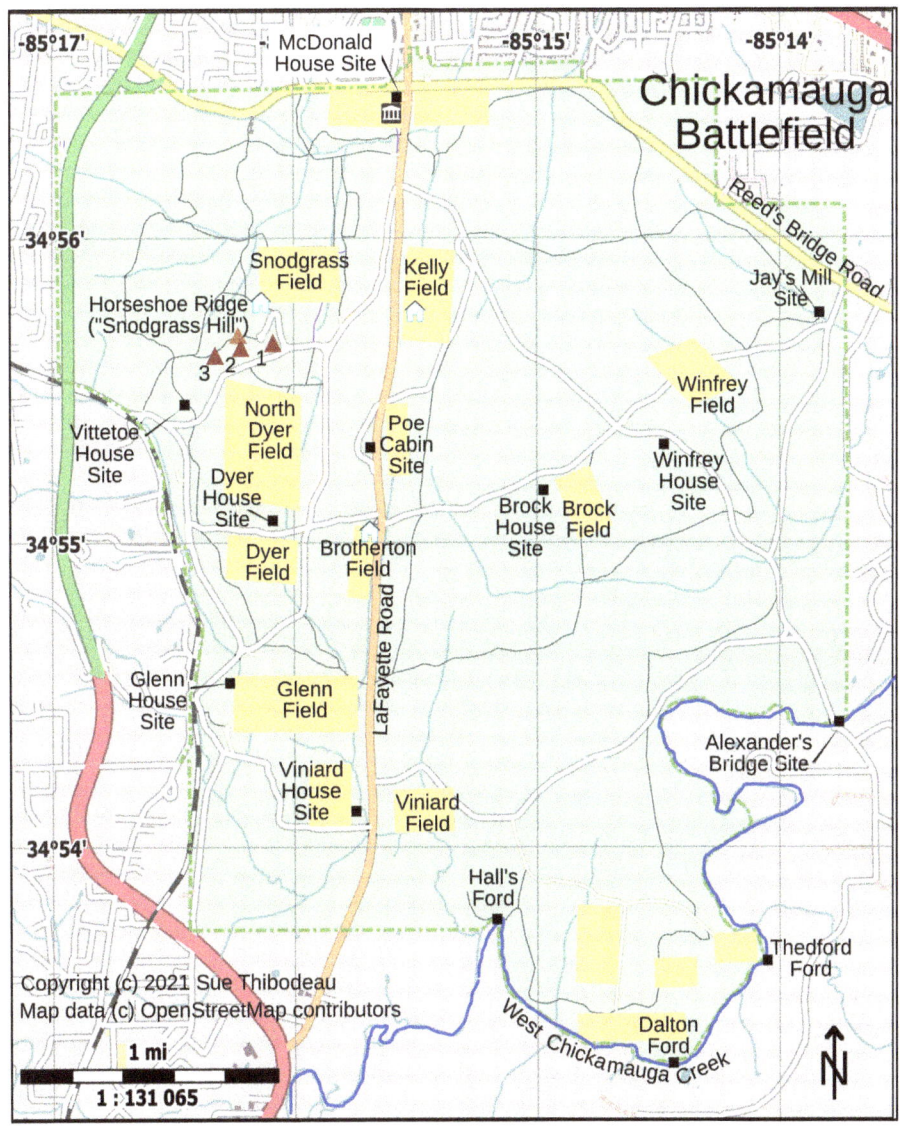

Map 7. Chickamauga Family Farms

Winfrey Field

> *The gallant Lieutenant Van Pelt was shot down at his guns, having fired 64 rounds into the midst of the enemy as they came charging down the hill ... The nature of my line, being in a right angle, the intricacies of the woods, overwhelming numbers, and the impetuosity of the charge rendered it impossible to withdraw in order, and not until they had reached a point near the road could order be restored.*[47]
> ~ Col. B.F. Scribner, 1st Brigade, Baird's Division, USA

Winfrey Field, Looking East from Northwest Corner

By the morning of September 19, Bragg's Confederate army had crossed Chickamauga Creek and pushed Rosecrans' Union army in a southwesterly direction. Fighting that day would move from Winfrey to Brock, Brotherton, and Viniard Fields. Thomas' 14th Corps anchored the Union left. They faced the Confederate right wing under Lt. Gen. Leonidas Polk. The conflict unfolded on the property of Mr. and Mrs. George Winfrey and their five children, Chap, Sampson, Adaline, May, and Minnie.[48]

Soldiers from Georgia and Mississippi forced Union Brig. Gen. Absalom Baird's midwesterners and U.S. Regulars out of the woods (visible in the photo, above) and into George Winfrey's small cornfield at an elevation of 730–40 feet. The fighting pit Baird against Confederate Brigs. Gen. St. John R. Liddell and S.R. Gist (both units from Walker's Reserve Corps). Liddell flanked Scribner's Brigade, and in the onslaught, Lt. George Van Pelt (1st Michigan Battery) fell dead. Col. Philemon Baldwin (USA) and Brig. Gen. Preston Smith (CSA) died around the same time. Adding to the melee, a nighttime flare-up tragically produced "friendly fire" deaths in Winfrey Field.[49]

Brock Field

> Before moving, I went to General Bragg himself... He informed me that... I must be governed by circumstances. Moving by the right flank in the direction indicated, from half a mile to a mile, we arrived near a corn-field, beyond which the heaviest firing was heard.[50]
> ~ Maj. Gen. Alexander P. Stewart, CSA

Brock Field, Looking South from Brotherton Road

From the woods on the left side of the photo, Confederate Maj. Gen. Benjamin F. Cheatham's division (men mostly from Tennessee, but also Georgia and Mississippi) attacked into John Brock's 740–50' elevation cornfield, which was larger than it is today.[51] Fortunately, by this point, the Brock family had fled to the Snodgrass ravine. Here, they joined the Brotherton, Kelly, McDonald, Mullis, Poe, Snodgrass, and Winfrey families. Notably, brothers William and John Brock arrived at Chickamauga as Confederate soldiers.[52] Union Maj. Gen. John M. Palmer's division of midwesterners fought Cheatham to a draw in what Woodworth called "a vicious close-range firefight."[53]

On Cheatham's left, Confederate Maj. Gen. Alexander P. Stewart's division (men mostly from Tennessee and Alabama) also attacked from the woods. Further south, one of Johnson's brigades breached a 600-yard gap in the Union line between the divisions of Brig. Gen. Jefferson C. Davis and Brig. Gen. Horatio P. Van Cleve, where "dense blackjack thickets reduced visibility in the woods to no more than fifty yards."[54]

Viniard Field

> *... It was here that some of the hardest fighting of the first day took place. Little is known of the Viniard family, they having come to the house only a short time before the battle.*[55]
> ~ Charles W. Lusk, *Chattanooga Times*, September 1923

In Viniard Field, an unassuming set of Union monuments marks one of the deadliest parts of Chickamauga Battlefield. Although the field's tragic and bloody history is like the back-and-forth fighting in The Cornfield (Battle of Antietam) and The Wheatfield (Battle of Gettysburg), Viniard Field is less well known. From the wooded line northwest of the Viniard house and field, Wilder's Lightning Brigade rained a blistering fire on Hood's Confederates who were attacking through the field. They were trying to cross LaFayette Road in an area now called the "Ditch of Death" due to the impact of Wilder's withering fire on September 19, 1863.

Most of Viniard Field is located on the southeast corner of LaFayette and Viniard-Alexander Roads. In the first photo, you can see monuments in the distance; these commemorate the service of Union soldiers from Illinois, Indiana, Michigan, Minnesota, Ohio, and Wisconsin. The second photo shows the field's extension to the west side of LaFayette Road, near where the Viniard house once stood. You can spot the Heg Monument, named for Col. Hans Heg, the Norwegian commander of the 15th Wisconsin. He received a mortal wound at this location.[56]

Looking Southeast over LaFayette Road to Viniard Field (in the distance, 710' elevation)

Looking West Beyond Heg Memorial to Wilder's Brigade Position (in the distance)

Chickamauga on a Bicycle

Brotherton Field

> *The Brothertons had four cows which somehow escaped the hunger of the foragers and the fury of the battle. Adaline Brotherton went once each day, after the battle, to their home and milked these cows, and turned the milk over to the nurses to be fed to the wounded soldiers who filled their yard and home.*[57]
> ~ Charles W. Lusk, *Chattanooga Times*, September 1923

Brotherton Cabin
750' elevation

Cannon and Marker, Left Wing of the Army of Tennessee

Nearly four years prior to the Battle of Chickamauga, George and Mary Brotherton moved to this area from Virginia. They lived in this (now reconstructed) 21' x 20' single-room log cabin with a stone foundation with their seven children. Another daughter, Sarah, had married Larkin H. Poe and lived nearby. One son, Thomas, "knew every pig trail through these woods," and so served in the Confederate army as a scout for Lt. Gen. James Longstreet. Another son, James L., also fought with the Confederate army at Chickamauga. When the battle ended, the Brothertons found and buried in one grave nine Union soldiers on their property.[58]

Before 11:00 a.m. on Sunday, September 20, Longstreet's Confederates were assembling in columns on the east side of LaFayette Road, where dense thickets and vines threatened to choke their efforts. Confederate skirmishers around and in the Brotherton cabin harassed soldiers in Brig. Gen. Thomas J. Wood's division. But the Union line was holding on the west side of LaFayette Road on the small ridge that was the Brotherton cornfield, which stretched "about 600 yards along the road and perhaps 150 feet back from the road to the western woodline."[59]

Then around 11:00 a.m.—behind the cabin and toward the woods on the cabin's west side—a 700-yard gap opened in the Union line around the same time that Longstreet ordered an all-out assault across LaFayette Road. Rosecrans mistakenly ordered Wood to move out of line for the purpose of helping Thomas on the left. At 11:10 a.m., the Confederate left wing broke through the gap and drove the Army of the Cumberland westward and northward through Dyer Field. Here, they held a defensive position on the hills of Horseshoe Ridge, including Snodgrass Hill.

Often called, "Longstreet's Breakthrough," this action was the turning point of the Battle of Chickamauga. According to an NPS wayside exhibit near the Brotherton Cabin, "so overwhelming was the assault that nearly one-third of the Union army was driven from the field, including its commander General Rosecrans."[60]

Looking South at the Brotherton Cabin from Dyer Road

In this general area, you will find regimental and artillery battery monuments or markers for the following states: Arkansas, Indiana, Illinois, Kansas, Michigan, Pennsylvania, and Tennessee. For a walking tour, Robert L. Carter's guidebook, *Longstreet's Breakthrough at Chickamauga: Accidental Victory*, is highly recommended.[61]

Poe Field

> *I began to see dead soldiers, yet unburied, lying in and near the road. I rode on, turning my horse first to the right and then to the left to avoid the thick-strewn bodies. In places I saw where great trees had been splintered by shells and riddled by bullets.*[62]
> ~ Larkin H. Poe, *Chattanooga Times*, September 1923

Looking West Over LaFayette Road from Poe Cabin Site

When Pvt. Larkin Poe returned to his property, the battle had ended three days earlier. Bivouacked nearby with Co. K, 4th Georgia Cavalry, Poe took leave to find his family. He rode to the Brotherton cabin, found his father-in-law, and then rode to the Poe property to find "the house in ashes and his family gone." Later that night, Poe found his wife Sarah and two young children, Hilliard and Gussie, camped in the Snodgrass ravine with about sixty other refugees.[63]

According to Confederate Maj. Gen. Simon B. Buckner, Poe's house was burning on September 20. When shells hit Union artillery near the house, it caught fire.[64] Today, a historic marker identifies the Poe House Site on a commemorative era road named Poe Road. The road cuts through a 760' elevation field that marks the continuation of the Union position along Battleline Road. The fighting in Poe Field was terribly chaotic. According to NPS historian James R. Sullivan, after Longstreet's breakthrough and turn to the right, the Confederate batteries in Poe Field were "so situated that it would appear they must have fired into their own infantry."[65]

Glenn Field

> *The brigade was halted and faced the rapidly approaching assault of the enemy from the east, the battery coming into position under a most destructive fire of musketry. ... Casualties: Men killed 1, wounded 3; officers captured 1; limbers lost 2.*
> ~ Tablet for Battery G, 1st Missouri Light Artillery, USA

Cannons and cast-iron marker: Battery G, 1st MO Light Artillery.

The Union cannon, shown above, points southeast over Glenn Field to the tree line from which Longstreet's Confederate columns attacked west over LaFayette Road on September 20, 1863. The marker is on the south end of Chickamauga-Vittetoe Road, where the Missouri battery withdrew around noon. This is the south slope of Lytle Hill (740–50' elevation), named for Union Brig. Gen. William H. Lytle, who was shot in the spine and face while his brigade and that of the Missouri battery (both in Sheridan's Division) fought to hold the line. Lytle died about 300 yards north of here.[66]

Rosecrans' headquarters at the Widow Glenn's house was also nearby, to the northwest and closer to Dyer Road.[67] For more about the Glenn family, see p. 39.

Dyer Field

> *The hospital of the First Division was established on the morning of the 19th at Dyer's house, which at that time was located in the rear of the right of this corps. A fine spring, a number of outbuildings, and plenty of straw near by rendered this a desirable locality for hospital purposes.*[68]
> ~ Surgeon Ferdinand H. Gross, U.S. Army, Medical Director

When the Union line collapsed at the Brotherton Farm and Longstreet's Confederate left wing charged over LaFayette Road and into Dyer Field, Ellen Dyer and her children were not at home. Like their neighbors, they fled northwest to a wooded area on the Snodgrass property so that they could survive the battle. The commemorative marker for the house site is on the north side of Dyer Road, which bisects the field. The family cemetery was due west.

On the morning of September 19, the Union 14th Corps (Thomas) established its 1st Division (Baird) hospital on the Dyer property, elevation 760–70'. By around 5:00 p.m., Confederate grape and canister fire made the hospital "entirely unsafe for the wounded," so medics evacuated wounded men to Crawfish Springs. After the evacuation, surgeons returned to Dyer Field hospital for the balance of the day. On the morning of September 20, medics evacuated about forty remaining wounded soldiers prior to the Union line collapsing under Longstreet's attack through a gap at the Brotherton Farm.[69] The Confederates shattered the Union line, and the Dyer property fell to Bragg's army, which scrambled to regroup and focus their attack to the northern hills of Horseshoe Ridge and the Snodgrass farm.

Ellen's husband, Spill B. Dyer, was the prosperous head of the family farm that expanded to support fifteen children, and eventually eleven sets of grandchildren. Dyer sold his farm to the U.S. government in 1890. This closed a significant chapter in his life, having previously served in the Confederate army as a courier for Gen. Bragg and a guide for Maj. Gen. Preston.[70]

Spill's brother, John also fought for the Confederate army at Chickamauga. However, their father, Robert was "picked up by Gen. Rosecrans and used as a guide." Being "much averse" to the Union general taking him to Chattanooga, the elder Dyer "managed to escape after accompanying the general about a mile from the field."[71]

Snodgrass Hill

> *The heights extending from the Vidito [sic] house across to the Snodgrass house gave the enemy strong ground upon which to rally. Here he gathered most of his broken forces and re-enforced them.*[72]
> ~ Lt. Gen. James Longstreet, Left Wing Commander, CSA

Snodgrass Cabin

This 26' x 20' reconstructed single-room log cabin was once the property of Virginia natives George and Elizabeth Snodgrass and their large family (his third wife) and their seven children at home. The cabin stands in an 800–820' elevation field on Snodgrass Hill.[73]

The wooded area northwest of the Snodgrass cabin is the ravine to which Chickamauga families fled the battle for eight days. While the family camped deep in the woods without shelter, one of Mr. Snodgrass' sons, Charles, fought at Chickamauga as a soldier in the Confederate army. Too old for military service, the sixty-year-old George Washington Snodgrass had planted crops in their fields, and hungry soldiers foraged everything edible. The Snodgrass property was so damaged by wounded soldiers that the family, now destitute, never lived there again. The cabin had been repurposed as a Union field hospital. "[N]othing remained but broken and bloodstained furniture and other fearful evidences of the agony of the wounded."[74]

Grazing farm animals kept clean the underbrush of the field's surrounding trees, making visibility in these wooded areas about 200–300 yards.[75] Farther south and more thickly wooded, Horseshoe Ridge includes three hills (elevation 850-940') that run in a longitudinal direction. This is where the Union army had dug in after Longstreet's men routed them there at around 11:15 a.m. on Sunday, September 20, 1963.

The Confederates continued their attack by moving north through the Dyer Field and trying repeatedly to conquer the ridge. In Robert L. Carter's excellent tour book, *The Fight for Snodgrass Hill and the*

Chickamauga on a Bicycle

Rock of Chickamauga, he writes that "the confounding series of hills and ravines, the curvature of the ridge crests, and the lack of visibility in the woods created a tactical nightmare for the Confederates trying to take Horseshoe Ridge."[76]

Looking Northeast from Snodgrass Cabin Area

Union Brig. Gen. John M. Brannan's 3rd division (Thomas' 14th Corps), plus fragments of the following divisions occupied the ridge: Maj. Gen. James S. Negley's 3rd division (Thomas' 14th Corps); Brig. Gen. Thomas J. Wood's 1st division (Crittenden's 21st Corps); and Brig. Gen. Horatio P. Van Cleve's 3rd division (Crittenden's 21st Corps). At about 2 p.m., Brig. Gen. James B. Steedman's 1st division (Granger's Reserve Corps) arrived with much-needed reinforcements and ammunition. At dusk, however, the Army of the Cumberland began to withdraw toward McFarland's Gap and into Rossville.

If you explore the Snodgrass Hill area on foot, you will find these Union monuments: Illinois, Indiana, Kentucky, Michigan, Minnesota, Ohio, Tennessee, and U.S. Regulars. These states erected Confederate monuments on the hill: Alabama, Kentucky, North Carolina, and South Carolina. Unfortunately, there are currently no bicycle racks in this area of the battlefield (and in fact, the only racks are at the Visitor Center).

Kelly Field

> *Here the conflict again renewed—a terrible conflict, with artillery and small-arms; a hand-to-hand fight, lasting far more than one and a half hours, the streams of smoke and fire from the enemy's guns reaching our lines, throwing missiles of death in every direction; and just at the going down of the sun their works were forced, and the enemy fled in wild confusion in every direction, giving a complete victory to our arms.*[77]
> ~ Col. George H. Nixon, 48th Tennessee Infantry, CSA

Kelly House

Elisha Kelly rented the 750-acre farm from his brother, Elijah, and lived in what was a 24' x 20' single-room cabin with his wife and five or six children. According to the NPS, newspapers used as insulation in the walls of the Kelly Cabin indicate that the family built the structure "shortly after the war," and so the exact location of the original structure cannot be confirmed.[78]

In the early evening of September 20, Confederate Col. Nixon's Tennessee regiment attacked the Union left flank on the east edge of Kelly Field, a 760' elevation ridge on Elijah Kelly's farm. Col. Nixon's command was part of a much larger force in Brig. Gen. Lucius E.

Polk's brigade, Cleburne's Division. Moreover, this was the second day that the right wing of the Confederate army repeatedly struck the Union line that extended from Kelly Field southward along modern-day Battleline Road. But the line would not break. "[B]reastworks erected of logs and rail picketing, covered with green brush" protected Union soldiers as they punished Confederate attackers with artillery and small-arms fire that Col. Nixon described as "one of the most destructive fires ever witnessed by any troops during the war."[79]

It would not have been possible for the Kelly family to stay here during the battle. One son, George Kelly, fought in the 1st Georgia Infantry (CSA) alongside his neighbors, William C. McDonald and John Ingraham. Without George at home, the entire Kelly family sought refuge on the Snodgrass property with other neighboring families.[80] As the conflict on Snodgrass Hill ended, at about 4:30 p.m., Thomas issued orders for the Federal men in Kelly Field to retreat and leave the field.

McDonald Field

> *[It was] a mad, irregular battle, very much resembling guerilla warfare on a vast scale, in which one army was bushwhacking the other, and wherein all the science and the art of war went for nothing.*[81]
> ~ Brig. Gen. John B. Turchin, USA

Turchin's description of the Battle of Chickamauga applies particularly well to the wildly chaotic fighting in McDonald's Field on September 20, 1863. Thomas ordered Turchin to clear this 760' elevation field to open a pathway for soldiers in Kelly Field to retreat. But Turchin did not know at first what direction to turn and face his Confederate opponents in Liddell's Brigade of men from Arkansas and Louisiana (under Col. Daniel C. Govan). David C. Powell quoted Pvt. Rob Abney of the 36th Ohio as saying, "So sudden was our [Turchin's Brigade] attack that we had our bayonets in their teeth before they knew it and in 15 seconds the whole plain was a mass of fleeing butternuts."[82]

With Brig. Gen. Edward C. Walthall's Mississippi brigade thus exposed and under fire from multiple directions, Walthall fell back. And that forced Capt. William H. Fowler's Alabama Battery to do the same. In the end, the Army of the Cumberland successfully left the field to rejoin its commander in Chattanooga. Here is how

Chapter 1

Bicycling Chickamauga Battlefield

Confederate Brig. Gen. St. John R. Liddell described the aftermath of the engagement in McDonald Field:

> The Federals had left their works at this time in retreat from the field and our whole line was moving upon them. After reforming my command I moved it to the position on the Chattanooga road near McDonald's house, where it bivouacked on the ground it was ordered to hold. At 10 o'clock Sunday night my scouts reported that the enemy had entirely withdrawn from the field and disappeared...[83]
> ~ Brig. Gen. St. John R. Liddell, CSA

McDonald Field (Fowler's Alabama Battery)

This closing drama on the Chickamauga battlefield played out on the property of Tennessee natives John and Pricilla McDonald. At the time of the battle, the family had lived here for seventeen years, and three children were at home in 1863: William C., Amanda L., and Charles. William would marry Adaline Brotherton and share his memories of the battle with the *Chattanooga Times* in 1923. Notably, William Calvin McDonald had enlisted in the Confederate army in 1861 as a soldier in the 26th Tennessee Infantry and later transferred to the 1st Georgia Infantry. During the Battle of Chickamauga, William worked as a teamster and after the battle transported wounded soldiers to hospitals in Dalton and Ringgold.[84]

What Next?

Chapter 1, "Chickamauga on a Bicycle," provides an overview of the battlefield road network; a high-level summary of three different sets of bicycle routes; and a lengthy visual presentation of significant physical and natural landmarks at Chickamauga Battlefield. The chapter's objective is to provide a solid introduction to what a bicyclist can see, feel, and learn on a 12.6-mile ride. It also sets the stage for mastering the high-level battle chronology that Chapter 2 "The Battle of Chickamauga," outlines.

Chapter 2 is a concise summary of 1863 battlefield events that relies heavily on maps and photos so that it is easier to learn on two wheels. But before turning to Chapter 2, please first familiarize yourself with the next three tables. Collectively, these tables give a "who's who" introduction to the names of Union and Confederate officers who appear on park wayside exhibits and other mini histories, including this guidebook. As you read Chapter 2, you may want to refer to Tables 2–4 to confirm your understanding of the Battle of Chickamauga.

Table 2. State Affiliations for Each Army

STATES AT THE BATTLE OF CHICKAMAUGA

USA / Federal / Union (7 states + 3 divided + 1 other*):

Indiana	Minnesota	Tennessee
Illinois	Missouri	*United States Regulars
Kentucky	Ohio	Wisconsin
Michigan	Pennsylvania	

CSA / Confederate (9 states + 3 divided):

Alabama	Kentucky	North Carolina
Arkansas	Louisiana	South Carolina
Florida	Mississippi	Tennessee
Georgia	Missouri	Texas

An italicized state name indicates that the state mustered soldiers to fight for both the USA and CSA at the Battle of Chickamauga.

Table 3. USA Abbreviated Order of Battle

ARMY OF THE CUMBERLAND, MAJ. GEN. WILLIAM S. ROSECRANS

14th Corps, Maj. Gen. George H. Thomas

1st Div., Brig. Gen. Absalom Baird	[Scribner, Starkweather, J.H. King]
2nd Div., Maj. Gen. James S. Negley	[J. Beatty, Stanley, Sirwell]
3rd Div., Brig. Gen. John M. Brannan	[Connell, Croxton, Van Derveer]
4th Div., Maj. Gen. Joseph J. Reynolds	[Wilder detached, E. King, Turchin]

20th Corps, Maj. Gen. Alexander McDowell McCook

1st Div., Brig. Gen. Jefferson C. Davis	[Post, Carlin, Heg]
2nd Div., Brig. Gen. Richard W. Johnson	[Willich, Dodge, Baldwin]
3rd Div., Maj. Gen. Philip H. Sheridan	[Lytle, Laiboldt, Bradley]

21st Corps, Maj. Gen. Thomas L. Crittenden

1st Div., Brig. Gen. Thomas J. Wood	[Buell, Wagner, Harker]
2nd Div., Maj. Gen. John M. Palmer	[Cruft, Hazen, Grose]
3rd Div., Brig. Gen. Horatio P. Van Cleve	[S. Beatty, Dick, Barnes]

Reserve Corps, Maj. Gen. Gordon Granger

1st Div., Brig. Gen. James B. Steedman	[Whitaker, J.G. Mitchell]
2nd Div., Col. Daniel McCook	[D. McCook]

Cavalry Corps, Brig. Gen. Robert B. Mitchell

1st Div., Col. Edward M. McCook	[Campbell, Ray, Watkins]
2nd Div., Brig. Gen. George Crook	[Minty, Long]

Key: Brackets indicate brigade commanders.

Note: At the Battle of Chickamauga, Maj. Gen. William S. Rosecrans' Chief of Staff was James A. Garfield, the future 20th president of the United States. In July 1881, after only four months in office, an assassin shot President Garfield in a Washington, DC train station. He died on September 19, 1881, at the age of forty-nine from an infection associated with his wounds.

Table 4. CSA Abbreviated Order of Battle
ARMY OF TENNESSEE, GEN. BRAXTON BRAGG

Lt. Gen. Leonidas Polk's Command (Right Wing)

    Maj. Gen. B.F. Cheatham's Div.   [Jackson, Maney, Smith, Strahl, Wright]
    Lt. Gen. Daniel H. Hill's Corps
        Maj. Gen. P.R. Cleburne's Div.   [Deshler, L.E. Polk, Wood]
        Maj. Gen. John C. Breckinridge's Div.   [Adams, Helm, Stovall]
    Maj. Gen. W.H.T. Walker's Reserve Corps
        Brig. Gen. S.R. Gist's (Walker's) Div.   [Ector, Wilson]
        Brig. Gen. St. John R. Liddell's Div.   [Govan, Walthall]

Lt. Gen. James Longstreet's Command (Left Wing)

    *Maj. Gen. T.C. Hindman's Div.   [Anderson, Deas, Manigault]
    *Maj. Gen. Simon B. Buckner's Corps
        *Maj. Gen. Alexander P. Stewart's Div.   [Bate, Brown, Clayton]
        *Brig. Gen. William Preston's Div.   [Gracie, Trigg, Kelly]
        **Brig. Gen. Bushrod R. Johnson's Div.   [Fulton, Gregg, McNair]
    Maj. Gen. John B. Hood's (Longstreet's) Corps
        Brig. Gen. J. B. Kershaw's (McLaws') Div.   [Humphreys, Kershaw]
        Brig. Gen. E.M. Law's (Hood's) Div.   [Benning, Sheffield, Robertson]
    Col. E. Porter Alexander's Corps Artillery
    Maj. Felix H. Robertson's Reserve Artillery
    Brig. Gen. Nathan B. Forrest's Cavalry Corps
        Brig. Gen. Frank C. Armstrong's Div.   [Dibrell, J.T. Wheeler]
        Brig. Gen. John Pegram's Div.   [Davidson, Scott]
    Maj. Gen. Joseph Wheeler's Cavalry Corps
        Brig. Gen. John A. Wharton's Div.   [Crews, T. Harrison]
        Brig. Gen. William T. Martin's Div.   [Morgan, Russell]

Key: Brackets indicate brigade commanders.

* Matching Sullivan and Cozzens.[85] Powell lists Hindman, Buckner, Stewart, and Preston under Polk's Corps. (Longstreet was in-transit on Sept. 18–19).
** Matching Sullivan and Cozzens.[86] Powell lists Johnson under Hood's Corps. (Created in mid-September, Johnson's Division was provisional).

Note: At Chickamauga, Maj. Gen. John C. Breckinridge commanded a division. But from 1857–1861, he was Vice President of the United States.

2. The Battle of Chickamauga

> It seems to me that the élan of the Southern soldier was never seen after Chickamauga—that brilliant dash which had distinguished him was gone forever. ... He fought stoutly to the last, but, after Chickamauga, with the sullenness of despair and without the enthusiasm of hope. That "barren victory" sealed the fate the Southern Confederacy.[87]
> ~ Lt. Gen. Daniel H. Hill, CSA

A Concise Overview of Battlefield Events

In September 18–20, 1863, Gen. Braxton Bragg's Army of Tennessee scored a Confederate victory in northwest Georgia. After three days of skirmishing, attacks, and counterattacks through forests and fields, Bragg forced Union Maj. Gen. William S. Rosecrans' Army of the Cumberland to retreat to Chattanooga and submit to a siege that threatened to choke the Union army. For the Confederacy, the Battle of Chickamauga was a costly but important reversal of momentum. Afterall, Rosecrans had been outmaneuvering Bragg all summer—even taking with ease the critical river and railroad hub of Chattanooga. Further, these losses in Tennessee aggravated the morale-crushing failures from eleven weeks earlier, at Gettysburg and Vicksburg. But September turned the Confederate tide when the Army of Tennessee delivered to the Union army its greatest defeat in the western theater. After the Battle of Chickamauga, Rosecrans vacated Georgia; Bragg held the mountains surrounding Chattanooga; and the battle claimed 16,170 Union and 18,545 Confederate casualties, second only to Gettysburg's count.[88]

But Bragg's victory at Chickamauga faded quickly. He did not destroy or pursue the Army of the Cumberland. In October, Maj. Gen. Ulysses S. Grant broke Bragg's siege, fortified the city's supply chain, and consolidated the Union armies now under his control. Then in November 23–25, Grant won a series of victories with the help of Gens. Thomas, Sherman, and Hooker. In retrospect, the Battle of Chickamauga marked the "death knell of the Confederacy."[89]

With seventy-five total brigades on the battlefield, and so much confusion due to poor visibility and garbled orders, historians often identify the Battle of Chickamauga as the most confusing battle of the

U.S. Civil War. According to historian Glenn Tucker, the battle was "more of a series of desperate struggles between groups in the thickets than grand sweeps over which generals of corps or divisions had control."[90] The following sections summarize the battle in both narrative and map form. See pp. 68–69 for help remembering the names and roles of commanders.

Friday, September 18, 1863

[See map, p. 76]. Bragg's plan was to cross Chickamauga Creek from the east side and drive Rosecrans' army southwest, away from Chattanooga. However, on September 18, starting in the late morning and lasting until around 4 p.m., Union Col. Minty's brigade delayed Confederate Brig. Gen. Bushrod R. Johnson's division at Reed's Bridge. Johnson eventually prevailed against Minty. About the same time, Col. Wilder's Union mounted infantry—equipped with Spencer repeating rifles—held-off the Confederates at Alexander's Bridge; that is, until Brig. Gen. Liddell's division crossed the creek.

Rosecrans aimed to protect the roads north to Chattanooga when he sent two divisions of Maj. Gen. George H. Thomas' 14th Corps on an all-night march north to the Kelly Farm. There, Brig. Gens. Brannan and Baird secured the Union left flank on the east side of LaFayette Road.[91] By the next morning, Bragg's Army of Tennessee had crossed Chickamauga Creek. They were surprised to find the Union army anchored that far north behind formidable breastworks along modern-day Battleline Road.

Saturday, September 19, 1863

[See map, p. 77]. Around 7 a.m., the battle ignited when Brannan and Baird engaged an unexpectedly large Confederate force (under Brig. Gen. Nathan B. Forrest) on the north end of the battlefield. The 1st Georgia Cavalry captured skirmishers in Col. Daniel McCook's brigade from Illinois and Ohio. Then for six hours, the battle grew as each army incrementally added brigades in a desperate effort to control a fight that waxed and waned. They fought in the deep woods of the northeast sector of the battlefield, but also in Winfrey Field. The following infantry units, among others, joined the contest: Croxton, Connell, Van Derveer, Palmer, and R.W. Johnson (for Rosecrans); and Wilson, Ector, Liddell, and Cheatham (for Bragg).

The Battle of Chickamauga

By the early afternoon, fighting rolled into Brock Field, where Cheatham's Confederates attacked Palmer's Federals. Farther west on the Brotherton Farm, "Stewart's Attack" pitted Stewart's Confederates against Van Cleve. Further south, the Confederate left attacked the Union right at the Viniard Farm.

Union Maj. Gen. Thomas L. Crittenden (21st Corps) commanded the line on the Viniard Farm. His command included elements of McCook's 20th Corps (Davis) and Thomas' 14th Corps (Wilder). In the afternoon, Wilder's Lightning Brigade repeatedly repulsed the Confederates from behind log-and-rail breastworks, 400 yards west of LaFayette Road. Wilder's chief artillerist, Eli Lilly, reported that his battery "opened lively, the pieces being double-shotted with canister;" and that when Benning and Robertson's men reached the ravine, "they fell back in disorder."[92] Here, soldiers hid in the "Ditch of Death."

The back-and-forth fighting at Viniard Farm was among the bloodiest in U.S. Civil War history. Crittenden attacked eastward through the field to attack Johnson and Law. But Johnson moved north to flank Van Cleve on the Brotherton Farm, only to be driven back. Historian Steven E. Woodworth described events this way:

> ... in all the confusion and the shuffling of divisions from different corps past and around each other and up the LaFayette Road, Rosecrans had gotten his army tangled up with itself, and south of Van Cleve a yawning gap in the Union line left a half mile of countryside devoid of Union troops. Ordinarily an error such as this would have been obvious to both sides, but in these woods and thickets, officers could only stumble on the truth.[93]

By 4:30 p.m., Hood's Confederates (Benning, Robertson) routed Davis (Heg, Carlin). Heg fell with a mortal wound. Around 5:30 p.m., Negley's Union division drove back Stewart. Except for "Cleburne's Night Attack" in Winfrey Field, the fighting ended for the day. Brigade commanders Baldwin, Deshler, and Smith fell with mortal wounds. The Union maintained a strong defensive line anchored at the Kelly Farm that extended south through the Viniard Farm.

Around 11 p.m., Lt. Gen. James Longstreet and his divisions arrived on the battlefield to form the left wing of Bragg's Army. Lt. Gen. Leonidas Polk would command the right wing. The Confederate fighting force now outnumbered that of the Federals.

Sunday, September 20, 1863

[See map, p. 78]. Bragg ordered Polk to attack early in the morning, but his attack did not begin until 9:30 a.m., which was long after Longstreet was ready to commit six divisions to the fight. His left wing command included Maj. Gen. Thomas C. Hindman's division and Brig. Gen. Bushrod R. Johnon's provisional division (both of the Army of Tennessee); Maj. Gen. Simon B. Buckner's Corps (Stewart and Preston's Divisions, formerly of the Army of East Tennessee); and Longstreet's Corps (McLaws/Kershaws' and Hood/Law's Divisions, Army of Northern Virginia).

For one-and-one-half hours, Bragg's army pounded Thomas' line. From Polk's right wing, two divisions from Lt. Gen. D.H. Hill's Corps attacked. Men from Alabama, Louisiana, and Kentucky delivered "Breckinridge's Assault," and men from Arkansas and Tennessee formed "Cleburne's Assault." Later, about one hour into the fight, Longstreet's left wing entered the fray, starting with Stewart's Division.

Then came the fateful moment of the day. After repeated requests from Thomas to move reinforcements to the army's left flank anchored at the Kelly Farm, Rosecrans ordered Brig. Gen. Thomas J. Wood (Crittenden's Corps) to leave the line near the Brotherton Farm. But rather than affect a move to strengthen the Union left, the order was part of a communication mix-up that caused an immediate 700-yard gap in the Union line, just west of Longstreet's massive columns of Confederate infantry. At 11:00 a.m., the gap opened about the same time that Longstreet ordered Hood and Hindman to attack from the woods on the east side of LaFayette Road. Johnson's men (Buckner's Corps) lined up first in the column, and yet, without detracting from Johnson's full participation, Longstreet credited Hood.

By 11:15 a.m., "Longstreet's Breakthrough" drove five Union divisions west through Dyer Field and then north to the high ground of Horseshoe Ridge. The routed divisions included Brannan from the 14th Corps; Davis and Sheridan from the 20th Corps; and Wood and Van Cleve from the 21st Corps. The Confederates drove Rosecrans, the commanding general of the Army of the Cumberland, off the battlefield. Chief of Staff and future President of the United States, James A. Garfield, accompanied Rosecrans.

[See map, p. 79]. Thomas assumed command and rallied the remnants of the Army of the Cumberland on Snodgrass Hill. As the

The Battle of Chickamauga

Union army regrouped, the Confederates captured fifteen cannons in Dyer Field. Union Col. Harker's brigade from Kentucky and Ohio slowed the advance of the Texas Brigade, thus providing valuable time for Thomas to build a line on the ridge. During this time, Maj. Gen. John B. Hood sustained a serious leg wound (at a site identified by a park sign on the west side of Glenn-Kelly Road). Shortly after that, and at about 1:00 p.m., Brig. Gen. Joseph B. Kershaw's South Carolinians made the first of several back-and-forth attacks that would continue until at least 7:00 that evening.

At about 2:00 p.m., another hero of Chickamauga arrived on the scene. This time, it was Union Maj. Gen. Gordon Granger, commander of the Reserve Corps, and his 1st division under Brig. Gen. James B. Steedman. Without orders, Granger arrived from the north after following the sound of the battle and bringing ammunition and men from Illinois, Indiana, Michigan, and Ohio.

As soldiers attacked and counterattacked each other on Horseshoe Ridge, Thomas ordered a Union retreat from Kelly Farm, even as Confederates kept attacking. By 6:00 p.m., the Federals had vacated Kelly Field, and Brannan's Division was retreating from Horseshoe Ridge. When the battle ended about one hour later, Bragg's army had captured three Union regiments. They captured one regiment from Negley's Division (Lt. Col. Stoughton's 21st Ohio) and two regiments from Steedman's Division (Col. Le Favour's 22nd Michigan and Col. Carlton's 89th Ohio). The rest of the Army of the Cumberland was on its way to Chattanooga through the gaps of Missionary Ridge.

On this day, three brigade commanders suffered fatal wounds: Helm (10 a.m.), Lytle (noon), and King (5 p.m.). Thomas earned the moniker, "Rock of Chickamauga," for having withstood repeated Confederate follow-up assaults on Horseshoe Ridge, holding the hill until after dark—and for enabling the army's ordered retreat to Chattanooga, where Rosecrans and two corps commanders (McCook and Crittenden) were waiting.

Thus victorious, Bragg's army took the battlefield but did not pursue Rosecrans or Thomas.

A Visual Summary of the Battle Phases

The next four maps summarize the Battle of Chickamauga.

Phase 1—Crossing Chickamauga Creek

> *[Mrs. Reed] remembers the roar of the battle on Friday when Wilder at Alexander's Bridge, and Minty at Reed's Bridge, were disputing the crossing of the Confederates. Her father refused at that time to leave the home...*[94]
> ~ Charles W. Lusk, *Chattanooga Times*, September 1923

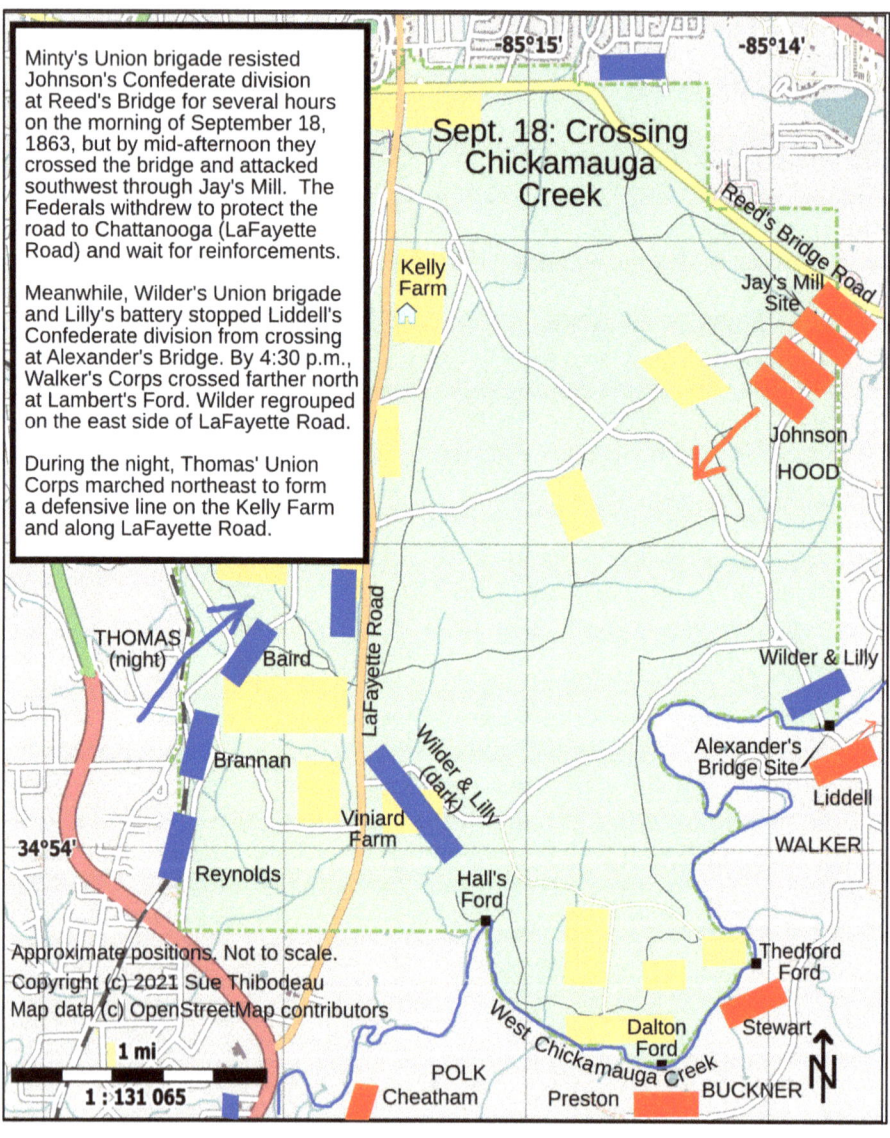

Map 8. September 18—Crossing Chickamauga Creek

The Battle of Chickamauga

Phase 2—The Fight East of LaFayette Road

> *All covered with dust... every soldier in that night's march knew that the confederate army was moving on the other side of the Chickamauga to gain the road [to Chattanooga].*[95]
> ~ Cpl. James Fenton, 19th Illinois Infantry, USA

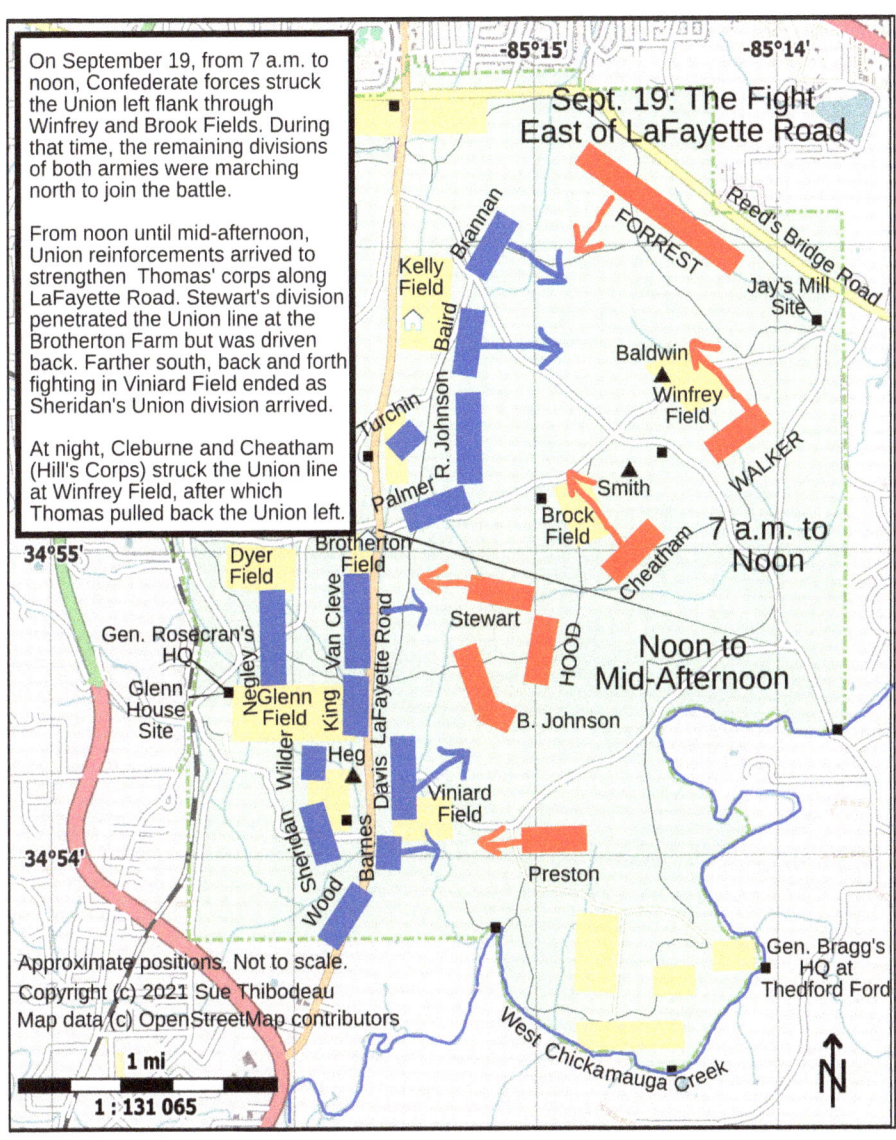

Map 9. September 19—The Fight East of LaFayette Road

Chapter 2

Phase 3—Longstreet's Breakthrough

The battlefield was in a rough and broken country, with trees and undergrowth, that ever since the creation had never been disturbed ... It looked wild, weird, uncivilized.[96]
~ Cpl. Sam Watkins, Co. H, 1st Tennessee Infantry, CSA

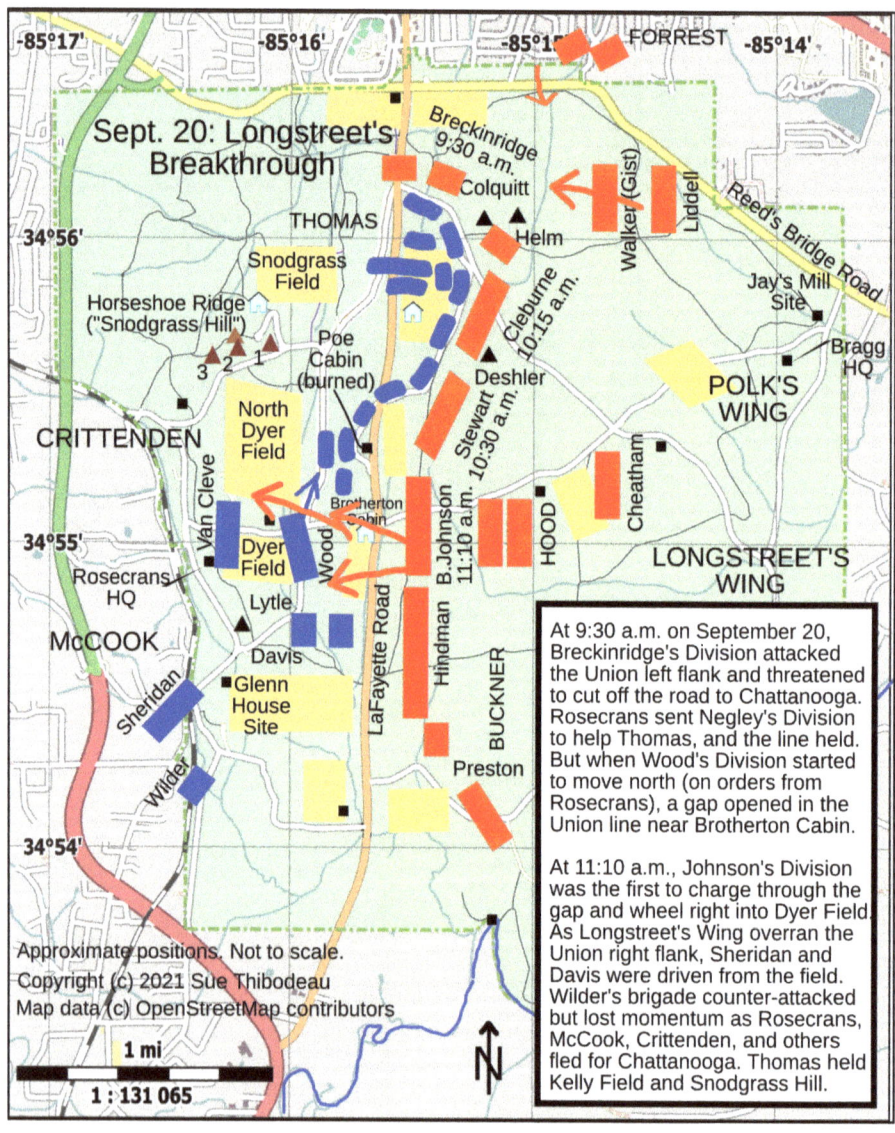

Map 10. September 20—Longstreet's Breakthrough

The Battle of Chickamauga

Phase 4—Stand-Off at Snodgrass Hill

Four desperate assaults and charges were made upon us, hurling upon us their immense columns, line after line, but as stubbornly were resisted.[97]
~ Col. R.H. Keeble, 23rd Tennessee Infantry, CSA

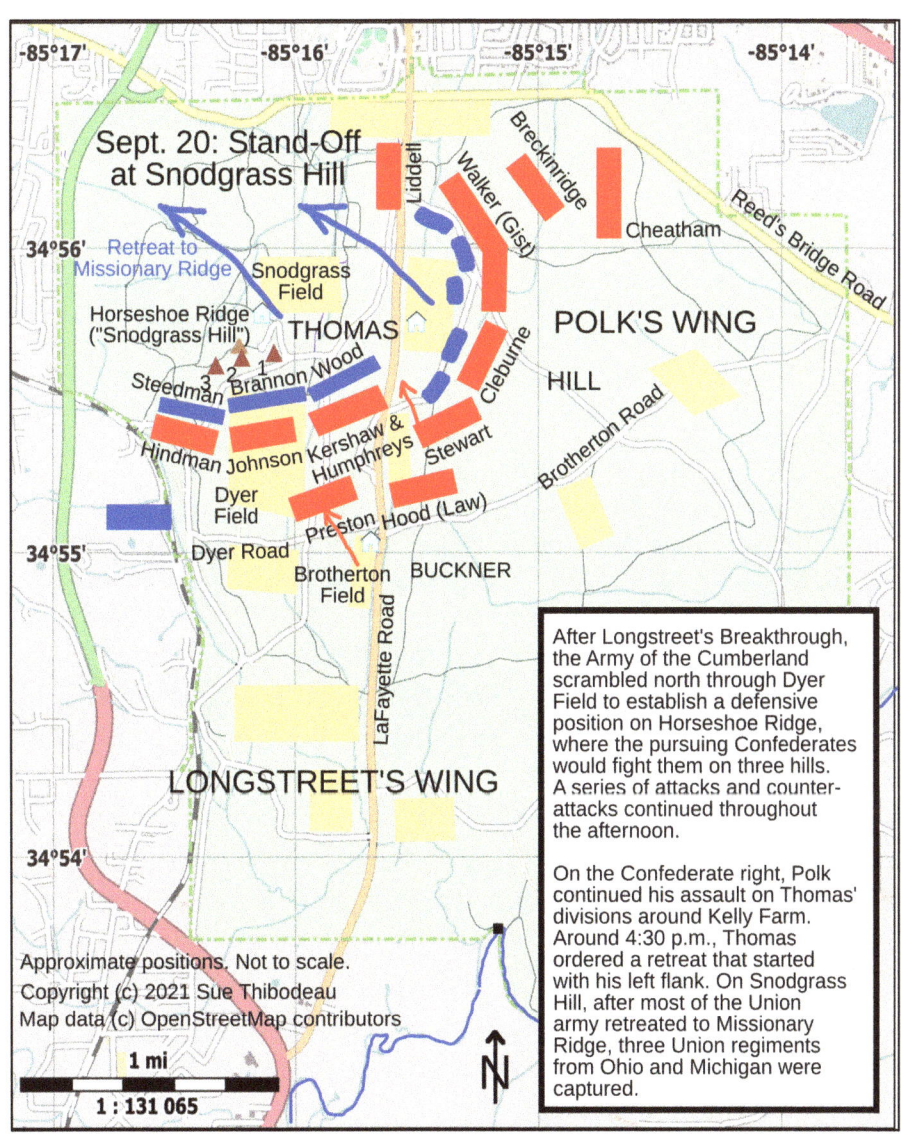

Map 11. September 20—Stand-Off at Snodgrass Hill

Battle Results

	Union	Confederate	Total
Dead:	1,657	2,312	3,969
Wounded:	9,756	14,674	24,430
Missing/Captured:	4,757	1,468	6,225
Total:	16,170	18,454	34,624

Table 5. Chickamauga Casualties

Source: American Battlefield Trust, https://www.battlefields.org/learn/civil-war/battles/chickamauga

After Longstreet's left wing of the Army of Tennessee broke through the Union line at the Brotherton Farm and sent the Army of the Cumberland reeling in disarray, the only Union corps commander that remained on the field was Thomas. The army's commander, Maj. Gen. Rosecrans, evacuated with two army corps and their commanders, McCook and Crittenden. Historian Bruce Catton called the Federal departure a "wild rout." Had it not been for Thomas' leadership on Snodgrass Hill and his orchestration of an orderly but dangerous retreat in the late afternoon, the entire Union army would have been destroyed. In the end, Gen. Braxton Bragg failed to pursue and crush the army, but instead, claimed the mountains around Chattanooga and put the Federals under a siege that threatened to starve the Army of the Cumberland. According to Catton:

> Supplies could reach Thomas only by the river itself, by the railroad which ran along the river's southern bank, or by the roads which similarly lay south of the river, and all of these were firmly controlled by Bragg. The Union army could not even retreat.[98]

The Battle of Chickamauga was a disastrous loss for the Union. But Bragg's siege failed when Grant leveraged his generals to open a supply line. Within weeks, Grant replaced Rosecrans with Thomas as the commander of the Army of the Cumberland. And then in late November 1863, Grant defeated Bragg's army in and around Chattanooga, which forced a Confederate retreat to Georgia.

The war in the western theater had taken a fatal turn for the Confederacy.

Human Consequences

After the Battle of Chickamauga, the U.S. Civil War would continue for another nineteen months, by which time the war claimed 1,125,453 casualties (killed, wounded, missing, or captured), according to the National Park Service. The count includes 204,100 soldiers killed in action, about 40 percent of whom no one could identify. According to one recent study, the war claimed 750,000 total deaths (up from the long-standing consensus of about 620,000).[99]

Subsumed by these national numbers is the local impact of death and destruction on Chickamauga's families. Georgia seceded from the Union on January 19, 1861,[100] so it is not surprising that Chickamauga's sons fought for the Confederacy and near their family homes. Notably, the singular marked military grave on the Chickamauga battlefield is for a local man named Pvt. John Ingraham—1st Georgia Infantry, J.K. Jackson's Brigade, Cheatham's Division—who died on September 19, 1863, "in heavy fighting that claimed the lives of more than 2,600 other Confederates." According to the nearby NPS wayside exhibit, "after the battle, friends searched for him, found his body, and buried it here."

Pvt. John Ingraham's Gravestone (Erected in 1959)

Ingraham's grave stands alone in a small patch of forest. A 4' x 8' black cast iron fence (c. 1974) surrounds the site. Look for a well-marked hiking trail lined with cedar chips on the south end of Alexander's Bridge Road (south side). On your way to Ingraham's grave, read the wayside exhibit entitled, "The Cost of Chickamauga."

Pvt. John Ingraham's Grave Site

It can be jolting to come across a solitary grave in a battlefield that claimed 34,624 casualties. With such a high casualty count, the battle's victors remained on the field to bury their dead in mass graves. Only later could families or states claim the bodies for re-burial elsewhere. Union dead, on the other hand, lay exposed to weather and foraging animals for three months; that is, until the army could recapture and subsequently move the bodies to what is now the Chattanooga National Cemetery.[101] Of the 13,000 total Civil War burials at the national cemetery, 1,789 graves are from the Chickamauga battlefield. There are exceptions. The Brotherton family buried nine Union soldiers on their property, but their identities are unknown, as is whether or where the men were reinterred.[102]

The battle resulted in a great loss of life. It also destroyed the land, homes, and livelihood of Chickamauga's farming families. The Poe house burned to the ground during the battle, and the McDonald house burned unexplainably a few days later. Most houses were torn apart and bloodstained by wounded men and the work of surgeons. The battle left families destitute, and they abandoned Chickamauga to build a new life elsewhere in Georgia, Tennessee, and Alabama. By 1891, when the federal government started buying (and later condemning) land for a national military park, most landowners no longer lived on battlefield land.[103]

The Battle of Chickamauga

> ### *Did you know ... ?*
>
> The Medal of Honor was awarded to nine soldiers for their actions at the Battle of Chickamauga.[104]

William J. Carson – Musician, Co. E, 1st Battalion, 15th U.S.. On September 19, Carson used his bugle to rally troops to check an attack. Awarded January 27, 1894. Born in Pennsylvania.

Orville T. Chamberlain – 2nd Lt., Co. G, 74th Indiana. On September 20, Chamberlain exposed himself to fire to gather ammunition. Awarded March 11, 1896. Born in Indiana.

Clinton A. Cilley – Capt., Co. C, 2nd Minnesota. On September 20, Cilley seized the colors of a retreating regiment and then led an attack. Awarded June 12, 1895.[105] Born in New Hampshire.

George S. Myers – Pvt., Co. E, 101st Ohio. On September 19, Myers saved the regimental colors. Awarded April 9, 1864. Born in Ohio.

Horace Porter – Capt., Ordnance Dept., U.S. Army. On September 20 and while under heavy fire, Porter rallied men to help wagons and batteries escape. Awarded July 8, 1902. Born in Pennsylvania.

Axel H. Reed – Sgt., Co. K, 2nd Minnesota. On September 19 and while under arrest, Reed secured a rifle and gallantly fought for two days. Awarded April 2, 1898. Born in Maine.

William E. Richey – Cpl., Co. A, 15th Ohio. On September 19, Richey single-handedly captured a Confederate major who was armed and mounted. Awarded November 9, 1893. Born in Ohio.

Anthony Taylor – 1st Lt., Co. A, 15th Pennsylvania Cavalry. On September 20, Taylor held ground to the last against overwhelming numbers. Awarded December 4, 1893.[106] Born in New Jersey.

William G. Whitney – Sgt., Co. B, 11th Michigan. On September 20, Whitney retrieved cartridge boxes from the dead and wounded at great risk to his safety. Awarded October 21, 1895. Born in Michigan.

Bicycling Chickamauga Battlefield

PART II: PLANNING YOUR TRIP

Bicycling Chickamauga Battlefield

3. Gathering Your Gear

To bicycle Chickamauga Battlefield, you need gear for a half-day ride on paved roadways through a densely wooded landscape. Your gear should make sense for Chickamauga's unique geography and weather. You need a bicycle, safety equipment, emergency supplies, food, water, and athletic clothing. (This chapter reproduces, and adapts for Chickamauga, content from *Bicycling Gettysburg National Military Park*, the first volume in Civil War Cycling's travel guide series).[107]

What Kind of Bicycle?

You need a bicycle that is in good repair and that fits your body. Beyond those basic requirements, a bike that has sophisticated gearing is far less important than installing rear red blinkies and front white lights. The reason is that visibility in the Chickamauga battlefield is sometimes difficult on shoulderless roads that wind through wooded park land. And unlike the Gettysburg and Antietam battlefields, Chickamauga's roads are mostly flat. Although the ride up Snodgrass Hill is a challenging ascent, it is the only significant climb where you need to know how to downshift without losing your chain. (Of course, you can always walk your bike).

Safety Equipment

Not surprisingly, daytime rides through Chickamauga Battlefield require a short list of basic safety gear. First, you need a bicycle helmet that fits your head.[108] Second, a bicycle mirror is helpful for sharing the road with motor vehicles. And finally, a front-mounted white light helps drivers to see your bicycle in shady areas or when the sky becomes overcast. Red blinkies mounted to your saddle or back rack provides extra visibility when cars moving 25–35 mph approach from your rear.

Emergency Supplies

You will also want to carry emergency tools like a portable tire pump and a bicycle lock. Here are some additional supplies that you could pack and carry on a routine basis:

Basic First Aid Kit
Small bandages
Antiseptic wipes
First aid cream
Antihistamine
Pain medication
Zinc oxide cream

Tiny Tools
Pocket knife or razor blade
Small flashlight
Tire patch kit, tubes
Tire levers, pressure gauge
Foldable toolkit
Duct tape, zip ties

Misc
Touring book, maps, pen
Insect (tick) repellent
Comb, hand sanitizer
Sunscreen, lip balm
Eyeglass wipes, eye drops
Sunglasses
Plastic bags for trash

Neck gaiter or wet cloth
Fluorescent ankle bands
Extra red LED lights
Cell phone, extra power
Camera, extra batteries
Identification, keys, cash
Extra plastic baggies

One straightforward way to protect your wallet and electronics from unexpected rain is to carry extra plastic baggies. For long rides on sizzling summer days, consider carrying a small container of zinc oxide cream to prevent chafing behind your knees. Packing small amenities like insect repellent and eyeglass wipes (for bugs that smash into your eyeglasses) can go a long way toward supporting a comfortable ride.

Due to the rural character of the Chickamauga battlefield, bicyclists should consider applying tick repellent to shoes and clothing before beginning a ride. It is a personal decision whether to use

Gathering Your Gear

essential oils (e.g., lemon eucalyptus, cedarwood, citronella, or lemongrass) or an insecticide like permethrin, but this guidebook recommends protection of some type.

The night before you begin a ride, check that you have fully charged your electronics. Have a plan for protecting your cell phone from extended, direct exposure to heat (so that your phone works in an emergency). Consider carrying a USB power core or, lacking that, preserving your cell phone's battery for emergency use only. Because cell tower signals can be intermittent, paper maps are highly recommended.

Food and Water

If you are bicycling for longer than 2-3 hours, you need a plan for replenishing your body with food, especially carbohydrates. Most bicyclists pack and carry complex carbohydrates, especially hardy fruits and vegetables, and a small amount of protein (nuts).

More important than food, however, is a way to carry water. Refillable water bottles or backpack hydration systems are good options. Except for the Visitor Center restrooms, you will not find water on the battlefield.

Restrooms and Portable Toilets

The Chickamauga Battlefield Visitor Center has a restroom that is normally open from 8:30 a.m. to 5:00 p.m., although hours can vary due to weather conditions, or as we learned in recent years, global pandemics. There is also a restroom at the Recreation Field down the hill from the Wilder Brigade Monument. As of this writing, and unlike Gettysburg and Antietam, there are no portable toilets installed for tourist use.

In the normal course of planning your ride, please check the NPS website at https://www.nps.gov/chch/planyourvisit/hours.htm and more generally, https://www.nps.gov/chch/planyourvisit/basicinfo.htm.

Bicycle Racks

As of this writing, Chickamauga Battlefield has only one bicycle rack, which you will find at the Visitor Center entrance patio. If you want to enter the building for a restroom or water break, this is an easy place to lock your bicycle. More likely, though, you will be parking your car in the Visitor Center parking lot, and your car's rack will be more convenient.

During your bicycle tour you may feel tempted to abandon your bike for a short hiking excursion (for example, at Snodgrass Hill). Unfortunately, the park does not have any structures to which you can chain and lock your bike. (Historic structures like cannons are obviously off-limits for this). If you are touring with a companion, one option is to chain together two or more bicycles, which makes it more difficult for honest people impulsively to steal. But in the end, it is all about what risks you are willing to carry and what not. The fact that this author is not aware of any bicycle thefts at Chickamauga does not mean that there have been no incidents or that the risk is minimal.

Pack and Carry

Your emergency supplies should fit into a front-mounted bag or bicycle trunk. Since a full battlefield tour is only 12.6 miles, you could lighten your load by leaving heavy foods, tools, and clothing locked in your parked car.

If you might extend your ride for whatever reason, lightweight panniers can offer a very convenient place to store food, water, and an extra shirt or windbreaker. Of course, you could also use a student-size backpack, but please anticipate that this set up can become uncomfortable on daylong rides.

Although Chickamauga battlefield has four picnic areas (see the map on p. 26), if you are touring on a hot day—which can be any day between May and October—please consider the possibility that park trash cans may be infested with flies. This may be an unavoidable consequence of the Georgia climate, but it does not mean that you cannot have a contingency plan that allows you to eat without the convenience of a picnic table.

Clothing

For a half-day ride through the Chickamauga battlefield, it is unlikely that you will get surprised by a change of weather on that day. However, a tip worth remembering is that Chickamauga can get hot in the spring, summer, and fall months. Fortunately, there is ample

Gathering Your Gear

shade. On the day of your ride, as you dress and pack your bicycle bags, ask yourself four questions:

1. If I get hot, what can I take off?
2. If I get cold, what can I put on?
3. If it starts to rain or snow, how will I keep dry?
4. If it starts to get cloudy or dark, how will I be seen?

The goal is to select weather-appropriate clothing you assemble into layers. Inexperienced bicyclists often underestimate the value of fluorescent, athletic shirts and windbreakers that contain moisture-wicking (synthetic) fibers. Cotton can get wet and stay wet for a long time, which can be uncomfortable and irritate your skin. For the extra expense of athletic clothing, your body will stay dry, and your body temperature will be better regulated. When worn in layers, air pockets generate extra warmth and keep you dry.

Maps

Pack and carry this guidebook so that you can look up monument histories in Part IV as you tour the battlefield using the book's maps. For your extra (optional) convenience, you can also purchase digital PDF companion maps from www.civilwarcycling.com. For a fraction of the cost of a paperback book, you can download and print companion maps for personal use without the hassle of license keys or passwords. Also, if your cell phone or mobile device has a PDF reader, you can consult a map during a break in your ride. (The maps are *not* intended for use while pedaling your bicycle).

4. Transportation and Lodging

The U.S. Congress authorized the establishment of Chickamauga and Chattanooga National Military Park in 1890. The U.S. government dedicated the park in 1895. Although the Chickamauga battlefield is today located in Fort Oglethorpe, Georgia, no such town existed in the nineteenth century. In 1902, the U.S. government established Fort Oglethorpe as an army cavalry post, but it is better known as a World War II training camp. The city incorporated in 1949 and its citizens live on the north end of the battlefield.

More than half of Fort Oglethorpe is the Chickamauga battlefield, which the National Park Service administers. This small city is in northwest Georgia on the Tennessee border. It is part of the Chattanooga metropolitan area. Not to be confused with the city of Chickamauga seven miles away, Fort Oglethorpe is your bicycling destination. (The city of Chickamauga is southwest of Fort Oglethorpe and home to Lee and Gordon's Mill, where Union and Confederate soldiers crossed Chickamauga Creek prior to the Battle of Chickamauga).

When planning a tour of the Chickamauga battlefield, bicycle rentals, transportation, storage, and lodging accommodations are important considerations. We will cover each of these topics in this short chapter.

Bicycle Renting Options

If you want to rent bicycles, the most convenient option is to find a business that is close to a park's Visitor Center. This can minimize the need to transport bicycles by car (if the public roads to a battlefield are safe). It also opens options for arranging for the delivery of bicycles to the battlefield, because sometimes area businesses offer services that cater to tourists.

With respect to Fort Oglethorpe in particular, as of this writing there is a friendly bike and kayak shop less than one mile north of the Chickamauga Visitor Center. The shop is in a plaza next to a local diner that offers local charm. If you are lodging outside of Fort Oglethorpe, you will find bicycle shops in Chattanooga and the wider Chattanooga area. You can begin your search by pointing your web browser to https://www.yellowpages.com/chickamauga-ga/bicycle-shops. (This guidebook does not make specific business recommendations other than to suggest options for you to research).

Transporting Your Bicycle

If you are driving to Fort Oglethorpe and bringing your own bicycles, you will most likely mount them on your car. For safety, consult your car dealership and a local bicycle shop for advice. Make sure that the rack fits the car, and the bicycles rest solidly in the rack, and then test your setup before you take your trip. Although not strictly necessary, you might use bungee cords to prevent the front wheel tires from moving. It is also smart to slip an inexpensive plastic cover over each bicycle's seat since rain can damage the seat and it can take a long time for the seat to dry. If it rains, towel-dry the bicycle and be sure to apply chain lube sometime before your ride.

If you do not want to purchase a car bicycle rack, another option is to slide the bicycles into the back of a large car (with middle seats down). Use a blanket for cushioning and bring repair tools in case you accidentally dislodge something. Minimally, you will need to re-adjust your mirrors, which requires an Allen wrench. If your hands touch your chains, you will want a rag to wipe them.

Storing Your Bicycle

If you are staying at an inn, it is highly likely that in policies will limit your bicycle storage options. In the author's experience, most inns want to be accommodating, but they may require you to store bicycles in a storage room or shed that is accessible to other patrons. Hotel policies are more predictable and usually allow you to bring your bicycle to your room.

Alternatively, ask about keeping your bicycle in a storage area that is accessible only to staff. You can also lock your bicycle to the rack on your car. As a theft deterrent, remove the front wheel and the seat and store them inside your locked car. And of course, if your car is large enough, you could also lock your bicycle in your car. You may prefer a strong bicycle lock system, like the popular but heavy Kryptonite New York Fahgettaboudit Ulock paired with a Kryptonite Kryptoflex Cable.

Lodging

Because the Chickamauga battlefield is a short drive from several small and large cities, selecting a hotel or other lodging is not much different than what you would do for any other vacation in the United States. Since individual budgets and requirements for what types of amenities will vary widely, this guidebook does not offer specific lodging recommendations.

Start your research in one of these locations: Fort Oglethorpe, Chickamauga (6 miles), Chattanooga (10 miles), and Ringgold (10 miles). Likely, you will select a location based on whether you are transporting your own bicycles (versus renting them).

Parking

Although the Chickamauga battlefield has many (mostly small) parking lots, as of this writing there is only one bicycle rack and that is outside of the Visitor Center. This situation does not seem to in any way hinder local bicyclists from riding through the battlefield, especially on weekends or after work, but it can be a challenge for bicycling tourists. Fortunately, having a bike rack outside of the Visitor Center helps when you need to use the restroom.

If you are touring with a companion, you may want to take turns watching your bikes while, for example, the other person walks up the stairs of the Wilder Brigade Monument. Other decision points include wanting to hike to the South Carolina State Monument on Snodgrass Hill; tour the fields around the Snodgrass or Brotherton Cabins; or search for memorial shell monuments in the woods along Battleline Road. A second option is to chain your bicycles together, which usually deters impulsive thefts but will not stop people who have a plan to steal.

This guidebook simply recommends that you think about what you will do if you feel like you need a bike rack, but none is available.

Bicycling Chickamauga Battlefield

PART III: ENJOY YOUR RIDE!

Bicycling Chickamauga Battlefield

5. How to Read Bicycle Cues

Segment Maps

A segment map is a detailed map of *part* of a bicycle route. When segment maps are sequenced one after the other, they describe a complete bicycle route. Route 1 for bicycling Chickamauga Battlefield consists of Segments A, B, and C. (See the map key on p. 28).

Bicycle Cue Sheets

In this book, each segment map has bicycling directions, called "cues," where distances are in miles. These abbreviations will help you to navigate the park:

L	Turn Left	R	Turn Right
QL	Quick Left	QR	Quick Right
BL	Bear Left	BR	Bear Right
PoL	Pass on Left	PoR	Pass on Right
CS	Continue Straight	X	Cross
U	U-Turn		
N	North	E	East
S	South	W	West

Table 6. Bicycle Cue Key

Tip 1: If you do not want to read bicycle cues, please skip over them. For most people, the maps in this book are sufficient to complete a loop through the Chickamauga battlefield. The cues are mostly helpful for people who want to find specific monuments along the route.

Tip 2: The cue sheets in this guidebook identify *optional* stopping points to visit monuments. It is highly unlikely that you will want to stop at all of them, mostly due to time restrictions. If you read this book before your trip, you can set a comfortable riding cadence that is based on your own unique touring needs and interests.

Tip 3: Battlefield park road signs are often not located or visible at a point at which a bicyclist needs to make a turning decision. The maps and cue sheets in this book should bridge that gap for you.

Start at the Visitor Center

If this is your first visit to the Chickamauga battlefield, stop at the Visitor Center before your bicycle tour. You will enjoy a high quality, thirty-minute introductory video presentation about the Battle of Chickamauga. For more information about the Visitor Center Museum and the Fuller Gun Collection, see p. 50.

The NPS consistently posts timely and helpful information on its website that may prompt you to adjust your touring plans. Go to https://www.nps.gov/chch/planyourvisit/basicinfo.htm for the Visitor Center's hours of operation, and for current park conditions, go to https://www.nps.gov/chch/planyourvisit/conditions.htm.

Note that park roads have gates that close in the evening or due to weather-related circumstances. For example, there is currently a gate on the south end of Glenn-Viniard Road, near LaFayette Road; and another gate is on Vittetoe Road on the way up to Snodgrass Hill.

Here is an interesting side note: According to the NPS, three U.S. presidents have visited Chickamauga Battlefield: Theodore Roosevelt (1903), William H. Taft (1911), and Franklin D. Roosevelt (1943).[109]

Selecting Your Chickamauga Route

For help selecting a bicycle route, please see "Chickamauga Bicycle Routes," p. 46. This book recommends that first-time visitors to Chickamauga and Chattanooga National Military Park select Route 1. To complete the route, the next chapter provides detailed navigational instructions (in visual, tabular, and narrative form) and periodic references to historical material. See:

Chapter 6: Route 1, the "Half Day Loop" (12.6 Miles).

For additional riding time, as well as an opportunity to explore the battlefield park without making specific plans to stop, you have these additional options:

Chapter 7: Route 2, "Fields of Chickamauga Loop" (12.9 Miles).

Chapter 8: Route 3, "Eastern Woods Loop" (8.8 Miles).

6. Route 1 Loop (12.6 Miles)

Route 1 ("Half Day Loop") offers a safe, 12.6-mile ride that extends beyond the official NPS auto tour to include sites on the eastern half of the park.

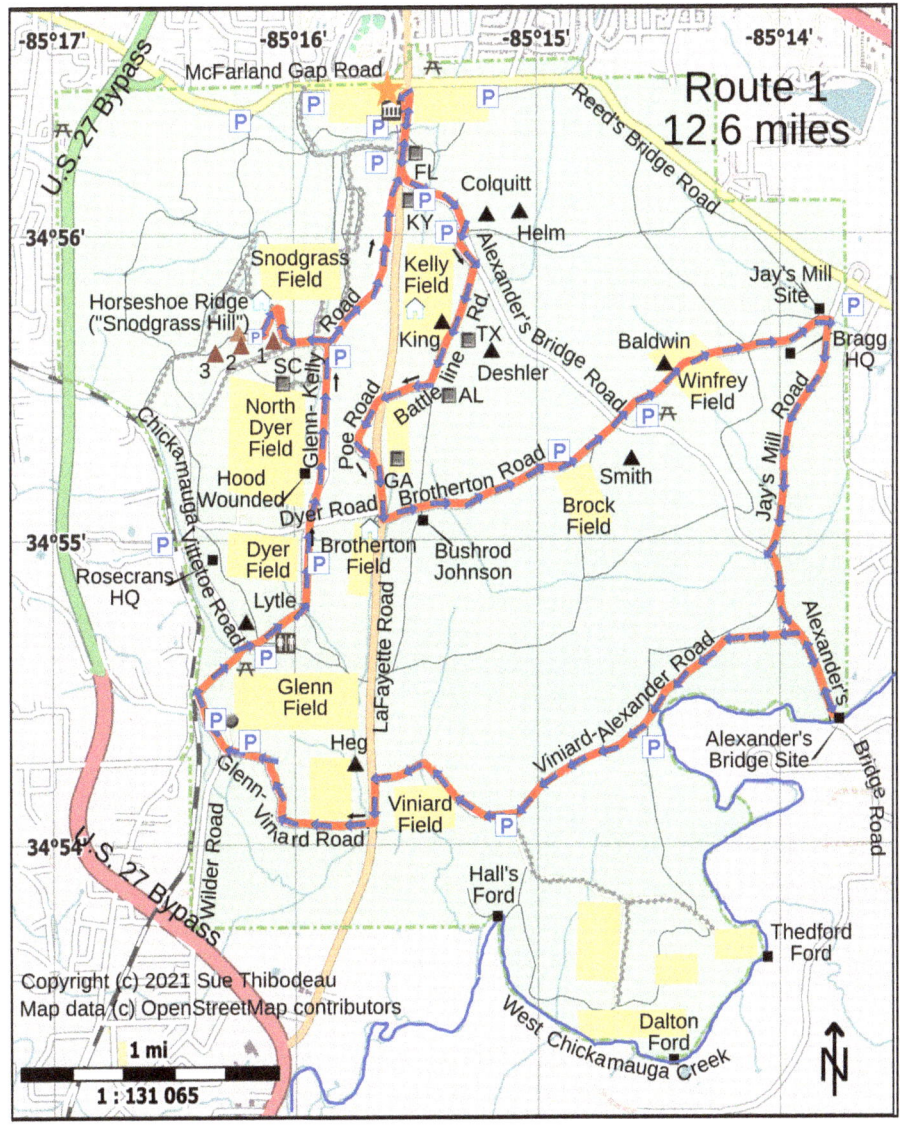

Map 12. Route 1 "Half Day Loop" (12.6 Miles)

Self-Directed Learning

Route 1's bicycling maps, cues, and cross-references to historical summaries are designed for self-directed learners. With that in mind, this guidebook does not include pre-defined "tour stops." Instead, it identifies and describes opportunities for you to visit Chickamauga's monuments and historic sites. This means that you will make stopping decisions based on your own educational objectives and interests—and not those of the author. You will take an active role in planning your battlefield tour, and optionally adjusting touring details when new learning opportunities present themselves.

Route 1 Segments

This 12.6-mile bicycle route consists of three segments, named Segments A, B, and C. Each segment ends at a convenient rest stop. For park amenities, refer to the Route 1 map on the previous page.

Segment A (5.6 miles) begins at the Visitor Center and follows Battleline Road to the Brotherton Cabin, and then northeast to Jay's Mill Site for a ride down to Alexander's Bridge Site. The 1863 bridge is gone, but its modern replacement is a convenient place to view West Chickamauga Creek. Although cars use the bridge, it is a remote and rural spot from which to enjoy the eastern-most edge of the battlefield park. For more details about Segment A, see p. 104.

From the bridge, Segment B (5.5 miles) follows the densely wooded Viniard-Alexander Road west toward LaFayette Road to cross over to Glenn-Viniard Road, and then continues with a tour of the western half of the park. The segment includes stops at the Wilder Brigade Monument and Snodgrass Hill. For more details about Segment B, see p. 109.

Depending on the degree to which you studied this book's historical material before starting your ride, you can still learn a lot by bicycling Segments A and B without stopping. Segment B ends at Snodgrass Hill, which most people will want to tour on foot. Monumentation in the field on the north side of Snodgrass Cabin tell veterans' stories of what they did here in the final hours of the Battle of Chickamauga. Hiking paths south of the cabin lead to other monuments associated with military actions on Horseshoe Ridge (also called Hills 1, 2, and 3).

Route 1 Loop (12.6 Miles)

Finally, Segment C (1.5 miles) directs you back to the Visitor Center to complete the circuit. For more details about Segment C, see p. 114. If you want to keep riding after completing Route 1's 12.6 miles, you can always ride again, this time stopping at more or different historic sites. Alternatively, explore the park in a looped fashion by following Route 2 (p. 117) or Route 3 (p. 121).

Before Your Ride

To get the greatest educational experience from your tour, read Parts I and IV of this book before your ride. Beyond that, confirm that your bicycle and safety gear are working properly. And finally, depending on the weather, apply sunscreen on your body and insect repellent on your clothes. (See Chapter 3, "Gathering Your Gear.").

For your safety, please plan to ride defensively around motor vehicle traffic. In the author's experience, cars at Chickamauga move faster than cars at Gettysburg and Antietam. The reason for Chickamauga's faster pace might be that many monuments are difficult to see from the road (but that is only a guess). In any case, safety-conscious bicyclists with road experience will feel comfortable touring Chickamauga, because park traffic is usually light.

Also, even though Route 1 avoids all but two short sections of LaFayette Road—0.3 miles from the Visitor Center to Alexander's Bridge Road, and 0.2 miles from Poe at LaFayette to Brotherton Road—commuter traffic moves especially fast on LaFayette Road. This is a 35-mph double-yellow-lined road that connects Chattanooga, Tennessee and LaFayette, Georgia. It is smooth pavement but has no shoulders for the entire north-south axis of the battlefield park. In recent years, the state built a bypass highway around the battlefield on its west side, which has helped to reduce commuter traffic.

Finally, as you use the maps and bicycle cues in this guidebook, keep this in mind: Distances are rounded to the nearest tenth of a mile and can vary based on your cyclometer's calibration and your personal riding style (straight or meandering). As mentioned earlier in the section entitled, "How to Use This Guidebook and Maps" (p. 22), most people will use maps for navigation, and bicycle cues to confirm one's location or to find a specific monument. The next sections provide both maps and bicycle cues.

Bicycling Chickamauga Battlefield

Segment A (to Alexander's Bridge)

Segment A (5.6 miles) is a mostly flat ride that begins at the Visitor Center and ends at the Alexander's Bridge Site.

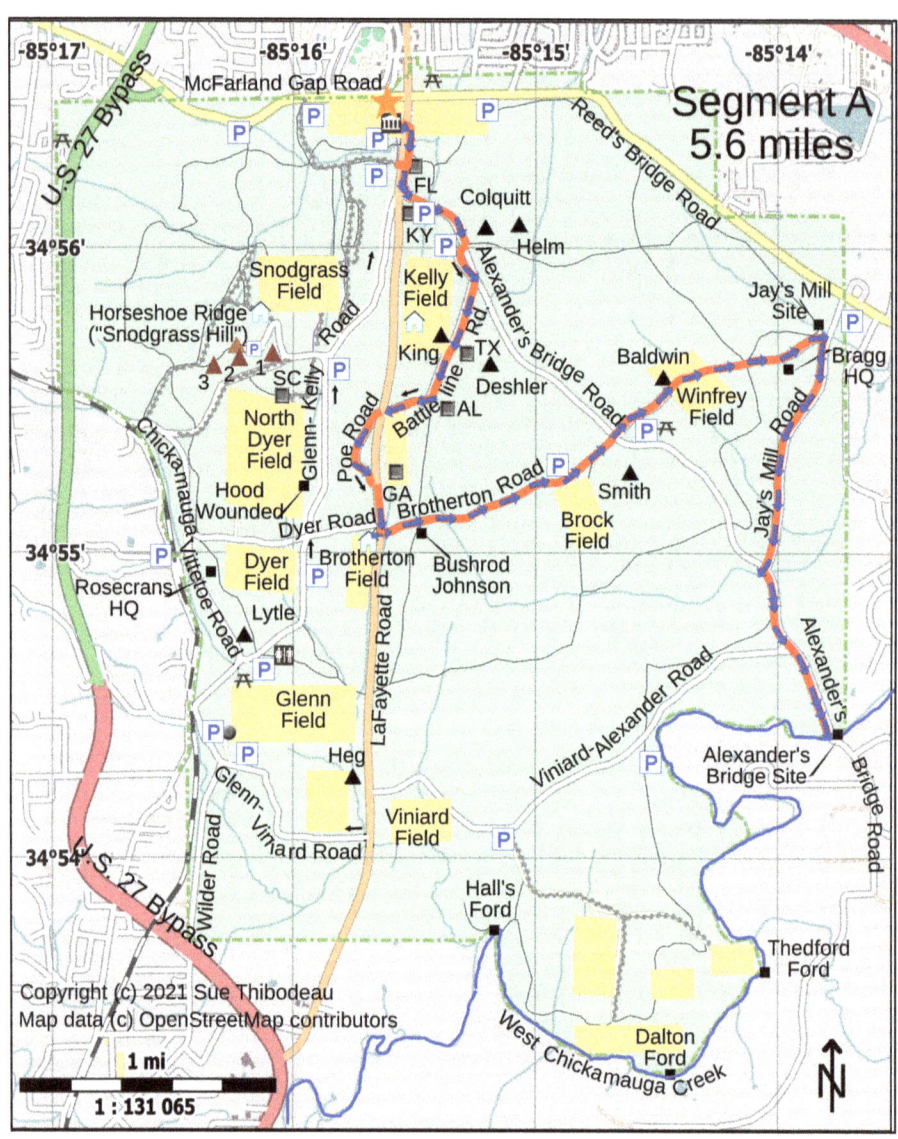

Map 13. Segment A Map (to Alexander's Bridge)

Tip: Use maps for general navigation. Refer to cue sheets for details.

Route 1 Loop (12.6 Miles)

A	Segment Cue Sheet (to Alexander's Bridge)		
Start	Visitor Center. See cue key, p. 99. No bike racks!		End
0.0	R	LaFayette Road for 500 feet (commuter road)	
	R	Into gravel lot, Stovall's Brigade, CSA p. 153	
0.2	R	South on LaFayette Road	0.3
0.3	BL	Alexander's Bridge Road (25 mph park road)	
		To gravel lot, Kentucky Monument p. 135, (map p. 77 has Sept. 19 battle line) 152	0.3
0.3	CS	Alexander's Bridge Road into woods	
	PoL	CSA monuments, east side p. 145	
	PoL	Colquitt and Helm CSA memorials, in woods (map p. 78 has context) p. 182 185	0.6
0.6	BR	Battleline Road, map p. 77 p. 36	
	PoR	King USA memorial, map p. 180 p. 186	
1.2	PoL	Texas Monument p. 172, 137	1.2
1.3	PoL	(In field) Alabama Monument p. 142, 132	1.3
1.3	CS	To stop sign at LaFayette Road	1.5
		Map p. 78 shows Stewart's attack	
1.5	X	LaFayette Road to Poe Road	
1.5	CS	Poe Road into woods to stop sign p. 59	1.8
	X	Walk to Georgia Monument, return p. 134	
1.8	S	LaFayette Road for about 0.15 miles	
	PoR	Dyer Road and coast 0.05 miles to park	
	BR	Brotherton Cabin (Sept. 20 map p. p. 57, 78 shows Longstreet's Breakthrough) 160	2.0
2.0	L	Brotherton Road and east 0.1 miles p. 45	2.1
2.1	PoR	Bushrod Johnson Monument p. 171	2.1
2.1	CS	0.5 miles to Brock Field, on right p. 55	2.6
2.6	PoR	Smith CSA memorial, map p. 77, 180 p. 188	2.9
2.9	CS	Stop at Alexander's Bridge Road p. 43	3.0
	X	Straight on Brotherton Road	
3.0	PoL	Baldwin USA memorial in Winfrey Field, maps pp. 77 and 180 p. 181	3.4
3.4	CS	To dead-end at Jay's Mill Road p. 44	4.0
4.0	R	Jay's Mill Road for 0.9 miles to dead-end	4.9
4.9	L	Alexander's Bridge Road, left p. 51, at fork, to Chickamauga Creek 156, 159	5.6

Table 7. Segment A Cue Sheet (to Alexander's Bridge)

Tip: Photocopy route cue sheets and clip to your bike handlebars.

Bicycling Chickamauga Battlefield

The following pages provide optional additional detail for navigating Segment A. They augment the visual (map) and tabular (table cues) provided above. Our intent is to appeal broadly to different touring preferences, where some bicyclists will use maps or cues, but others may expect more traditional narrative instructions.

Memory check. Look again at the maps on pp. 27, 76–79. This will help you to get oriented on the battlefield so that it is easier to understand the battle. During your ride, you may also want to consult the Orders of Battle on pp. 68–69 as you try to remember "who's who" among the senior officers of both armies.

0.0 Miles. From the Visitor Center parking lot, turn RIGHT (south) onto LaFayette Road. This double-yellow-lined road is a busy 35 mph commuter road that has no shoulders. There will be trees on your left and a field on your right. As you cross a small stone bridge, you will notice the Florida State Monument on your left, in the distance. It is more convenient to visit this monument on your return to the Visitor Center in Segment C when you will not need to cross the road.

Take your first RIGHT (west) into a gravel lot to visit NPS Tour Stop 1 and four Confederate cannons that mark the September 20 (10:00 a.m.) position of Maj. Gen. John C. Breckinridge's division. At this location near the center of Breckinridge's line, Marcellus Augustus Stovall's brigade faced south and then advanced into Kelly Field, flanking the Union line and "gaining its rear," according to a marker on the other side of the road. For an abbreviated visual of Breckinridge's Assault, see the troop block on Map 10, p. 78. For a summary of Kentucky's role in the assault, see the text on p. 153.

0.2 Miles. Turn RIGHT (south) again on LaFayette Road for 0.1 miles and bear LEFT into the woods at Alexander's Bridge Road, yielding the right of way to oncoming traffic (25 mph). Before you turn, you will see the tall Kentucky State Monument (p. 135) to your front. There is a small parking lot here. You are at the left flank of the Union line, specifically Maj. Gen. George H. Thomas' 14th Corps of the Army of the Cumberland. The map on p. 77 shows the battle lines drawn on September 19, 1863.

0.3 Miles. Continue STRAIGHT (southeast) along the flat, shaded roadway. On your left, notice a series of monuments shaped like pup tents. They mark the battlefield positions of Georgia infantry, artillery, and cavalry units (p. 145). The Colquitt and Helm memorial

Route 1 Loop (12.6 Miles)

shell monuments, which are labeled on the Segment A map (p. 104), are not visible from the road. Also, in the woods on the east side of Alexander's Bridge Road are two CSA division markers (for Walker and Breckinridge) and two CSA brigade markers (for Gist and Helms).

0.6 Miles. Bear RIGHT (west) onto Battleline Road to NPS Tour Stop 2. Battleline Road is a one-way, 20 mph paved road that is flat, well-shaded, and has narrow gravel shoulders. For a description of the military significance of this modern road, see pp. 36–39. After your turn, a monument that depicts a prone rifleman (15th US Infantry) will appear at your front. You will also begin to see monuments that have acorn ornamentation, a symbol for Thomas' 14th Corps (p. 165). All along this 0.8-mile stretch, you will pass by monuments that stand only a few yards from the road, but there are also monuments in the woods. For example, a white-on-brown NPS sign across the road from the Texas State Monument points to a trail to the King (right) and Deshler (left) memorial shell monuments (see pp. 186 and 183, respectively).

Although Union monuments dominate this area, there are exceptions. For example, you will find monuments that mark battle positions for the 2nd, 3rd & 5th, and 35th Tennessee, and the 4th Georgia Battalion Sharpshooters, as well as Confederate red-on-white (versus Union white-on-blue) cast iron brigade markers. As for cannons, those that face east are Union, because they point to Confederate targets. When you come upon cannons, look for their corresponding battery monuments (e.g., Indiana and Ohio batteries).

About 0.1 mile beyond the Texas State Monument, look for the Alabama State Monument in a field on your left. For more details, see pp. 137 and 172 (Texas), and pp. 132 and 142 (Alabama). As you pass the Alabama State Monument, enjoy a pleasant downhill glide to a stop sign at LaFayette Road.

1.5 Miles. Stopped now between the 1.4 and 1.5-mile-mark, you are looking toward Indiana infantry and artillery monuments associated with King's Brigade, which was attacked from the east (your position) by Stewart's Confederate division at about 10:30 a.m. on September 20, 1863 (see the map on p. 78).

CROSS LaFayette Road to Poe Road, and follow this one-way, tree-lined road south until it dead-ends. As you ride, scan the sparse woodlot to find the Georgia State Monument (p. 134) in a field on the east side of LaFayette Road. You will notice markers for artillery batteries (and cannons) from Indiana, Ohio, and Michigan. Also, look for a white cast-iron sign that says, "Site of Poe House Burned During the Battle Sept. 20, 1863," near the end of the road's bend left. At the southernmost end of Poe Road, you will find several Confederate monuments (e.g., Tennessee and Georgia infantry regiments) and nearby, battery markers and guns for Georgia, Alabama, Mississippi, Florida, and South Carolina. (You might want to walk your bike across the road to visit the Georgia State Monument on foot; this is NPS Tour Stop 3).

1.8 Miles. Turn RIGHT (south) on LaFayette Road and continue for about 0.15 miles, passing Dyer Road on your right. Ride safely in this area, because cars will pass at 35 mph over double-yellow lines even when cars are coming from both directions. Park in the pull-out area in front of the Brotherton Cabin (p. 57). Note that the September 20, 1863, headquarters monument for Confederate Maj. Gen. Simon B. Buckner is located across the road. You are at NPS Tour Stop 4, the site of Longstreet's Breakthrough (map, p. 78), when the Confederates attacked westward through the Brotherton property. You can read more about Longstreet's Breakthrough here: Alabama (p. 142), Arkansas (p. 143), Missouri (p. 160), South Carolina (p. 170), and Texas (p. 172). Brotherton Field is one of the most popular sites to explore, so if you can manage a walk through the property, you will not regret it.

2.0 Miles. Take your next LEFT (east) on Brotherton Road. You will pass the Bushrod Johnson Monument about 0.1 miles on your right (p. 171). Continue STRAIGHT (northeast) for 0.5 miles to Brock Field. Look for the Smith memorial monument a short distance farther down the road (in a field, p. 188). You may see a mowed pathway to the monument. Continue STRAIGHT to the intersection of Brotherton Road and Alexander's Bridge Road (p. 43). Continue STRAIGHT toward Winfrey Field (p. 54). The Baldwin memorial monument is on the left side of the road in the back corner of the field (p. 181). For fighting related to Smith and Baldwin, see the map on p 77. Continue STRAIGHT to dead-end at Jay's Mill Road.

4.0 Miles. Turn RIGHT (south) on Jay's Mill Road (p. 44). For 0.9 miles until you dead-end on Alexander's Bridge Road. Turn LEFT (southeast) for 0.7 miles to arrive at the Alexander's Bridge Site at West Chickamauga Creek (pp. 43, 51). See the map on p. 76. Segment A ends at the **5.6 mile-point**.

Route 1 Loop (12.6 Miles)

Segment B (to Snodgrass Hill)

Segment B (5.5 miles) begins at the Alexander's Bridge Site and ends at Snodgrass Hill. Except for Snodgrass Hill, the ride is mostly flat and is entirely over paved park roads.

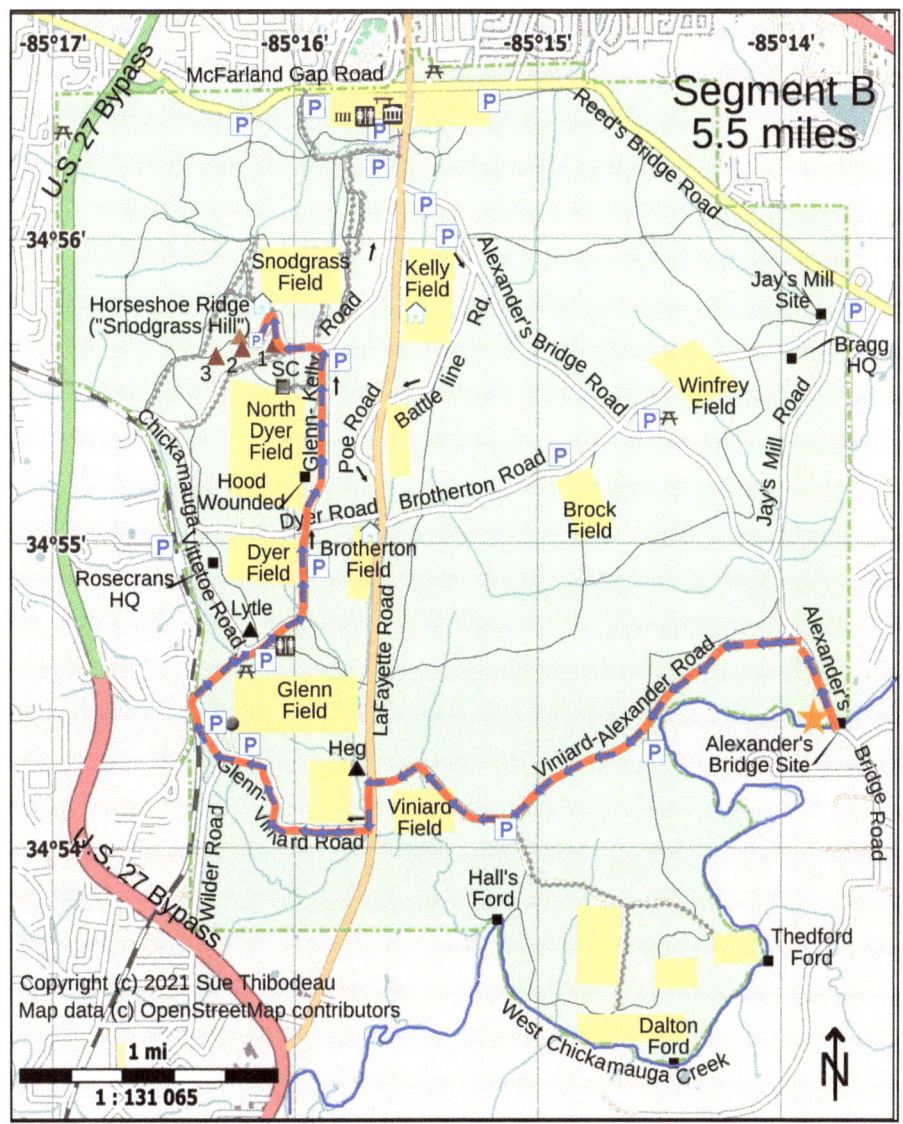

Map 14. Segment B Map (to Snodgrass Hill)

Bicycling Chickamauga Battlefield

B — Segment Cue Sheet (to Snodgrass Hill)

Start			End
		Alexander's Bridge. No bike racks!	
0.0	CS	Alexander's Bridge Road for about 0.35 miles	
0.35	L	Viniard-Alexander Road p. 42	
1.0	PoL	(In woods, not visible) Chickamauga Creek	1.0
1.0	PoR	Parking lot and trail to Thedford Ford	1.7
2.2	PoL	Viniard Field, maps pp. 76, 77; also p. 56, 151	2.4
	CS	To dead-end at LaFayette Road near p. 184, Heg Memorial Shell Monument 176	2.4
2.4	L	LaFayette Road (busy commuter road)	2.4
2.5	BR	Glenn-Viniard Road, one-way p. 39	3.0
3.0	CS	Glenn Field comes into view p. 60	
3.1	CS	Bend west on Glenn-Viniard Road	
3.2	BL	Veer left at fork to bypass car lot	3.3
	PoL	Wilder Road, watch two-way traffic	3.3
3.3	CS	Slight uphill, note cavalry monuments	3.5
3.5		Park and visit Wilder monument p. 147	3.5
3.75	X	Cross small stream, stone bridge	
3.8	BR	Glenn-Kelly Road, slight downhill p. 39	
	PoL	(Not visible) Lytle USA memorial, p. 187, map p. 78, 180 177	
	PoR	Recreation Field, north end of Glenn Field	3.9
3.9	CS	Bend north, coasting down tree-lined p. 41 road to intersection at Dyer Road	4.4
4.4	X	Dyer Road. Watch for cars on your right.	
4.4	CS	Glenn-Kelly Road, Dyer Field on left p. 61	4.9
	PoL	(Not visible) Hood Wounded Marker p. 172	
4.9	PoL	South Carolina Monument (hill) p. 136, 170	4.9
5.0	BL	Vittetoe Road (unmarked) uphill, 15 mph	5.2
5.2	BR	At fork, uphill to see Snodgrass Field	5.4
5.4		Stop at Snodgrass Cabin p. 62	5.4
5.4	CS	South, uphill to circle on hilltop p. 144, 157, 161, 164, 170, 174	5.5

Table 8. Segment B Cue Sheet (to Snodgrass Hill)

Route 1 Loop (12.6 Miles)

In the following pages, segment miles appear first and match the mileage numbers in the above cue sheet. Cumulative miles appear second, in parentheses. If you take a spontaneous detour on Segment A, this means that you can "reset to 0.0" to begin Segment B without having to do mental math.

0.0 Miles (5.6 Miles). From the Alexander's Bridge Site, return north on Alexander's Bridge Road for about 0.35 miles. (Note that a Chickamauga park road sign might not be visible to bicyclists at the time a turn is required). Turn LEFT on Viniard-Alexander Road (p. 42). Continue STRAIGHT (southwest) around Chickamauga Creek (not visible, on your left), and pass a small parking lot to a hiking trail near the creek. At about 1.0 (6.6) miles, pass a second small parking lot and the entrance of a trail entrance to Thedford Ford. Continue STRAIGHT.

~2.2 Miles (7.8 Miles). Pass Viniard Field on your left (maps, pp. 76, 77; also p. 56, 151). The back-and-forth fighting in Viniard Field was particularly brutal and deadly. If you want to visit the monuments in this area, park your bicycle (there are no racks) and walk to your left (south). In the field, you will find regimental and battery monuments for Indiana, Illinois, Michigan, and Minnesota. On your bicycle, continue STRAIGHT until Viniard-Alexander Road dead-ends at LaFayette Road.

2.4 Miles (8.0 Miles). Stop briefly at LaFayette Road and note that Viniard Field extends to the other side of the road. Also, slightly northwest of your current position, is the Heg Memorial Shell Monument. Wisconsin Col. Hans C. Heg received a mortal wound in Viniard Field on September 19, 1863 (p. 184). Across the road, a white-on-brown NPS sign points 200 yards to the monument. If you visit the Heg monument, walk your bicycle there, while watching for cars moving 35+ mph in both directions on LaFayette Road. When you are ready to continue your ride, carefully turn SOUTH on LaFayette Road for 0.1 miles and immediately bear RIGHT on Glenn-Viniard Road. (The road sign is not visible to bicyclists).

2.5 Miles (8.1 Miles). Continue STRAIGHT on Glenn-Viniard Road (p. 39), which is one-way at this point, but not marked as such on the official NPS park map. Warning: The author has encountered cars driving down this one-way road, despite signage to the contrary, so please stay alert and careful. On your left are woods, and on your right, an open field that has monuments for Illinois infantry, Indiana

Infantry, and Ohio artillery. In about 0.5 miles, Glenn Field is on your right and straight ahead. Continue STRAIGHT, following the road's bend westward, for another 0.1 miles until you reach a fork in the road.

3.2 Miles (8.8 Miles). Unless you want to use the restroom in the car parking lot, bear LEFT at a fork to bypass the lot. Although it might seem counter-intuitive, follow signs to Bus/RV parking. This is the most convenient path for bicyclists to visit the Wilder Brigade Monument. Go STRAIGHT and up a slight hill, passing Wilder Road on your left. Watch for two-way traffic in this area. Now at 3.3 (8.9) miles, continue STRAIGHT as you pass monuments for midwestern regiments (Indiana, Kentucky USA, Kentucky CSA, Pennsylvania, Michigan, Wisconsin, and Ohio). You will also pass by cavalry monuments (Pennsylvania, Michigan, Indiana, Wisconsin, Tennessee USA, and Ohio), as well as Indiana mounted infantry monuments.

3.5 Miles (9.1 Miles). Stop to visit the Wilder Brigade Monument (p. 147) on your RIGHT. This is NPS Tour Stop 6. You are now in the southeast corner of Glenn Field (p. 60). Unfortunately, there are no bicycle racks, so if you want to climb the stairs inside the Wilder monument and observe the battlefield from its observation tower, you need a plan to secure your bicycles. (The author's approach is to take turns with riding partners). The parking lot here has flat rectangular barrier stones that you can sit on if you need to rest or wait. Then ride STRAIGHT (north) for about 0.3 miles, crossing a small stream over a stone bridge along the way. This is a slight uphill ride followed by a gentle glide downhill.

3.8 Miles (9.4 Miles). At the fork, bear RIGHT on Glenn-Kelly Road (p. 39), where you will see the guns of the 1st Missouri Battery G on your right. (Chickamauga-Vittetoe Road was on the left part of the fork). In 0.1 miles and riding slightly downhill, pass the park recreation field on your right. Look for a white-on-brown NPS sign that points to the Lytle Memorial Shell Monument 600 feet into the woods on the left side of the road (pp. 187, 177). See the maps on pp. 78 and 180. Continue STRAIGHT on this 25-mph road. There are no one-way signs, but without any lines down the middle of the pavement, this road functions as a one-way road north. Continue bending north and then coast down the tree-lined road. Dyer Field will come into view on your left. As the road flattens out, there are occasional small car pull-off areas, like at NPS Tour Stop 7. Note the old (unmarked) bicycle lane on the left side of Glenn-Kelly Road. At

Route 1 Loop (12.6 Miles)

the 4.4 (10.0) mile point, you will arrive at the intersection of Glenn-Kelly and Dyer Roads (p. 41).

4.4 Miles (10.0 Miles). CROSS Dyer Road but watch for cars coming from your right. (As of this writing, you have the right of way, because traffic on Dyer heading west has a stop sign). Continue STRAIGHT on Glenn-Kelly Road (25 mph) into the woods where the road has a mix of grass and gravel on the shoulder. You will pass on your right a shell pyramid that marks Maj. Gen. John B. Hood's headquarters on September 20, 1863. Not far from here, near the edge of the woods and a short hike on the left side of the road, is the Hood Wounded Marker (p. 172). As the road bends slightly to the left, you will begin to see a clearing (North Dyer Field, p. 61). Watch out for deer jumping out of the woods in this area. On the distant ridge on your left stands the South Carolina State Monument.

4.9 Miles (10.5 Miles). At the worm fence on your left is a pedestrian trail up to the hill on which the South Carolina State Monument stands (p. 136 and 170). There are no bicycle racks in this area, and the NPS forbids off-road riding at Chickamauga battlefield park. Trees line Glenn-Kelly Road at this point, and the road is mostly flat.

5.0 Miles (10.6 Miles). At the fork, bear LEFT on Vittetoe Road (unmarked, 15 mph), and ride uphill for 0.2 miles through a heavily wooded area. At the next fork, bear RIGHT and continue uphill. After another 0.2 miles, you will begin to see Snodgrass Field straight ahead of you.

5.4 Miles (11.0 Miles). As you round the bend, you will arrive at Snodgrass Cabin (p. 62). This is NPS Tour Stop 8. There is a gravel pull-off area and paved side-road parking. In and around Snodgrass Field you will notice monuments and markers all over the field. Continue STRAIGHT (south) on the Vittetoe Road. The road is steep but manageable. Of course, you can always walk your bicycle if you cannot make it up the ridge.

5.5 Miles (11.1 Miles). Arrive at the hilltop, where the road circles around a small parking lot at NPS Tour Stop 8. You are on Horseshoe Ridge. For historical background, see pp. 144, 157, 161, 164, 170, and 174.

Segment C (return to Visitor Center)

Segment C (1.5 miles) begins at Snodgrass Hill and returns to the Visitor Center with no touring stops other than the Florida State Monument on the east side of LaFayette Road.

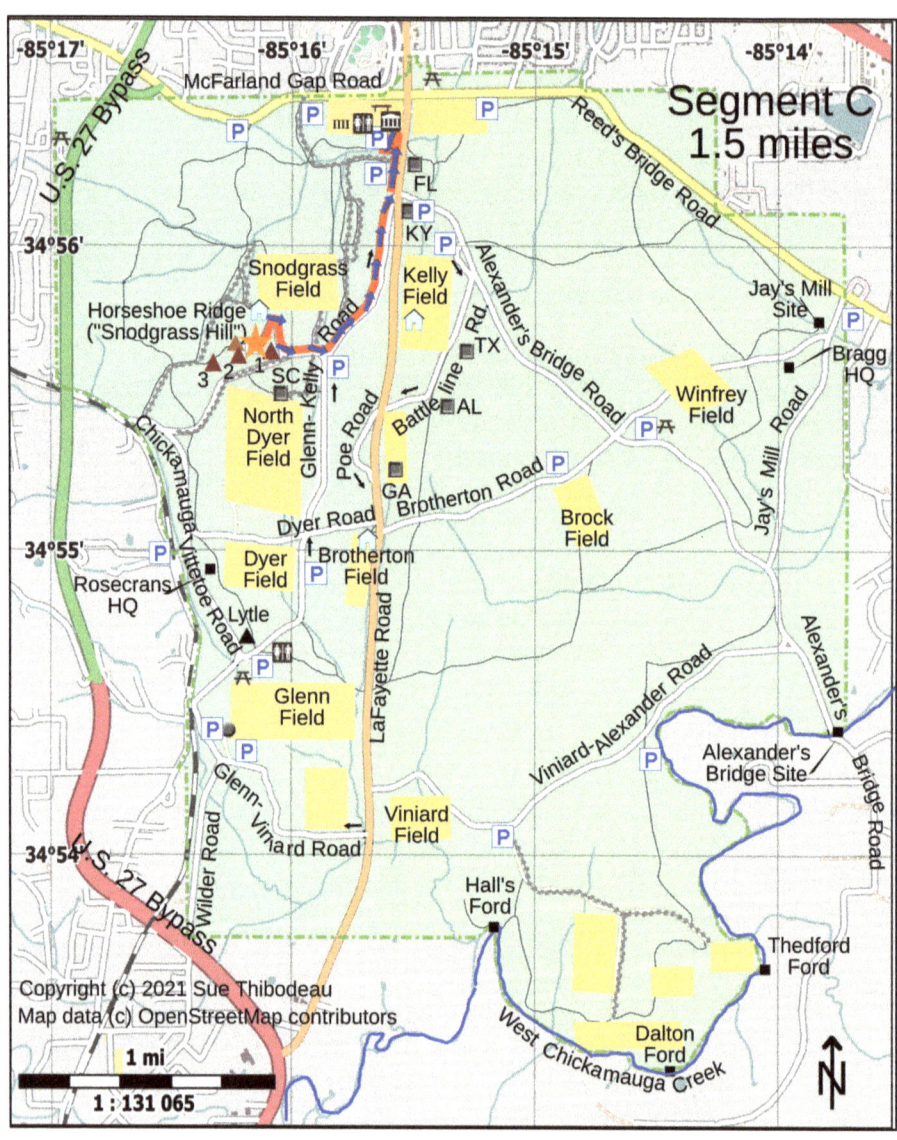

Map 15. Segment C Map (return to Visitor Center)

Route 1 Loop (12.6 Miles)

C	Segment Cue Sheet (return to Visitor Center)	
Start	Snodgrass Hill. No bike racks!	End
0.0	U North, downhill to Snodgrass Cabin	0.1
0.1	CS South, downhill on Vittetoe Road	
0.15	BL Vittetoe Road, downhill	
0.25	BL To Glenn-Kelly Road, one-way north	1.1
1.1	L LaFayette Road to Florida Monument p. 133	1.2
1.2	CS North to Visitor Center	1.5

Table 9. Segment C Cue Sheet (return to Visitor Center)

Having completed your tour of Snodgrass Hill and Horseshoe Ridge, Segment C directs you back to the Visitor Center. You can visit the Florida State Monument along the way.

0.0 Miles (11.1 Miles). From the Horseshoe Ridge parking lot, ride north and downhill for 0.1 miles to the Snodgrass Cabin. Round the bend and continue south and downhill on Vittetoe Road. In about 260 feet, bear LEFT and then LEFT again at the 0.25-mile mark to ride north on Glenn-Kelly Road. This tree-lined road has a rough, grassy shoulder and is one-way at this point. Continue STRAIGHT (north) on Glenn-Kelly Road, which has a gentle downward slope, until the road dead-ends on LaFayette Road. You can see the Kentucky State Monument across the road on the Kelly Farm.

1.1 Miles (12.2 Miles). While riding STRAIGHT (north) on LaFayette Road, you will see the Florida State Monument (p. 133) about 0.1 miles in the distance, on the right side of the road. There is a paved pull-off in front of the monument. Next, continue STRAIGHT for about 0.3 miles, turning LEFT into the park entrance near Reed's Bridge Road.

1.4 Miles (12.6 Miles). Arrive at the Visitor Center.

Bicycling Chickamauga Battlefield

7. Route 2 Loop (12.9 Miles)

Route 2 ("Fields of Chickamauga Loop") combines two loops to assemble a 12.9-mile circuit through most of the battlefield.

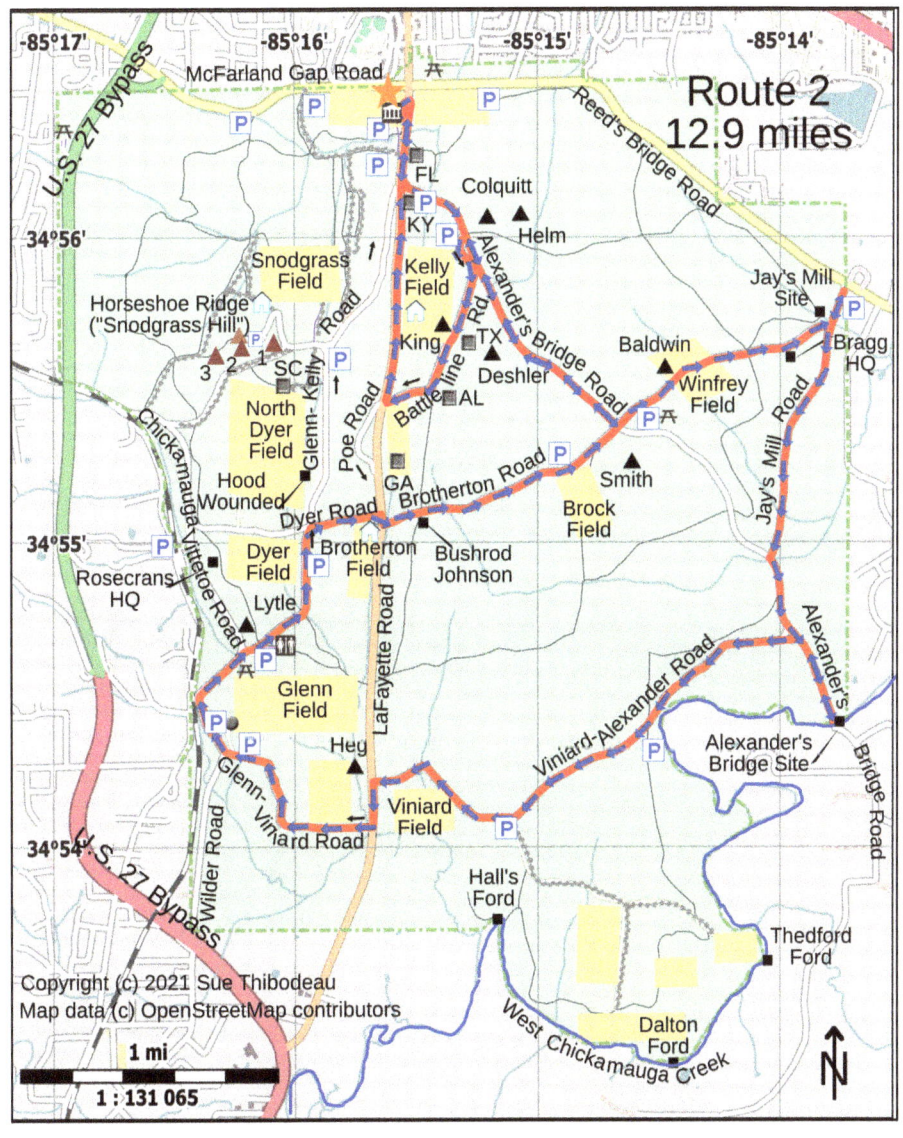

Map 16. Route 2 "Fields of Chickamauga Loop" (12.9 Miles)

Why Route 2?

Routes 1 and 2 cover a comparable number of miles (12.6 versus 12.9), and they also share common pathways. So why include Route 2 in this guidebook? This guidebook provides two reasons.

First, some bicyclists may find Route 2 more appealing because it is flat. Route 2 substitutes the relatively flat ride southeast on Alexander's Bridge Road (from Battleline Road to Brotherton Road) for Route 1's steep ride uphill to Snodgrass Cabin and Horseshoe Ridge. It also opens the opportunity to explore the Snodgrass Hill area separately, on foot, since there are hiking trails and monuments in that area. Note: One significant downside of Route 2 is that it adds an additional 0.8 miles on highly trafficked LaFayette Road (from Poe Road to the Kentucky State Monument).

For bicycling historians, Route 2 provides more time to explore Confederate positions on the eastern half of the battlefield. You will see Confederate cannons that point in a northwesterly direction. The cannon in the next photo stands near two cast-iron tablets—Calvert's Arkansas and Semple's Alabama Batteries. Around Winfrey Field, trails lead to tablets that describe Cleburne's Confederate attacks.

Confederate Cannon in the Winfrey Field Area

Route 2 Loop (12.9 Miles)

Second, our primary reason for including Routes 2 (and 3) in this guidebook is to provide bicyclists with an opportunity to ride freely through the battlefield without excessive stopping. Once you successfully complete Route 1—which includes reading the historical summaries and viewing the maps and photos that go with it—you are ready to introduce more spontaneity into your ride. With that in mind, the intent of the Route 2 (and 3) overview maps is to give you visual *examples* of how to design your own looped rides.

More than the Gettysburg and Antietam battlefield parks, Chickamauga's road network consists of several "closed circuits" that a bicyclist can easily use to build a variety of touring routes. Route 1 will have introduced you to the Chickamauga road network. After following Route 1, on your next ride it will be easier to anticipate where you are going, and why. But also, Route 1 introduces historical lessons that you can recall on later rides through the battlefield.

Besides Route 1 touring experience, you only need two additional things. First, you must carefully consider the one-way roads that the maps in this book identify. Map 2 on p. 26 will be particularly helpful. Second, you need the physical stamina for another ride.

Although the overview map for Route 2 (p. 117) is normally sufficient to complete a second tour through the Chickamauga battlefield, the map's use of blue double arrows requires explanation. Double arrows indicate that at some point in the route, you will travel in both directions on that road. Route 2 begins at the Visitor Center, where you will turn RIGHT on LaFayette Road, and then LEFT on Alexander's Bridge Road until you reach the intersection with Brotherton Road. You will repeat this entire stretch of road near the end of your ride, which concludes at the Visitor Center.

8. Route 3 Loop (8.8 Miles)

Like Route 2, Route 3 ("Eastern Woods Loop") combines two loops to build a circuit. But unlike Route 2, it is an 8.8-mile ride over only one-third of the battlefield.

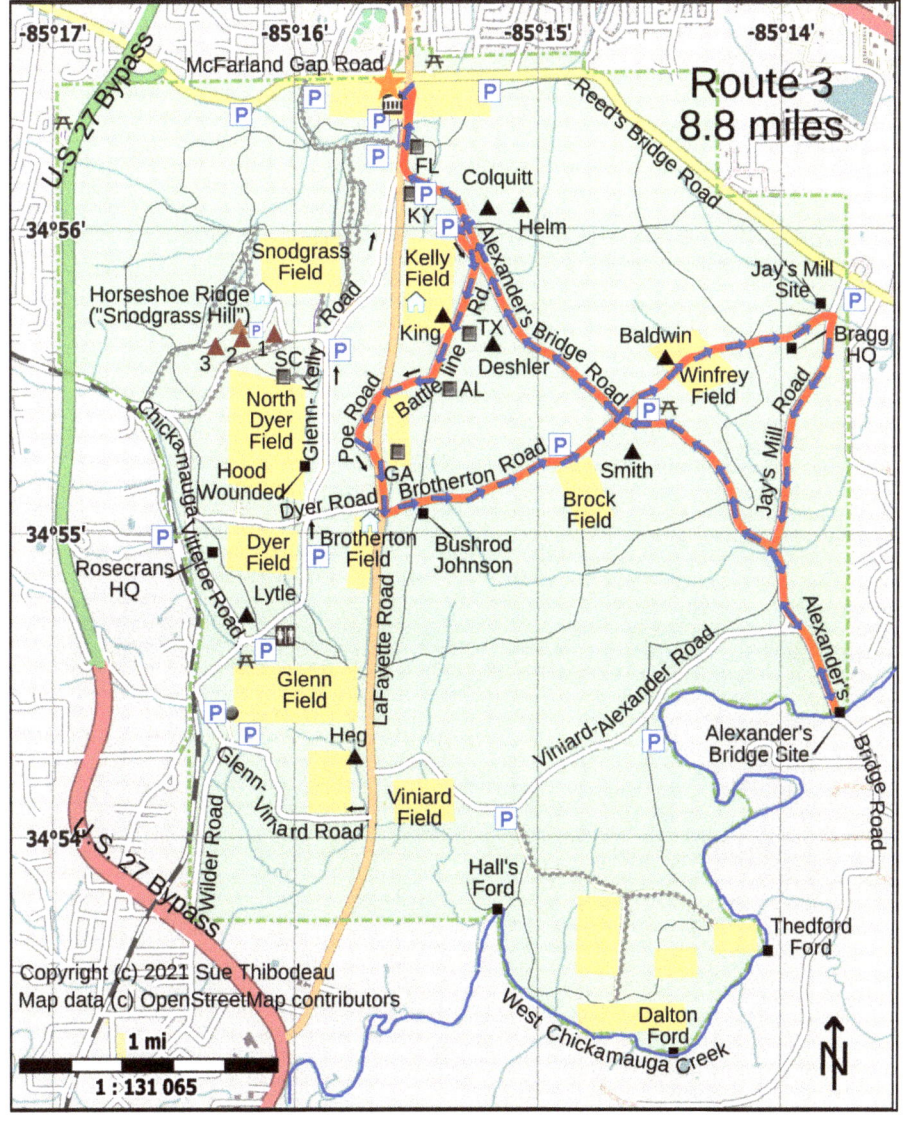

Map 17. Route 3 "Eastern Woods Loop" (8.8 Miles)

Why Route 3?

Route 3 spends very little time on LaFayette Road. In total, the distance from the Visitor Center to Alexander's Bridge Road (round-trip) is 0.6 miles, and then we add another 0.2 miles between Poe Road and Brotherton Road. Route 3 is a shoulderless, paved and flat ride through Chickamauga's scenic woods and fields. Moreover, the butterfly shape of this route, which you can see clearly in Map 17, means that you can ride the butterfly and add 6.5 more miles with each iteration.

This guidebook encourages you to explore Chickamauga on another ride *after* you complete Route 1. Once you learn from experience that the park is easy to navigate in loops, Route 3 emerges as an interesting way to focus on battlefield events that occurred on September 19, 1863. (The NPS auto tour skips most of the historic sites that you will encounter on Route 3).

Like the maps for Routes 1 and 2, double arrows indicate that you will ride in both directions sometime while following the route. You will begin at the Visitor Center, turn RIGHT on LaFayette Road, LEFT on Alexander's Bridge Road, and then RIGHT on Battleline Road.

Picnic Area on Alexander's Bridge Road Near Winfrey Field

Route 3 Loop (8.8 Miles)

Federal Cannon on Battleline Road, Pointing East
(Near the 4th Indiana Battery Monument)

Confederate Cannon Pointing to Alexander's Bridge Road
(Near the Site of Brig. Gen. Helm's Mortal Wounding)

PART IV: MONUMENTS AND STRUCTURES

Chapter 9 Listing

	Page
1. Alabama State Monument	132
2. Florida State Monument	133
3. Georgia State Monument	134
4. Kentucky State Monument	135
5. South Carolina State Monument	136
6. Texas State Monument	137

9. State Monuments

> *In no book was it ever recorded that the battle-scarred soldiers of two opposing armies ever before met as brethren on such a field of strife to mark with enduring monuments where they shed each other's blood.*[110]
> ~ Alabama Gov. William C. Oates, 15th Alabama Infantry

This guidebook tells the Chickamauga battlefield story using the natural and physical structures that a bicyclist would encounter while touring the park. Previous chapters put the narrative in the context of roadways, farmsteads, woodlots, and of course, Chickamauga Creek. The next three chapters provide a thematic introduction to commemorative features of the national military park, especially its state and regimental battle monuments.

Chapter 9 provides an overview of Chickamauga's six state monuments. These mostly large, impressive structures are easily accessible to the bicycling tourist—one obvious reason to include them in this travel guide. More importantly, though, Chickamauga's state monuments put forward the voices of thousands of Civil War veterans, organized by home state. It therefore makes sense that this guidebook selects "state monuments" as a helpful theme for learning about the Battle of Chickamauga. However, Chickamauga's state monuments are all Confederate structures—except for the border state of Kentucky—and not every Confederate state has a monument dedicated to whole sets of regiments. This obviously means that the "state monument" learning theme would imperfectly tell only "half" of the battle story.

Chapter 10 will obviate this shortcoming by surveying *every* state that mustered military units to fight for either side. To make this work, the chapter will expand its source material beyond physical battlefield structures. This approach is necessary, because a "perfect" and complete (by state) sequencing of structures would require too many tour stops for too many small markers and cast iron signs.

Chapter 11 represents a return to a cleanly thematic learning approach. The chapter covers Chickamauga's eight memorial shell monuments, each of which honors a mortally wounded or killed officer.

Six State Monuments (1899–1964)

On your ride through the Chickamauga battlefield, you will visit six state monuments: Alabama (1913), Florida (1912), Georgia (1899), Kentucky (USA/CSA, 1899), South Carolina (1901), and Texas (1964).[111] These large, prominent structures commemorate the service of all soldiers hailing from a common Confederate state—or in the case of Kentucky, both its Confederate and Union members. For the tourist, these six monuments merit special attention partly for their size, but also for their breadth of commemorative coverage. Notably, Union veterans did not elect to build large monuments that honored Union soldiers, by state, and instead focused on monuments and markers that defined battle lines and advanced the battle narrative based primarily on military structures and actions, not state affiliation.

Veterans erected Chickamauga's Confederate state monuments in the years *after* the park's dedication in September 1895. This was due to financial challenges in the southern states in the decades after the U.S. Civil War. Northern states and veterans' groups had larger budgets. The first so-called "state monuments" at Chickamauga honor Union state *regiments*, not the states themselves. Before providing an overview of Chickamauga's six Confederate state monuments, let us back up for a brief history of the establishment of Chickamauga and Chattanooga National Military Park.

The Nation's First National Military Park

Ohio Congressman Charles H. Grosvenor advanced the work of fellow Chickamauga veterans, Henry Van Ness Boynton and Ferdinand Van Derveer, by introducing a bill to preserve and commemorate the Chickamauga and Chattanooga battlefields. H.R. 6454 authorized the establishment of Chickamauga and Chattanooga National Military Park on August 19, 1890, and President Benjamin Harrison (a former Union general) signed the bill into law on the following day. It stipulated that Union and Confederate veterans together design and construct the country's first national military park. These states contributed to the project, which commemorated both the Chickamauga and Chattanooga campaigns: Alabama, Connecticut (late), Georgia, Illinois, Indiana, Iowa (late), Kansas, Kentucky, Louisiana, Maryland (late), Massachusetts, Michigan, Minnesota, Missouri, New Jersey, New York, North Carolina, Ohio

State Monuments

(the first), Pennsylvania, South Carolina, Tennessee, Texas, and Wisconsin.[112]

Pursuant to the Act of Congress, Secretary of War Redfield Proctor formed the Chickamauga Memorial Commission and appointed its members. The commission's charter was to procure and restore battlefield land; mark battle lines; coordinate with states on the design and installation of monuments; and plan the dedication ceremonies. Its members included Joseph F. Fullerton (Union Missouri veteran); Alexander P. Stewart (Confederate Tennessee veteran); active-duty servicemember Sanford C. Kellogg (5th U.S. Cavalry); and others, especially commission secretary Boynton. The challenge was a large one:

> To achieve this ambitious end, the commission called in groups of veterans to reconstruct the history of the battles and locate troop positions so that the lines would be accurately marked. After thirty years, the battlefield had been obscured by overgrown vegetation and destructive farming practices, and veterans often disagreed on the locations of various battle-era events and landmarks. Roads, buildings, fences, and other features from the battle period were restored and more recent additions removed.[113]

The law provided for the erection of monuments and markers funded not only by the federal government (for U.S. Regulars), but also state commissions and private veterans' groups. Although the park commission set the standards for monument design, construction, and inscriptions, final approvals issued from the Secretary of War after 1893. Prominent companies received contracts to build park monuments. Among them were the Smith Granite Company (Rhode Island); E.F. Carr and Van Amringe Companies (Massachusetts); Muldroon Company (Kentucky); and McNeel Marble Company (Georgia). The monument sculptors were also well-known and included, for example: Lorado Taft, Roland Hinton Perry, C.H. Niehaus, Fred Moynihan, and Caspar Buberl.[114]

Dedication Ceremonies (September 18–20, 1895)

The work of the commission culminated in a three-day dedication ceremony on the battle's 32nd anniversary, September 18–20, 1895. Secretary of War Daniel S. Lamont had appointed Fullerton to plan the dedication event in his role as grand marshal. About 40,000 to

50,000 visitors, fifteen state governors, and military officers participated in the ceremonies, which included speeches from leaders on both sides of the bloody conflict. Congressman Grosvenor said in his speech that, the park's completion was "the achievement of which we are proudest ... that we are no longer enemies, but brothers." Tennessee Governor and Confederate loyalist Peter Turney framed the character of the commemoration in this way: "You are welcome now. Perhaps thirty-two years ago you were not; but you are broad, true, and chivalrous men, and as such we welcome you."[115]

On September 18, 1895, and at various locations throughout Chickamauga and Chattanooga National Military Park, eight states dedicated what the program loosely identified as "state monuments." This was an umbrella term that included regimental monuments associated with a particular state, all of which fought for the Union: Indiana, Illinois, Massachusetts, Michigan, Minnesota, Missouri, Ohio, and Wisconsin. In other words, the first monuments erected on the battlefield were Union regimental monuments (due to funding challenges faced by the former Confederate states). As previously mentioned, in later years six Confederate states erected monuments specifically to honor the state's full, multi-regiment contribution to the Battle of Chickamauga.

On September 19, a forty-four-gun salute opened the dedication exercises on Snodgrass Hill, where the dedication focused on the Chickamauga section of the park. Chairman Fullerton announced that the day's celebration on Snodgrass Hill "marks the beginning of a regenerated national life" where there is peace.[116] Fullerton then introduced U.S. Vice President Adlai E. Stevenson, who like other speakers that weekend, invoked the spirit of Lincoln by quoting the Gettysburg Address. Notably, Union generals Rosecrans and Thomas were not in attendance since Rosecrans was "struggling with age and disease" and Thomas had died in 1870. On the Confederate side, Gen. Bragg died in 1876, but Lt. Gen. James Longstreet was at the dedication to deliver an address. Finally, on September 20, dedication ceremonies moved to the Chattanooga.[117]

State Monuments

State Monuments at Chickamauga Battlefield

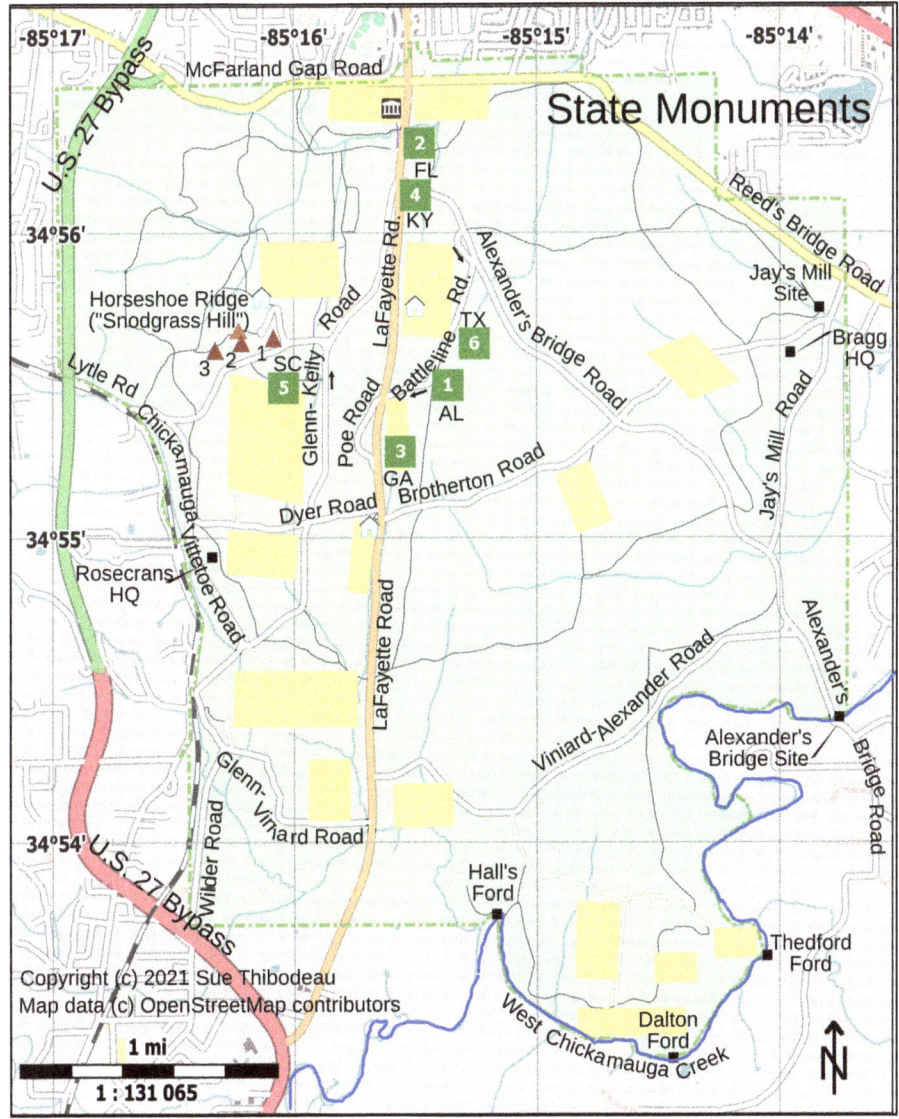

Map 18. State Monuments at Chickamauga

The green numbers on Map 18 correspond to an alphabetized listing and description of Chickamauga's state monuments, below.

1. Alabama State Monument (CSA)

Erected: May 28, 1913, by the Ladies Aid Memorial Association of Montgomery, Alabama[118]
Designer: Toca Cozart
Contractor: E.C. Rammage[119]
Location: Battleline Road
GPS (lat, lon): 34.92450, –85.25703

These Confederate brigades fielded at least one unit from Alabama:[120]

Alabama State Monument

  Daniel W. Adam's Brigade
  Patton Anderson's Brigade
  William B. Bate's Brigade
  Henry D. Clayton's Brigade
  Zach C. Deas' Brigade
  Matthew D. Ector's Brigade
  Archibald Gracie's Brigade
  Benjamin Helm's Brigade
  Arthur M. Manigault's Brigade
  James Sheffield's (Law) Brigade
  Sterling A.M. Wood's Brigade
  Army Reserve Artillery
  Cleburne's Division Artillery
  Liddell's Division Artillery
  Stewart's Division Artillery
  Charles C. Crews' Cavalry
  John T. Morgan's Cavalry
  Col. Alfred A. Russell's Cavalry

After the U.S. Civil War, societies of Confederate women helped to bury soldiers and to memorialize their service and cause by erecting monuments. The Ladies Aid Memorial Association of Montgomery, Alabama raised the funds to design and erect Alabama's only monument on the Chickamauga battlefield. They dedicated this simple 32' 6"-high granite obelisk during a United Confederate Veteran reunion in 1913. The monument's south face has the words "Here We Rest" and its west face bears this inscription:

> In tender memory of Alabama soldiers who fought and fell on Chickamauga battlefield. This shaft shall point to those exciting scenes and visions long since flown, for memory is the only friend that grief can call its own.

2. Florida State Monument (CSA)

Erected: 1912–13 by the State of Florida
Sculptor: L. Milinn
Fabricator: McNeel Marble Works, Marietta, Georgia[121]
Location: LaFayette Road, near Visitor Center
GPS (lat, lon): 34.93788, –85.25890

Florida State Monument

At Chickamauga, Florida soldiers fought in the three brigades: Buckner's Corps reserve artillery and the infantry commands of M.A. Stovall and R.C. Trigg. The Florida State Monument is Florida's only monument on the battlefield. It is a domed, twelve-column structure erected by the state and dedicated on May 28, 1913, during a reunion of the United Confederate Veterans. Each corner has three Doric columns made of Mt. Airy granite that support a canopy over a bronze statue of a Confederate soldier. Its west face inscription broadly honors all Florida soldiers who fought at the Battle of Chickamauga:

> This monument has been erected in memory of the soldiers of the State of Florida who took part in the battle fought here September 19–20, 1863 whether they fell in battle or lived to render further services to their state and country.

3. Georgia State Monument (CSA)

Erected: May 4, 1899, by the State of Georgia
Sculptor: Frederick Moynihan (1843–1910)
Granite Work: Muldoon Monument Co., Louisville, Kentucky
Bronze Work: Gorham Manufacturing Co. (New York)[122]
Location: Poe Field, east side of LaFayette Road
GPS (lat, lon): 34.92093, –85.26039

These Confederate brigades fielded at least one unit from Georgia:

Georgia State Monument

William B. Bate's Brigade
Henry L. Benning's Brigade
Henry B. Davidson's Brigade
J. Fulton's (Johnson) Brigade
John K. Jackson's Brigade
John H. Kelly's Brigade
Marcellus A. Stovall's Brigade
Claudius C. Wilson's Brigade
Army Reserve Artillery
Cheatham's Division Artillery
Preston's Division Artillery
Stewart's Division Artillery
Walker's Division Artillery
Charles C. Crews' Cavalry

The Georgia State Monument stands 87' high and is the tallest monument on the Chickamauga battlefield. A bronze statue of a Confederate soldier (a color bearer) tops the blue granite column immediately above four stone carvings of horses' heads. On the monument's three-tiered base stand bronze statues of an infantryman, artilleryman, and cavalryman. For the dedication ceremony, officials had draped a United States flag over the bronze statues and then lifted it. This inscription on the monument's west face defined the intent of the commemorative exercise:

> To the lasting memory of all her sons who fought on this field—those who fought and lived and those who fought and died, those who gave much and those who gave all. Georgia erects this monument.

State Monuments

4. Kentucky State Monument (USA, CSA)

Erected: May 3, 1899, by the State of Kentucky
Architect: J.H. Lowe
Contractor: Muldoon Monument Co., Louisville, Kentucky[123]
Location: LaFayette Road at Alexander's Bridge Road
GPS (lat, lon): 34.93594, −85.25932

Kentucky State Monument

Union brigades that fielded at least one unit from Kentucky:

Philemon P. Baldwin's Brigade
Sidney M. Barnes' Brigade
John Beatty's Brigade
Samuel Beatty's Brigade
John T. Croxton's Brigade
Charles Cruft's Brigade
William Grose's Brigade
William B. Hazen's Brigade
Charles G. Harker's Brigade
Eli Long's Brigade
John B. Turchin's Brigade
Louis D. Watkins' Brigade

Confederate brigades having at least one unit from Kentucky:

Benjamin Helm's Brigade
John H. Kelly's Brigade
Breckinridge's Division Artillery
Thomas Harrison's Cavalry Brigade
Wheeler's (Armstrong) Cav. Brigade

Kentucky's 43' 7" high state monument is the only Chickamauga structure dedicated to soldiers from both armies. Its state seal quotes Kentucky native Abraham Lincoln: "United we stand, divided we fall." The monument features a statue of Bellona, the Roman goddess of war. Granite eagles protect two national flags.[124] Its inscription says:

> Erected by the State of Kentucky in memory of her sons who fought and fell on this field. As we united in life, and they united in death, let one monument perpetuate their deeds, and one people, forgetful of all asperities, forever hold in grateful remembrance all the glories of that terrible conflict which made all men free and retained every star on the nation's flag.

5. South Carolina State Monument (CSA)

Dedicated: May 27, 1901, by the State of South Carolina[125]
Contractors: Winsboro Granite & Stewart Stone
Foundry: Ames Foundries, Chicopee, Massachusetts[126]
Location: Dyer Field, northeast corner via pedestrian path
GPS (lat, lon): 34.92518, −85.26769

These Confederate brigades fielded at least one unit from South Carolina:

Peyton Colquitt's (Gist's) Brigade
Joseph B. Kershaw's Brigade
Arthur M. Manigault's Brigade
Evander McNair's Brigade

The South Carolina State Monument stands on a hill over which South Carolina soldiers advanced to attack Maj. Gen. George H. Thomas' last line of defense on September 20, 1863. A tally of the casualty numbers inscribed on the monument indicate that the state suffered 134 killed; 40 mortally wounded; 736 wounded; and 13 missing.

South Carolina State Monument

Two bronze sculptures depict a Confederate infantryman and artilleryman. They stand on a 10'-tiered granite pedestal base that also supports a 25' high pointed obelisk. The obelisk replaces what was in 1905 a 13' high bronze palmetto tree whose fragile structure could not weather hilltop winds and rainstorms. The monument's original cost was $8,750 but the tree and obelisk renovations cost another $2,500.[127]

The front face of the South Carolina State Monument bears this inscription:

> To her faithful sons at Chickamauga South Carolina erects this monument to commemorate the valor they proved, and the lives they gave on this great battlefield.

State Monuments

6. Texas State Monument (CSA)

Erected: 1964 by the State of Texas[128]
Designer: Harold B. Simpson (1917–1989)
Location: Battleline Road
GPS (lat, lon):   34.92698, –85.25646

Texas State Monument

These Confederate brigades fielded at least one unit from Texas:

    James Deshler's Brigade
    Matthew D. Ector's Brigade
    John Gregg's Brigade
    Thomas Harrison's Brigade
    Jerome B. Robertson's Brigade
    Cleburne's Division Artillery

The Texas State Monument is a 7' high pink granite structure that stands (replicated) on eleven U.S. Civil War battlefields. The Texas state seal is on the top and near the bottom are these words: "A memorial to Texans who served the Confederacy."

The State of Texas erected this monument in time for Civil War Centennial celebrations, which is obviously long after the Commemorative Era in which veterans installed monuments on the Chickamauga battlefield. For decades, Texas state and federal officials declined to enact legislation for such a project. But in 1961, that changed, and Texans selected as the site for their monument to be near the mortal wounding of Brig. Gen. James Deshler, a brigade of mostly Texans in Cleburne's Division.[129] The inscription on the monument's front face includes this dedication:

> Texas remembers the valor and devotion of her sons who served at Chickamauga, September 19–20, 1863. Here in the Great Confederate Breakthrough Texans vied with each other to prove themselves worthy of fame won by their brothers on other fields.

Chapter 10 Listing

	Page
1. Alabama (CSA)	142
2. Arkansas (CSA)	143
3. Florida (CSA)	144
4. Georgia (CSA)	145
5. Illinois (USA)	146
6. Indiana (USA)	149
7. Kansas (USA)	151
8. Kentucky (USA, CSA)	152
9. Louisiana (CSA)	155
10. Michigan (USA)	156
11. Minnesota (USA)	157
12. Mississippi (CSA)	159
13. Missouri (USA, CSA)	160
14. North Carolina (CSA)	161
15. Ohio (USA)	163
16. Pennsylvania (USA)	168
17. South Carolina (CSA)	170
18. Tennessee (USA, CSA)	171
19. Texas (CSA)	172
20. Virginia (CSA)	174
21. Wisconsin (USA)	176

Reading Tip: Because this chapter contains a significant amount of military detail, it can be dense reading. The chapter works best as historical reference material because it provides additional context to the more general narrative presented in Parts I and II. Notably, the bicycle cues in Part III include references to state military actions described in this chapter.

10. The States at Chickamauga

> *Truth, crushed to earth, shall rise again;*
> *The eternal years of God are hers;*
> *But error, wounded, writhes with pain,*
> *And dies among his worshippers.*[130]
> ~ William Cullen Bryant (1794–1878), American Poet

Many tourists who visit U.S. Civil War battlefields enjoy learning about their own state's role in a particular battle. Sometimes this interest extends deeper into family connections and genealogical research. Whereas the previous chapter described Chickamauga's six state monuments, with brief mention of the state's military actions at the Battle of Chickamauga, this chapter expands the topic to include all twenty-three states that mustered troops that fought here. These include ten Union states, twelve Confederate states, and one border state (Kentucky).

There is obviously a great deal of subjectivity involved in deciding what subject matter to select for each state summary. Chapter 10 will present a varied mix of topical approaches, with an emphasis on military history. Examples include describing monument architecture and commemorative history, summarizing battle strategy and tactics, and telling human interest stories. The approach is like Chapter 1, "Chickamauga on a Bicycle," where park roads (p. 34) and natural and physical landmarks (p. 48) are the tactile components of the battle narrative. As reference material that summarizes the role of each state, Chapter 10's sections can be read in any order.

Chapter 10 will vary its presentation by alternating between the use of modern photos, monument inscriptions, and quotations of nineteenth century military sources. In this way, the chapter retells various aspects of the battle narrative from different perspectives. With each retelling, you will make new connections and develop new historical insights. Finally, the careful reader will want occasionally to refer to earlier, more chronological sections of this book while building a factual framework for understanding the battle:

> Pages 68–69: USA and CSA Abbreviated Orders of Battle
> Pages 71–75: A Concise Overview of Battlefield Events
> Pages 75–79: A Visual Summary of the Battle Phases

Army of the Cumberland (USA) at Chickamauga Maj. Gen. William S. Rosecrans[131]					
States		Infantry	Cavalry	Artillery	Totals
Illinois	*§	33	—	4	37
Indiana	*	33	3	8	44
Kansas	*	1	—	—	1
Kentucky	♦*	14	4	—	18
Michigan	*	5	2	2	9
Minnesota	*§	1	—	1	2
Missouri	*§	2	—	1	3
Ohio	*§	43	3	10	56
Pennsylvania	*	3	2	1	6
Tennessee	*	—	2	—	2
US Regulars	*	5	1	4	10
Wisconsin	*	5	1	3	9
	Totals:	145	18	34	197

Notes: Infantry totals include unmounted cavalry, sharpshooter battalions, and units guarding the army supply train. Counts include regiments, battalions, and batteries (but not detached companies).

Key:
- ♦ Erected state monuments (all regiments) at Chickamauga.
- * Erected regimental monuments at Chickamauga.
- § Dedicated regimental monuments at Chickamauga, Sept. 1895.

Table 10. USA Military Units at the Battle of Chickamauga

Of the eleven Union states that participated in the Battle of Chickamauga, only Kentucky erected a state monument. It honored soldiers from both sides of the conflict. All Union states erected regimental monuments, but only four states met the deadline for the September 1895 dedication of Chickamauga and Chattanooga National Military Park: Illinois, Minnesota, Missouri, and Ohio. In the next decade, veterans installed and dedicated monuments for Indiana, Kansas, Michigan, Pennsylvania, Tennessee, and Wisconsin.

Note: For this chapter, the author extracted GPS coordinates from photo metadata collected during a 2019 visit to the battlefield.

The States at Chickamauga

Army of Tennessee (CSA) at Chickamauga
Gen. Braxton Bragg (Sept. 20)[132]

States		Number of Regiments, Battalions, and Batteries			
		Infantry	Cavalry	Artillery	Totals
Alabama	♦	31	7	8	46
Arkansas	x	11	1	3	15
CSA Regulars	x	1	4	—	5
Florida	♦	5	—	1	6
Georgia	♦*	17	5	7	29
Kentucky	♦*	5	2	2	9
Louisiana	x	6	1	3	10
Mississippi	x	20	1	4	25
Missouri	*	—	—	2	2
North Carolina	x	4	1	—	5
South Carolina	♦*	8	—	1	9
Tennessee	*	42	12	6	60
Texas	♦	10	2	1	13
Virginia	x	2	—	1	3
Totals:		**162**	**36**	**39**	**237**

Notes: Infantry totals include unmounted cavalry and sharpshooter battalions. Counts include regiments, battalions, and batteries (but not detached companies). Combined regiments count as one (e.g., 12th + 47th Tennessee is one). This table is for September 20.

Key: ♦ Erected state monuments (all regiments) at Chickamauga.
* Erected regimental monuments at Chickamauga.
§ Dedicated regimental monuments at Chickamauga, Sept. 1895.
x Installed small granite or cast iron markers, but not monuments.

Table 11. CSA Military Units at the Battle of Chickamauga

Of the thirteen Confederate states that fought in the battle, only Georgia, Kentucky, and South Carolina erected both state and regimental monuments. In a different approach, Alabama, Florida, and Texas each erected a state monument but no regimental monuments. On the other hand, Arkansas, Louisiana, Mississippi, North Carolina, and Virginia did not erect any monuments at Chickamauga, but the states installed simple granite markers that identify the regiments' battlefield positions and their commanders' names.

1. Alabama (CSA)

Men from Alabama served in almost every division of Bragg's Army of Tennessee (see p. 132). They were infantrymen, artillerymen, and cavalrymen. Notably, Maj. Gen. Thomas C. Hindman's division included five Alabama infantry regiments in Deas' Brigade and three in Manigault's Brigade; three Alabama batteries (Garrity, Dent, Waters); and one Alabama battalion of sharpshooters. This section shines the spotlight on Deas' all-Alabama infantry brigade. Brig. Gen. Zach C. Deas was a wealthy Alabama cotton broker.

Deas' Brigade (Longstreet's Breakthrough)

On September 20, 1863, Deas' Brigade (in Longstreet's left wing) attacked through a gap that opened in the Union line at the Brotherton Farm. Union Brig. Gen. Brannan described the situation at 11:00 a.m.:

> [Brig. Gen.] Wood was now on my immediate right. Wood being almost immediately afterward ordered to the left, moved out of line, while Davis took ground to his left to fill the vacancy caused by Wood. In this movement a slight interval occurred in the line, which the rebels took advantage of with great rapidity, intercepting and breaking the line of battle of the army at that point.[133]

By 11:15 a.m., Longstreet had ordered three divisions to attack with Hood's men in front, but Johnson took the lead as Col. Fulton's Tennessee brigade crashed through Brotherton Field (see p. 57).[134]

Then at 11:30 a.m., Deas' Alabama brigade, now on the west side of LaFayette Road, drove through the woods to Fulton's left and flanked the weakened Union brigades of Cols. Carlin and Martin (who replaced Col. Heg, now dead; see p. 184).[135] The Alabamians sent the midwesterners reeling northward through Dyer Field and up to Horseshoe Ridge and Snodgrass Farm. While rallying the Federals in the chaos, Brig. Gen. Lytle also died (see p. 187).

Hindman reported that Deas' Brigade "swept like a whirlwind over the breastworks" and charged "at the double-quick through a storm of bullets, shot, and shell." The entire advance from the woods through fields and up to the ridge led to the capture of 17 guns; 1,400 small arms; 165,000 rounds of ammunition; and more than 1,100 prisoners, including 3 colonels.[136]

2. Arkansas (CSA)

At Chickamauga, the following units included soldiers from Arkansas (and none erected a monument on the battlefield):

> 1st AK, Lucius Polk's Brigade, Cleburne's Division
> 19th-24th AK, Deshler's Brigade, Cleburne's Division
> Calvert's Battery, Semple's Artillery, Cleburne's Division
> Humphreys' Battery, Eldridge's Artillery, Stewart's Division
> Daniel C. Govan's (Liddell's) Brigade, Liddell's Division
> Evander McNair's Brigade, Johnson's Provisional Division
> 3rd AK, Robertson's Brigade, Law's (Hood) Division
> Wiggins' Battery, Russell's Brigade, Wheeler's Cavalry
> 3rd AK, Armstrong's (Wheeler's) Brigade, Forrest's Cavalry

The brigades of Daniel C. Govan and Evander McNair had the most men from Arkansas. We highlight McNair's Brigade, below.

McNair's Brigade (Longstreet's Breakthrough)

A Mississippi businessman who moved to Arkansas, Brig. Gen. Evander McNair commanded a brigade until he fell at Chickamauga while fighting in Bushrod Johnson's division.[137] His brigade roster included these Arkansas units: 1st and 2nd AK Mounted Rifles (which fought as infantry, dismounted since 1862); 4th AK Battalion; 25th AK; and a patchwork unit of the 4th+31st Infantry. These men attacked with the weight of the left wing of Bragg's army under Longstreet and helped to route the Union right wing on September 20, 1863.

Before the Confederate breakthrough, Johnson described the Union line as having "two lines of breastworks made of rails and timber." His division, which included McNair's Arkansas brigade, "advanced about 600 yards through the woods under a heavy fire and crossed the road." Johnson wrote that their "charge was irresistible" and that "the Yankees who did not flee were killed and captured at the fences and out-houses."[138] According to Longstreet, who thought Hood attacked first, "Hood's column broke the enemy's line near the Brotherton house and made it wheel to the right." Longstreet also wrote that Hood fell with a severe leg injury while "Johnson's division [including McNair] followed the movement made by Hood ... having a full share of the conflict."[139] The brigade of 1,207 men suffered 35.2 percent casualties: 51 killed, 320 wounded, 54 missing (425 total).[140]

3. Florida (CSA)

Florida men fought in these units at Chickamauga (see p. 133):

> Robert P. McCants' Battery, Buckner's Reserve Artillery
> Marcellus A. Stovall's Brigade, Breckinridge's Division
> Robert C. Trigg's Brigade, Preston's Division

Trigg's Brigade (Capture of the "Lost Regiments")

When Robert C. Trigg received a brigade command, his Virginia regiment joined with three Florida units. On September 20, 1863, at 7:00 p.m., Col. Trigg's brigade captured the "Lost Regiments" of the 21st Ohio, 89th Ohio, and 22nd Michigan on the third hill southwest of the Snodgrass Cabin. Out of ammunition and refusing to retreat without orders, the midwesterners "continued the battle with gun butts and bayonets;" that is, until the men from Florida surrounded and captured them.[141] Trigg's Brigade marker is in the woods on the ridge and bears the following inscription, which lists the brigade's battle casualty rate as 25.85 percent, a devastating loss for Florida.

> Sept. 20, 1863, 7 p.m., Last Position
>
> 1st Florida Cavalry (Dismounted) Col. G. Troup Maxwell.
> 6th Florida – Col. J.J. Finley.
> 7th Florida – Col. Robert Bullock.
> 54th Virginia – Lieut. Col. John J. Wade.
>
> This Brigade being formed on the left of Kelly's on the opposite side of this ridge, swung to the right across the ridge into this ravine, and co-operating with Kelly then opposite to its line closed up on the knoll to the right of this point and captured most of the 21st and 89th Ohio and 22nd Michigan. These three regiments were serving temporarily on the left of Whitaker's Brigade.
>
> The movement of Trigg's Brigade to capture these troops was led by Capt. J.C.S. Blackburn of the Division staff, and about the time this had been accomplished, the brigade received a volley on its left flank from the right of Van Derveer's Brigade of Brannan's Division, ending the battle on this ground at 7:15 p.m. Strength in action 1091. Casualties: killed 46; wounded 231; missing 5; total 282. Percentage of loss 25.85.[142]

4. Georgia (CSA)

Series of Georgia Infantry Monuments

Three months after the September 1895 dedication of Chickamauga's national park, Georgia appropriated $25,000 for the Georgia Memorial Board to erect monuments that mark the state's battlefield positions. The state required that "the material used in the work shall, as far as practicable, be a product of Georgia."[143] Dedicated in 1899, the monument in Poe Field is the state's most impressive structure (pp. 134 and 59). Georgia's regimental monuments are distinctively shaped, five-sided granite monuments that each bears a symbol that identifies a branch of service: cartridge boxes (infantry), crossed cannon tubes (artillery), or horseshoe (cavalry). The monuments suggest the image of army pup tents.

The above photo shows the middle of a series of nine Georgia monuments that identify the positions of state infantry regiments and battalions on September 20, 1863. Specifically, they mark the noon–12:30 p.m. positions of Wilson's Brigade (Walker's Division) and the 5:30 p.m. positions of Jackson's Brigade (Cheatham's Division). Built in 1898–99, these monuments stand on the east side of Alexander's Bridge Road on the approach to Battleline Road. It was in this area that Georgians attacked the main Union line at Chickamauga.

5. Illinois (USA)

24th Illinois Infantry
Erected: 1899
Location: Battleline Road
GPS: 34.93108, -85.25453

Illinois mustered more than one-quarter-million of its citizens to the Union war effort overall. Chickamauga was its deadliest battle. On May 22, 1895, the State of Illinois appropriated $65,400 to mark the battlefield positions of ninety-two Illinois regiments and batteries that fought in the military campaigns of Chickamauga and Chattanooga. Then four years later (April 21, 1899), the state approved an additional $5,000 to cover the expense of monument dedication ceremonies.[144]

Illinois did not install a state monument on the Chickamauga battlefield, but instead elected to build large monuments on Missionary Ridge and Orchard Knob. At Chickamauga, you can identify Illinois' regimental monuments by their uniform construction. They are 7.5' x 4.3' x 4.5' beveled granite rectangular structures that include a prominent "ILLINOIS" heading and a polished front panel that names the military unit and its commander.

The 24th Illinois hailed from Chicago, a mostly German—but also Swiss, Swedish, and Hungarian—group of immigrants. The average age of a soldier in this regiment was twenty-seven years old and ranged from eighteen to fifty years of age. The older men had fought in the Revolutions of 1848 in Germany and the Austrian Empire.

At 5:30 p.m. on September 20, 1863, the 24th Illinois was part of the Union line along what is now Battleline Road. Col. Geza Mihalotzy commanded regiment, part of Starkweather's Brigade in Baird's Division. Georgians in Jackson's Brigade, Cheatham's Division, attacked the 24th Illinois from the northeast.

The Battle of Chickamauga was the regiment's last major fight. They had 23 killed, more than 80 wounded, and 50 soldiers captured. One captured man, Pvt. Christian Dressel (an eighteen-year-old German immigrant) died in 1864 while at the Confederate prison camp in Andersonville, Georgia.[145]

The States at Chickamauga

Wilder Brigade Monument (USA)

Wilder Brigade Monument Near Glenn Field

Dedicated: 1899
Location: Chickamauga-Vittetoe Road, east side
GPS: 34.90736, -85.27289

Named for Col. John T. Wilder (1830–1917) and his "Lightning Brigade" of mounted infantry—three regiments from Illinois and two from Indiana—the Wilder Brigade Monument is an 86-foot-high limestone structure that includes an interior staircase to an observation deck.[146] It stands on Rosecrans' headquarters before Longstreet's morning assault on September 20, 1863. Here, Wilder delayed Longstreet using rapid-fire Spencer repeating rifles (but the action stalled when Rosecrans, McCook, and Crittendon left the field). Invented in 1860 but not yet widely available, this .52-caliber breech-loading weapon could fire accurately seven shots in thirty seconds.[147]

Confederate soldier Benjamin Sawyer described the experience of the 24th Alabama regiment that morning when Wilder's Brigade unleashed the power of their Spencer rifles:

> A half mile, struggling through a tangle of scrubby brushwood, brought us to a field where, rising to the crest of a little ridge,

we saw the Federal lines on the opposite edge, strongly posted behind its hastily impoverished but efficient breastworks. We had scarcely gotten in range before they opened upon us a continuous sheet of fire. We had no time to pause for thought of dread or danger. We were in the very jaws of the monster. We could not retreat. ... One-fourth of my regiment was cut down. Never before had I, nor since have I, seen such terrible execution in so short a time. It was more than mortal nerve could bear...[148]

On the 36th anniversary of the Battle of Chickamauga, about 10,000 visitors traveled to northwest Georgia via rail, "private vehicles," and bicycles to participate in dedication ceremonies for the Wilder Brigade Monument and 113 Indiana monuments and markers.[149] Among the travelers was Smith D. Atkins, who led the 92nd Illinois, part of Wilder's Brigade. Atkins paid tribute to his former commander in a speech that noted Wilder's "inventive genius" in revolutionizing cavalry tactics for every army in the world. Notably, and for expediency, Wilder purchased the Spencer repeating rifles through personal loans. According to Atkins, these rifles were "the most effective and complete weapon for actual service ever placed in the hands of soldiers."[150]

Wilder also emphasized the importance of the Spencer rifles in his 1899 monument dedication speech when he said that the structure "marks the line where the bravest of brave Americans met in headlong conflict, each determined to win, and where the best armament proved successful." Armed with Spencer rifles against overwhelming force, Wilder claimed that his mounted infantry brigade "proved their manhood by driving their attack with irresistible power."[151] After crediting superior weaponry and his brigade's skillful use of its rifles and horses, he concluded his speech using the language of national reconciliation and commemoration. Addressing the secretary of the memorial commission, Wilder said:

> To you, General Boynton, I have the honor of turning over the custody of this monument as the representative of our great country. May it stand for ages to show the coming generations how their ancestors fought for their principles. It stands as a monument to the valor of those who fought on both sides. May its lessons be learned by all our descendants.[152]

6. Indiana (USA)

Indiana monuments are mostly rough-hewn structures built from limestone that has a pockmarked look. The monuments typically have a two-step base on which stands a rectangular block (as for the 4th Indiana Battery) or smooth granite shaft (as for the 5th Indiana Battery). The tops appear slightly angled or curved. A bronze state seal inset shows on the front face of each structure.

4th Indiana Battery (from Indianapolis)
Erected: 1897–98
Location: Battleline Road
GPS: 34.93186, -85.25459

5th Indiana Battery (from Indianapolis)
Erected: 1897–98
Location: Battleline Road
GPS: 34.92983, -85.25494

The 4th Indiana Battery Monument marks the unit's position from 9:00 a.m. until 5:30 p.m. on Sunday, September 20, 1863. Facing east, the battery was part of Thomas' defensive battle line that included, to their immediate left, units from Indiana and Ohio; and to their immediate right, units from Wisconsin and Pennsylvania. Farther southwest on that same line was the 5th Indiana Battery, which supported similar midwestern units, but also the 5th Kentucky U.S. Regulars. The 5th Indiana Battery has the distinction of having killed Chickamauga's Confederate right wing commander, Lt. Gen. Leonidas Polk, eight months later at Pine Mountain, Georgia.

Bicycling Chickamauga Battlefield

This page provides a sampling of images that collectively express the architectural design of Indiana's regimental infantry monuments at Chickamauga battlefield.

**6th Indiana Infantry
(from counties near Indianapolis)**
Erected: 1897–98
Location: Battleline Road
GPS: 34.92956, -85.25507

**31st Indiana Infantry
(from Terre Haute)**
Erected: 1897–98
Location: Brotherton Road, west
GPS: 34.91900, -85.25377

**35th Indiana Infantry
("The Irish Regiment")**

**38th Indiana Infantry
(from New Albany)**

Erected: 1897–98
Location: Battleline Road
GPS: 34.93359, -85.25612

Erected: 1897–98
Location: Battleline Road (p. 36)
GPS: 34.93207, -85.25479

7. Kansas (USA)

Kansas installed one monument at Chickamauga. Built between 1910 and 1919, the 8th Kansas Monument is an eight-foot-high rock-faced structure that consists of three simple granite tiers. Because the monument is located on the heavily trafficked LaFayette Road, north of Viniard Road, this book does not include it as a tour stop.

8th Kansas Infantry ("Hot Fighting" in Viniard Field)

The inscription and veteran reports of the 8th Kansas Monument describe in unusual detail Kansas' role in the "hottest fighting" of September 19, 1863, in Viniard Field. The monument describes briefly what happened after Kansas soldiers crossed LaFayette Road with Heg's Brigade of midwesterners to fight men from Tennessee:

> On Sept. 19th, *[the regiment]* went into action east of this point and was in the hottest part of the battle from 12:30 until 6:00 p.m.. Col. Heg was killed, Col. Martin assumed command of the brigade... The fighting during the day was severe. The ground where this monument stands was repeatedly occupied by the opposing forces. ... Sept. 20th, at 12:00 o'clock the brigade went into action on the Brotherton Farm, but was soon forced to retire to McFarland's Gap. ...[153]

The unit's two-day losses were staggering (from the monument):

> Total number engaged 406. Loss: 2 Commissioned officers killed. 9 Commissioned officers wounded. 28 Enlisted men killed. 156 Enlisted men wounded. 25 Enlisted men missing. Total Loss 220 = 54.19 percent.

The *Report of the Adjutant General of the State of Kansas* describes the regiment's actions on September 19 in this colorful way:

> ... a more terrible sound greeted our ears, the dull, heavy crashes of a dense musketry fire, rising and falling in sullen, resounding, deafening roars, like waves beating upon a shore. ... and our division came up just in time to check the impetuous advance of the rebels. We were moved rapidly ... on the double-quick, and after forming line of battle, advanced through the dense woods, "going in", as General Rosecrans after expressed it, "where the fight was the hottest."[154]

8. Kentucky (USA/CSA)

The Kentucky State Monument (p. 135) lists seventeen Union regiments, seven Confederate regiments, and two Confederate batteries that fought at Chickamauga. Although a granite marker or cast-iron tablet identifies each unit's battle position, they are not particularly easy for a bicyclist to find. None have monuments on the Chickamauga battlefield. For those reasons, this section is "pre reading" for your battlefield tour. For brevity and inclusiveness, we feature one Union and one Confederate Kentucky brigade.[155]

Union Kentucky Protecting Supplies and Wounded Men

Col. Louis D. Watkins' brigade in Mitchell's Cavalry Corps was the Union army's only all-Kentucky cavalry brigade (4th, 5th, and 6th regiments). According to Watkins' official report, on September 20, 1863, the brigade was protecting the army's supply train and 400 sick men, plus 4 prisoners, while moving northeast from Lookout Mountain to Crawfish Spring, still about five miles from the battle's center. Unfortunately, a communication breakdown between Col. Watkins and Brig. Gen. Mitchell threw the brigade into the path of Confederate Maj. Gen. Joseph Wheeler's cavalry. Also, unbeknownst to Watkins, the 5th Kentucky had already retreated through Cooper's Gap, where an officer traveling with a different supply train remarked that the regiment "came rushing up like bees swarming from a hive."[156]

Now, with only two (not three) regiments under Watkins' effective command, he described the clash with Wheeler's cavalry, as follows:

> Now commenced a running fight, but the wagons (as they only got as far as the foot of the mountain) blockaded the road and threw all into confusion. All efforts of the officers to form and rally the men proved only partially successful... [T]he enemy's column, flanking on my right, ran in and intercepted a portion of the Fourth and Sixth Kentucky Cavalry, and after considerable slaughter on both sides the enemy captured a large number of prisoners.[157]

The brigade lost 53 wagons but reached Chattanooga safely by 10:00 p.m. that night. Watkins' Brigade casualties were as follows: 4th Kentucky (288): 1 wounded, 94 missing; 5th Kentucky (363): 20 missing; and 6th Kentucky (524): 2 killed, 7 wounded, 122 missing.[158]

The States at Chickamauga

Confederate Kentucky in "Breckinridge's Assault"

At Chickamauga, Brig. Gen. Benjamin H. Helm commanded a brigade comprised of four Confederate Kentucky infantry regiments (2nd, 4th, 6th, and 9th) and the 41st Alabama. Born and raised in Kentucky, Helm was the son of a Kentucky governor, a Kentucky state legislator and state's attorney, and the half-brother-in-law of Mary Todd Lincoln. (Helm's wife was Mary's half-sister).

One famous Kentucky action at Chickamauga occurred at about 9:30 a.m. on September 20, 1863, when Helm's "Orphan Brigade" (named for its heavy casualties sustained at the Battle of Stones River in 1862) attacked the Union left flank and failed to turn it through Kelly Field. The brigade was fighting in concert with Breckinridge's Division, which included Adams' and Stovall's Brigades.

The morning attack on the Union left flank came to be known as "Breckinridge's Assault," named for former U.S. Vice President John C. Breckinridge (1857–1861), one of Bragg's division commanders at Chickamauga in 1863. The attack ended disastrously and with no effective support from Cleburne's Division on Breckinridge's left. Within thirty minutes, Helm received a mortal wound to the chest and was carried off the field (p. 185). According to historian David A. Powell, "The brigade's final losses would total nearly 500 men, almost all of them felled during the single desperate hour of fighting."[159] Aside: Col. Colquitt (Walker's Division) and Brig. Gen. Deshler (Cleburne's Division) also sustained mortal wounds in "Breckinridge's Assault." See pp. 182 and 183, respectively.

The Breckinridge Division Tablet is an 1890 red-on-white cast iron sign located in Kelly Field on the east side of LaFayette Road. The tablet provides summarizes "Breckinridge's Assault" and is easiest to understand when you read it while facing south:

> Breckinridge's Division - Hill's Corps.
> Maj. Gen. John C. Breckinridge.
> Sept. 20th, 1863, 11 a.m.
>
> Helm's Brigade – Brig. Gen. Benjamin H. Helm.
>   Col. Joseph H. Lewis.
> Adams' Brigade – Brig. Gen. Daniel W. Adams.
>   Col. Randall L. Gibson.
> Stovall's Brigade – Brig. Gen. Marcellus A. Stovall.

Adams' and Stovall's Brigades, advancing from the north, and marching with the LaFayette Road between them, Adams on the west and Stovall on the east of it, had penetrated to this point at 11 a.m.

The left of Helm's Brigade had been shattered by three unsuccessful assaults on the lines north and east of the Kelly Field. The right of Helm's Brigade had forced itself into a gap in John Beatty's Brigade, pushed a part of the latter back to the LaFayette Road, and captured two of its guns, being then repulsed.

Beatty, with portions of his force, first strongly resisted, and then with the help of Stanley's Brigade of Negley's Division checked the advance of Adam's Brigade – Gen. Adams being wounded and captured.

At this point Van Derveer's Brigade of Brannan's Division, on its way to assist Baird, emerged from the woods on the west side of the road, wheeled into the face of Stovall's Brigade, charged it and drove it back, pursuing to a point 100 yards north of Kelly Field. From this line, assisted by the Brigades of Grose, Dodge, parts of Willich, and Berry, detached from the Divisions of Palmer and Johnson, Breckinridge's Division was forced beyond the Union left. It was then further withdrawn and its place taken by Gist's and Liddell's Divisions of Walker's Corps. Late in the afternoon Breckinridge's troops again advanced, taking part in the last attack of the Confederate right wing, heavily assaulted Baird's position, followed that Division to the LaFayette Road, and bivouacked in this portion of Kelly Field.[160]

Kentucky Executive Leadership

Here is an interesting side note about Kentucky: Not only were Presidents Abraham Lincoln and Jefferson Davis from Kentucky, but the Blue Grass State fielded 79 Civil War generals, which is more than any other state except New York (120) and Virginia (101).[161]

9. Louisiana (CSA)

No Louisiana regimental monuments stand on the Chickamauga battlefield. Most men in the following units mustered from Louisiana:

> Adams' Brigade, Breckinridge's Division
> Robinson's Battery, Scott's Brigade, Pegram's Division
> Slocomb's Louisiana Battery, Breckinridge's Division
> 1st LA, Scott's Brigade, Pegram's Division
> 1st LA, Govan's Brigade, Liddell's Division
> 4th LA Battalion, Wilson's Brigade, Walker's Division
> Le Gardeur's Battery, Robertson's Battalion, Reserve Artillery

The Capture of Louisiana Brig. Gen. Daniel W. Adams

Brig. Gen. Daniel W. Adams commanded the 13th and 20th, 16th and 25th, and 19th Louisiana; 14th Louisiana Battalion; and 32nd Alabama. The brigade belonged to Breckinridge's Division of Lt. Gen. Daniel H. Hill's Corps. Born in Frankfort Kentucky in 1821, Adams was a Mississippi and Louisiana lawyer before the U.S. Civil War. During the Battle of Shiloh in April 1862, he assumed brigade command when Brig. Gen. Adley H. Gladden fell, but soon thereafter Adams was left for dead in the Hornet's Nest. Mississippi soldiers rescued Adams, who lost an eye but recuperated only to lose his left arm at the Battle of Stones River in December. At the Battle of Chickamauga—during "Breckinridge's Assault" on the morning of September 20, 1863—Adams suffered another arm wound, and the Federals captured him. Capt. Borden M. Hicks, 11th Michigan Infantry, recounted the following story of Brig. Gen. Adams' capture:

> We took up a new position in Kelley's [*sic*] field... and awaited the oncoming Confederates... When within two or three rods of our line, we opened fire on them... and we captured nearly all of the balance, including General D.W. Adams who was in command of the rebel forces making this charge—our regiment captured General Adams, yet there are no less than six regiments who claim the honor of having captured him, but as the best proof would say that I had his sword, other members of our regiment had his field glasses and revolvers, belt, and so forth. I carried his sword on the charge we now made to the McDonald field, going into this charge with a sword in each hand, and looking as savage as a meat ax.[162]

10. Michigan (USA)

4th Michigan Cavalry
Erected: 1895
Location: Near Jay's Mill Site
GPS: 34.93085, -85.22901

Michigan men fought in the following units at Chickamauga:

Baird's Division Artillery
Brannan's Division Artillery
Buell's Brigade
Campbell's Brigade
Lytle's Brigade
Minty's Brigade
Stanley's Brigade
Thomas' Provost Guard
Whitaker's Brigade

The 4th Michigan Cavalry was one of four cavalry units in Col. Robert H.G. Minty's brigade. At Chickamauga, the 489-man regiment reported 1 killed, 12 wounded, and 6 missing. The brigade included the 3rd Indiana Cavalry (in Chattanooga); 7th Pennsylvania Cavalry; and 4th U.S. Cavalry.[163]

Made from blue Westerly granite, the 4th Michigan Cavalry Monument is on the south side of Reed's Bridge Road, near Jay's Mill Road. The front-facing bronze relief panel depicts Union cavalry challenging Confederate infantry along Chickamauga Creek at Reed's Bridge on the morning of September 18, 1863. The scene captures the face-off between Minty's brigade and a much larger Confederate force under Brig. Gen. Bushrod R. Johnson, whose division pressed eastward from Peavine Ridge to Reed's Bridge.

Bragg's plan was to crush the left wing of the Union army, but Minty's Brigade thwarted that effort. The inscription on the 4th Michigan Cavalry Monument credits both the brigade and their regiment (led by Maj. Horace Gray) with having met the advance of Johnson's Division and blocking their crossing of Chickamauga Creek for ten hours.[164] While Minty's Brigade was thus engaged, a Confederate cavalry brigade under Brig. Gen. Nathan B. Forrest tried to flank the Union army at a point south (and east) of Jay's Mill.

11. Minnesota (USA)

At Chickamauga, two units fielded Minnesota soldiers:

2nd MN, Van Derveer's Brigade, Brannan's Division
2nd Battery Light Artillery, Carlin's Brigade, Davis' Division

This section highlights the battlefield actions of the 2nd Minnesota Infantry under the command of Union Col. James George in Thomas' 14th Corps. The regiment fought at three critical junctures at the Battle of Chickamauga. On September 19, 1863, the 2nd Minnesota repulsed a flanking attack at Reed's Bridge Road. On September 20, they repulsed Confederate Maj. Gen. John C. Breckinridge's attempt to turn the Union left at Kelly Field. And finally, later in the day, the regiment played a critical role in the defense of Horseshoe Ridge near the Snodgrass Cabin, which we summarize below.

In Defense of Horseshoe Ridge (Snodgrass Hill)

Having arrived on Horseshoe Ridge at about 2:30 p.m., the 2nd Minnesota faced south toward their Confederate attackers over a deep ravine.[165] (See the area photo on p. 63). Col. George reported that "the enemy charged repeatedly and desperately on our position here, but were always repulsed by the cool and deadly fire of our rifles."[166] Judson Wade Bishop (1831–1917), who claimed to be the longest serving member of the 2nd Minnesota Infantry, described his regiment's actions on Snodgrass Hill in this way:

> Arriving on the ridge, our regiment took the place of one already there (the 21st Ohio), which had exhausted its cartridge boxes, and immediately had a view of the assaulting columns of the enemy, just commencing the ascent of the southern slope in our front. Ranks followed ranks in close order, moving briskly and bravely towards us. It was theirs to advance, ours, now to stand and repel. Again the order was passed to aim carefully and make every shot count, and the deadly work began. The front ranks melted away under the rapid fire of our men, but those following bowed their heads to the storm of bullets and pressed on, some of them falling at every step, until, the supporting touch of elbows being lost, the survivors hesitate, halt, then turning, start back with a

rush that carries them to the rear—all who escape the bullets, as deadly in wild retreat as in the desperate and orderly advance. This was all repeated again and again, until the slope was so covered with dead and wounded men that looking from our position we could hardly see the ground. Never was any position more gallantly assaulted or more desperately defended.[167]

The regiment's brigade commander, Col. Ferdinand Van Derveer, described the seen at the end of the day:

The ammunition failing, and no supply at hand, except a small quantity furnished by Maj. Gen. Gordon Granger, our men gathered their cartridges and from the boxes of the dead, wounded, and prisoners, and finally fixed bayonets, determined to hold the position. ... For an hour and a half before dark the attack was one of unexampled fury, line after line of fresh troops being hurled against our position with a heroism and persistency which almost dignified their cause.[168]

According to Col. George, the firing was constant until 4:45 p.m., when two failed Confederate attacks followed. The contest ended at about 6:30 p.m..[169] Having held Horseshoe Ridge long enough to allow for the ordered retreat of the Army of the Cumberland, at 7 p.m., the Minnesota regiment joined the Union withdrawal to Chattanooga via Rossville Gap.

The 2nd Minnesota (384 men) suffered 42.2 percent casualties at the Battle of Chickamauga: 35 killed, 113 wounded, 14 missing.[170]

12. Mississippi (CSA)

Bragg's Army of Tennessee included Mississippi units assigned to the divisions of Cheatham, Cleburne, Liddell, and Walker, plus Buckner's Reserve Artillery. The state fielded two all-Mississippi brigades (and none erected monuments):

>Walthall's Brigade, Liddell's Division
>Anderson's Brigade, Hindman's Division

Walthall's Brigade

At Alexander's Bridge on September 18, 1863 (noon), Brig. Gen. Edward C. Walthall's five-regiment brigade of Mississippians in Liddell's Division challenged Wilder's three mounted infantry regiments from Indiana. Armed with Spencer-repeating rifles, Wilder denied Walthall his intent to cross Chickamauga Creek at Alexander's Bridge.[171] (See the photo of Chickamauga Creek on p. 51).

At Winfrey Field on September 19 (about 11:00 a.m.), Walthall's Brigade—with Brig. Gen. St. John R. Liddell's 3,800-man strong infantry—charged across Winfrey Field (p. 54) and overran the Union brigades of Scribner and Starkweather, which were part of Brig. Gen. Absalom Baird's division.[172] On the final day of the battle, the brigade was at McDonald's Field (p. 65).

Anderson's Brigade at Horseshoe Ridge

At 2:00 p.m. the next day, a Mississippi brigade under Brig. Gen. Patton Anderson made a "gallant and impetuous charge" against the 21st Ohio, which held the western hill on Horseshoe Ridge. Led by Lt. Col. Dwella M. Stoughton, the 21st Ohio "poured a volume of fire that speedily repulsed the charge." Anderson's Brigade fell back.[173]

Silas Chandler, Enslaved Mississippi Man

Enslaved Mississippi man, Mr. Silas Chandler (1838–1919), was one of thirty-six enslaved African Americans in the Chandler household. At the Battle of Chickamauga, Silas served Sgt. Andrew Chandler, 44th Mississippi Infantry. He got Andrew back home after Andrew suffered a bullet to his leg. Silas then also served the younger brother, Benjamin Chandler, 9th Mississippi Cavalry.

13. Missouri (USA/CSA)

For the Chickamauga and Chattanooga Campaigns, most Missouri monuments and markers stand on Missionary Ridge. On the Chickamauga battlefield, Missouri placed only one monument and four markers. Bledsoe's Missouri Battery Monument (CSA) is located near Brotherton Cabin. Of the four markers, one is for Hescock's Battery G, 1st Missouri Light Artillery (USA) and stands in a wooded area northeast of the Wilder Brigade Monument.

This section will summarize Missouri's contribution to the Battle of Chickamauga from the perspective of the Hescock (USA) and Bledsoe (CSA) batteries, both of which fought near the Brotherton Cabin on September 20, 1863. It is unclear what happened between the two. Glenn Tucker recounts that, because of Longstreet's Breakthrough, Hescock's Federal battery lost four three-inch rifled guns to Bledsoe's men. However, while David Powell acknowledges the Confederate claim, he also notes that Battery G reported that "all of its guns got off the field safely," a claim implicitly supported by the battery commander's official report.[174]

Hescock's Battery G, 1st Missouri Light Artillery, USA

Hescock's Battery was part of Col. Bernard Laiboldt's brigade (Sheridan's Division, McCook's Corps), but according to. Lt. Gustavus Schueler, on September 20 the battery supported Bradley's Brigade, which "formed on the edge of the cornfield to check the attack of the enemy... who poured deadly fire into our lines." The photo on p. 60 shows the battery's position overlooking Glenn Field. Lt. Schueler reported that Capt. Hescock was taken prisoner; one 12-pounder gun fired 215 rounds; and one 10-pounder Parrott gun fired 62 rounds.[175]

Bledsoe's 1st Missouri Battery, CSA

Lt. R.L. Wood commanded Bledsoe's Battery, part of Gregg's Brigade (Johnson's Division, Longstreet/Hood's Corps). Led by Col. Sugg, the brigade included Bledsoe's Battery, six Tennessee regiments, and one Texas regiment. According to Johnson's official report, Confederate soldiers captured Capt. Hescock near the Vidito [sic] house, where "the ladies of the family ... burst forth and greeted our soldiers with clapping hands and shouts of joy." Bledsoe's Battery fired 125 rounds of ammunition.[176]

14. North Carolina (CSA)

North Carolina's five regiments at the Battle of Chickamauga belonged to five different divisions and collectively represent about 2 percent of the total Confederate strength in terms of number of fighting units.[177] Four small North Carolina infantry monuments are tucked away in wooded areas. In the following list, parentheses mark brigade commanders:

> 6th NC Cavalry, Folk (Davidson), Pegram's Division
> 29th NC Infantry, Creasman (Ector), Walker's Division
> 39th NC Infantry, Coleman (McNair), Johnson's Division
> 58th NC Infantry, Palmer (Kelly), Preston's Division
> 60th NC Infantry, Ray (Stovall), Breckinridge's Division

On September 19, 1863, Col. George N. Folk led the 6th North Carolina Cavalry, whose 520 men suffered 5 killed, 6 wounded, and 18 missing.[178] On September 20, North Carolina's other four regiments fought mostly in two places. First, in Kelly Field was Lt. Col. Ray's 60th regiment. Second, on Snodgrass Hill was Col. Creasman's 29th, Col. Coleman's 39th, and Col. Palmer's 58th North Carolina infantry regiments. We spotlight Palmer's regiment, below.

Attack on Horseshoe Ridge (Snodgrass Hill)

John B. Palmer was born in New York State in 1826 and moved to Michigan and then North Carolina, where he led the 58th North Carolina Infantry. Col. John B. Palmer issued a detailed report on his regiment's September 20, 1863, attack on Horseshoe Ridge, specifically Hill #2 (which is accessible by foot along a trail that is southwest of the Snodgrass Cabin). According to Palmer, the attack was the regiment's first battle. He describes the terrain as follows:

> The enemy occupied a range of ridges, from which they had repulsed several assaults made by our troops. The approach to these ridges was along spurs and through intervening depressions, all more or less wooded, but more open and exposed opposite the right of the brigade. The line being again formed, my regiment, which was on the right, moved with steadiness through this comparatively open space till my extreme right arrived within 10 or 12 feet of the enemy. ...[179]

Next, the colonel describes the chaos that reigned on the ridge:

> ... a charge was about being made when directions were received from the colonel commanding brigade to cease firing, with a statement that we were firing upon our friends. Having discovered that no friends were in advance, firing was resumed by the center and left (the right had not ceased its fire) and continued with vigor. A deadly fire was, and had been ever since we came within range, poured into the ranks of our foe. ...[180]

The chaos claimed the lives of 3 officers and wounded 1 major, 1 captain, 3 lieutenants, and 1 adjutant. According to Col. Palmer, the 58th North Carolina's right flank was under immense strain:

> Two-thirds of my right flanking company, which was exposed to a most galling cross-fire from the enemy on our right and in front, had been killed or wounded. A longer continuance in this position seemed beyond human endurance, and in spite of my most strenuous exertions, my right wing was forced back a short distance and sought shelter. I, however, succeeded without difficulty in reforming it and in again advancing it in perfect good order, when, ascertaining that no charge was being made, I caused the men to lie down and fire upon the enemy.[181]

After commenting on the status of his left flank, Col. Palmer offered his summary of the regiment's performance:

> In the meantime, the left wing of my regiment had stood firm and continued to pour its fire into the foe. I desire to state here that the position against which the regiment under my command advanced was one of the very strongest occupied by the enemy during the battle of Chickamauga, and from which our troops had at least twice repulsed before our arrival upon the field, and as we pressed forward we met and swept over the retreating and shattered regiments that had preceded us in the attack. ... My regiment captured about 20 officers and men...[182]

Of the regiment's 322 men, its total Chickamauga casualties were: 46 killed, 114 wounded, 1 missing. The 58th North Carolina was on the field until at least 6 p.m. that evening.[183] Col. Palmer died in South Carolina in 1893.

15. Ohio (USA)

Ohio brought fifty-six regiments and batteries to the Battle of Chickamauga. That represents about 29 percent of the total Union strength. Indiana ranked second (23 percent) and Illinois third (19 percent). All other Union states fall in the single-digit percent range. At Chickamauga, Ohio served in every division of the Army of the Cumberland, except for Sheridan's Division.[184] Since Ohio placed fifty-four monuments and nearly as many markers on the Chickamauga battlefield, this section provides a brief overview of only some of them.

Ohio monuments commonly include on their front faces a bronze medallion of the Ohio State Seal. The first photo below shows the 1st Ohio Infantry Monument in the northwest corner of Winfrey Field, where the unit resisted an attack by Cleburne's Division on September 19, 1863. The second monument marks the September 20 Union main line battlefield position of Battery F, 1st Ohio Light Artillery, a scene that the bronze bas-relief panel captures. Two west facing cannons flank the monument.[185]

1st Ohio Infantry
Erected: 1894
Location: Winfrey Field
GPS: 34.92534, -85.24199

1st Ohio Battery F
Erected: 1894
Location: Battleline Road
GPS: 34.92720, -85.25642

Bicycling Chickamauga Battlefield

1st Ohio Light Artillery, Battery M

Erected: 1894
Location: North end of Dyer Field (looking southeast)
GPS: 34.92519, -85.26757

The above photo captures a southeasterly view from the South Carolina State Monument on the north end of Dyer Field. The wood line traces Glenn-Kelly Road (left) and Dyer Road (right). The tallest monument in the foreground marks the September 20, 1863, position of "Schultz's Battery" M, 1st Ohio Light Artillery, a German-speaking unit in Negley's Division. Its inscription says that the battery "opened fire from this position and maintained it for a short time."

That "short time" was the period of chaos that ensued after Longstreet broke the Union right flank and Confederate infantry poured through Dyer Field. Lt. Morris D. Template of Bridges' Illinois Light Artillery—part of the same artillery unit as "Schultz's Battery" M and "Marshall's Battery" G—described the scene in this way:

> Large columns of dust being discovered in the woods and fields to our left and front, General Negley ordered Captain Bridges to open, and at the same time Captain Schultz opened from the crest of the hill, firing over our heads. All this time there was heavy musketry firing in the woods to our front, which were so dense that it was impossible to see the enemy... [T]he ravine was full of rebels ... the infantry was retiring upon both our right and left, leaving the battery without support, while the musketry fire of the enemy was increasing and one of his batteries opened with shell.[186]

The States at Chickamauga

2nd Ohio Infantry

Erected: 1894
Location: Battleline Road near Alexander's Bridge Road
GPS: 34.93303, -85.25543

In the spring of 1863, the Union Army of the Potomac adopted corps badges that inspired Maj. Gen. Thomas to ask Maj. Gen. Daniel Butterfield what he might suggest for Thomas' Corps. Butterfield proposed an acorn, because the 14th Corps had "stood as firm as an oak at Chickamauga." Thomas agreed.[187] American artist Charles H. Niehaus (1855–1935) sculpted the acorn for the 2nd Ohio Monument.

According to the monument inscription for September 19, Lt. Col. Obadiah C. Maxwell led the regiment "on the left in the front line of battle" and advanced with its brigade one mile eastward, capturing "fifteen or twenty" prisoners. The inscription for September 20 reads:

> ...the regiment occupied this position throughout the day successfully holding the line, in the execution of the order to retire about sundown, it became involved on its flanks and lost some prisoners. Number engaged 18 officers; 394 men; total 412. Loss, killed 9; wounded 50; captured or missing 122; total 181. Among the wounded were Lieutenant Colonel Maxwell Major Beatty.

24th Ohio Infantry

Erected: 1894
Location: Brotherton Road
GPS: 34.91849, -85.25450

The Reverend Col. David J. Higgins suffered recurrent back problems, so he passed command of the 24th Ohio regiment to Maj. Thomas McClure, who struggled to hold the line after a surprise attack by Wright's Tennessee Brigade on September 19, 1863. In the area on which their monument stands, this 277-man regiment incurred its heaviest losses: 3 killed, 60 wounded, and 16 captured or missing.[188]

33rd Ohio Infantry

Erected: 1894
Location: Battleline Road
GPS: 34.932842, -85.255447

49th Ohio Infantry

Erected: 1894
Location: Brotherton Road
GPS: 34.92421, -85.24306

The States at Chickamauga

90th Ohio Infantry

Erected: 1894
Location: Battleline Road
GPS: 34.92826, -85.25571

The 90th Ohio was under the command of Col. Charles H. Rippey, a unit in Cruft's Brigade, Palmer's Division, 21st Corps. The colonel described his 4 a.m. September 20 preparations in his official report: "In less than one hour, without the aid of axes or other entrenching tools, a strong breastwork of logs and stones was built." Confederates attacked the Buckeyes at about 8 a.m. and "met with few casualties."[189]

94th Ohio Infantry

The 94th Ohio Infantry Monument includes a granite acorn that identifies the unit as part of the 14th Corps. From this location on September 20, Maj. R.P. Hutchins led the regiment. He wrote this in his official report:

"Notwithstanding the heavy losses of Saturday [19th] the men went forward Sunday cheerfully and willingly."[190]

Erected: 1894
Location: Battleline Road, at pull-out near 20 mph sign
GPS: 34.93243, -85.25517

16. Pennsylvania (USA)

Pennsylvania contributed five regiments and batteries, plus one regiment assigned to Department Headquarters. Although this count represents less than 3 percent of the total Union strength, Pennsylvanians fought in all three branches of service—infantry, cavalry, and artillery. Three Pennsylvania men received the Medal of Honor. A formerly enslaved man from Kentucky named Jack Hines was "severely wounded and nearly captured during the Union retreat from Chickamauga." He served with the 15th Pennsylvania Cavalry.[191]

In the following list, parentheses identify brigade commanders:

   7th PA Cavalry, (Minty) Crook's Division
   9th PA Cavalry, (Campbell) McCook's Division
   15th PA Cavalry, Department Headquarters
   77th PA Infantry, (Dodge) R.W. Johnson's Division
   79th PA Infantry, (Starkweather) Baird's Division
   Battery B, PA Light Artillery, Van Cleve's Division

7th Pennsylvania Cavalry
Erected: 1890–1899
Location: Reed's Bridge Road at Jay's Mill, north side of road
GPS: 34.93098, -85.22891

79th Pennsylvania Infantry
Erected: 1894
Location: Battleline Road, north end, west side
GPS: 34.93133, -85.25451

The States at Chickamauga

7th Pennsylvania Cavalry (September 18)

The 7th Pennsylvania Cavalry Monument stands on Reed's Bridge Road, near the park entrance on the east side. Its bronze relief panel depicts a cavalryman charging on horseback with his saber raised over his left shoulder. Organized in Harrisburg in 1861 and led by Union Cpt. James B. McIntyre, the 7th Pennsylvania Cavalry was part of Minty's Brigade.

The monument's inscription summarizes the regiment's actions on September 18, 1863, when the right flank of the Army of Tennessee tried to cross Chickamauga Creek at Reed's Bridge:

> Encountered the enemy, Johnson's Division of Hood's Corps, already in line of battle... three miles east of this point at 7 a.m. September 18th, 1863, there at that hour John Ward of Company F was killed. With the other regiments of the brigade engaged and retarded the enemy and prevented him from crossing Chickamauga Creek at Reed's Bridge until 3 p.m.. Reed's Bridge was partially dismantled but restored by the enemy. The Regiment retired with Wilder's Brigade toward Viniard's House, skirmishing until dark, where it dismounted and remained in line of battle throughout the night.[192]

79th Pennsylvania Infantry (September 20)

The 79th Pennsylvania Infantry Monument stands on what was in 1863, the main line of the Union army at the Battle of Chickamauga. It was here that the regiment—part of Starkweather's Brigade, Baird's Division, Thomas' Corps—built breastworks out of trees, brush, and even their own knapsacks in the defense of the ridge that runs along the east side of LaFayette Road. Lt. John Johnston had the idea to use knapsacks to help them more rapidly load and fire their rifles. After the war, he wrote that at the Battle of Chickamauga Confederate gray and butternut uniforms blended into the woody scenery, whereas their own bright blue uniforms made them stand out "in bold relief."[193]

The monument marks the battlefield position "from early Sunday morning September 20th until evening when ordered to retire," according to the monument's back-side inscription. Also called the "Lancaster Rifles," the unit mustered into service in Lancaster, 1861. Lt. Col. Henry A. Hambright commanded the regiment.

17. South Carolina (CSA)

Gen. Bragg's Army of Tennessee included nine South Carolina regiments and batteries assigned to the divisions of Walker (Gist), Hindman, Johnson, and McLaws. The South Carolina State Monument on the north end of Dyer Field honors their service. (See p. 136 and the landscape photo on p. 40).

Brig. Gen. Joseph B. Kershaw's brigade consisted entirely of men from the State of South Carolina. These are the same men who fought in Gettysburg's Peach Orchard, The Wheatfield, and finally the ill-fated Pickett-Pettigrew-Trimble charge on July 3, 1863. Kershaw's Brigade arrived on the Chickamauga battlefield with Longstreet's Corps. Gen. Robert E. Lee released them from the Army of Northern Virginia to fight in the western theater. With the left wing of the Confederate army, Kershaw's Brigade pierced the Union line and fought through Dyer Field to Horseshoe Ridge ("Snodgrass Hill").

Kershaw's South Carolinians attacked Horseshoe Ridge three times, but the Federals beat them back each time. Although the Union Army of the Cumberland held a strong defensive position, that advantage waned as they ran low on ammunition and as their line thinned to meet a Confederate threat on their right flank. Fortunately for Maj. Gen. Thomas, Maj. Gen. Gordon Granger's Reserve Corps arrived with ammunition to spare, and they secured the Union right so that Thomas could coordinate a quick but orderly withdrawal and retreat to Chattanooga.

Of the 1,591 men in Kershaw's Brigade at Chickamauga, 113 were killed, 390 wounded, and 1 missing, for a total loss of 504 men.[194] The brigade consisted of the 2nd, 3rd, 7th, 8th, and 15th South Carolina regiments, and the 3rd South Carolina Battalion. The commander of the 7th South Carolina regiment, Lt. Col. Elbert Bland died from his wounds. Bland had previously suffered injuries at Seven Pines, Fredericksburg, and Gettysburg.[195] His replacement, Maj. John S. Hard, died at the Battle of Chickamauga.

In 1901, the State of South Carolina installed rectangular granite markers that marked the September 20 battlefield position of each regiment. Located in the woods and fields along Horseshoe Ridge (mostly southwest of the Snodgrass Cabin), the markers are each roughly 3-feet wide, 2-feet high, and 1.5-feet deep.

18. Tennessee (USA/CSA)

Brig. Gen. Bushrod R. Johnson Monument

Erected: 1977 by the Sons of Confederate Veterans and United Daughters of the Confederacy of St. Louis, Missouri
Location: Brotherton Road, south side
GPS: 34.91849, -85.25706

The Brig. Gen. Bushrod R. Johnson Monument honors the men who fought in Johnson's Division, which included two all-Tennessee brigades. These men captured Reed's Bridge on September 18 and spearheaded "Longstreet's Breakthrough" on September 20, 1863.

Johnson was born in Ohio in 1817, graduated from West Point, and then served in the U.S. Army before working as an educator. In 1861, he joined with Tennessee to fight for the Confederacy. After the war, Johnson served as the co-chancellor of the University of Nashville until he retired to Illinois, where Johnson died in 1880. In 1975, his body was re-interred in Nashville, next to his wife, Mary.

At Chickamauga, Tennessee CSA regiments outnumbered Tennessee USA regiments 60 to 2 (the 1st and 2nd Tennessee Cavalry, USA). Notably, Tennessee fielded more regiments than any other state in either army. About 25 percent of the Confederate regiments and batteries at Chickamauga hailed from Tennessee.[196]

19. Texas (CSA)

At the Battle of Chickamauga, Texas fought in five infantry brigades, one artillery unit, and one cavalry brigade in Wheeler's Cavalry Corps that included two Texas regiments. Of the infantry brigades, five out of twelve Texas regiments fought as dismounted cavalry. The Texas State Monument on Battleline Road honors the service of all Texans (see p. 137 and the landscape photo on p. 38).

Rather than summarize the accomplishments of every Texas regiment, this section highlights the military actions of John B. Hood's Texas Brigade. At Chickamauga, the brigade was under the command Brig. Gen. Jerome B. Robertson, then part of Hood's Division under Longstreet. (For a photo of the wooded area occupied by Hood's Division on modern day Viniard-Alexander Road, see p. 42). According to historian David Powell, Texas regiments in the Texas Brigade suffered these losses at Chickamauga:[197]

> 1st Texas (490 men): 19 killed, 124 wounded, 12 missing
> 4th Texas (322 men): 26 killed, 102 wounded, 5 missing
> 5th Texas (247 men): 13 killed, 87 wounded, 12 missing

At the Battles of Fredericksburg, Gettysburg, and Chickamauga, Robertson commanded the Texas Brigade, which for those battles included the 3rd Arkansas infantry regiment. Fighting with men from Arkansas, these were the Texans who captured Devil's Den at Gettysburg. As Texas Brigade commander at Gettysburg, Hood suffered a severe wound to his left arm. Not three months later as division commander at Chickamauga, Hood received a bullet in his right leg, and the leg required amputation.

The following excerpts from the *Official Records* describe the scene during Longstreet's Breakthrough on September 20, 1863. Due to battlefield losses of officers, three captains issued these reports:

From the Report of Capt. R.J. Harding, 1st Texas Infantry:

> September 20, the regiment moved forward in line of battle about noon through a wood into a field, the enemy throwing both shells and grape upon us from a battery on an elevated position. After entering the field we changed front forward on first battalion, directing our march upon a wooded hill occupied by the enemy.[198]

The States at Chickamauga

From the Report of Capt. James T. Hunter, 4th Texas Infantry:

> [September 20] about noon, we again moved forward in the same position in line we had occupied the day previous. We moved immediately in rear of another line, and consequently had gone a considerable distance before we received a heavy fire, except from the enemy's batteries. On arriving at a field about 1 mile from where the advance commenced, the enemy appeared on our right flank. ... After our line was reformed, a temporary breastwork was constructed. We were here exposed to a heavy fire from the enemy's artillery, and here it was that Captain Bassett, who had ably and gallantly commanded the regiment since the wounding of Colonel Bane, received a severe wound by a fragment of shell, which deprived us of his services.[199]

From the Report of Capt. T.T. Clay, 5th Texas Infantry:

> Maj. J.C. Rogers and Capt. J.S. Cleveland having been wounded in the actions of the 19th and 20th instant, the duty devolves upon me, therefore, to make the report of the part taken by the Fifth Texas Regiment in the late engagement. ...
>
> [September 20 about 11 a.m.] We were moved forward in quick-time across a wooded flat, and, before we gained the hill beyond, the enemy hailed down upon us a perfect shower of shot and shell; but we pressed forward, and just after crossing a small field we found the enemy's first line of breastworks, but we encountered no one here, the enemy having fled precipitately. About 300 yards farther on we crossed the Chattanooga Road, and on entering a thick beyond we were hid for a time from the rest of the brigade... The regiment soon pressed forward, and by the time we had entered the field beyond the road before mentioned the balance of the brigade, assisted by a portion of the Fifth, had run over and captured a battery on our left.[200]

20. Virginia (CSA)

Like the states of Arkansas, Louisiana, Mississippi, and North Carolina, Virginia did not erect any monuments on the Chickamauga battlefield. Virginia fielded a small fraction of the Confederate fighting force, about 1 percent of the Army of Tennessee. In all, only three regiments from Virginia fought at the Battle of Chickamauga, but their contribution was significant. The Virginia regiments belonged to Brig. Gen. William Preston's division, Buckner's Corps, Army of Tennessee:

> 54th VA, Trigg's (Florida) Brigade
> 63rd VA, Kelly's Brigade
> Jeffress' VA Battery, 9th Georgia Artillery Battalion

54th Virginia Infantry (Horseshoe Ridge)

On Horseshoe Ridge, the 54th Virginia regiment fought with Trigg's Floridians to capture the "Lost Regiments" of the 21st Ohio, 89th Ohio, and 22nd Michigan at about 7:00 p.m. on September 20, 1863. (For more details, see p. 144). The 54th Virginia lost 4 killed and 43 wounded out of 477 men, nearly 10 percent casualties at the Battle of Chickamauga. Trigg's Brigade had 282 total casualties.

63rd Virginia Infantry (Horseshoe Ridge)

The 63rd Virginia regiment fought in Col. John H. Kelly's mixed brigade of men from Georgia, Kentucky, North Carolina, and Virginia. Kelly was from Alabama. In his official report on the actions of the Virginians, their commander, Maj. James M. French wrote that the 63rd Virginia occupied the center line (with the 5th Kentucky on their left and the 58th North Carolina on their right) before they attacked the Union defensive position on Horseshoe Ridge. This was the situation after Longstreet's Breakthrough when the Union right wing was "broken up and beaten back toward the foothills of Missionary Ridge in the rear."[201] Now pressing north through Dyer Field to the ridge, Maj. French described the events that led up to a friendly fire incident:

> The enemy occupied a range of ridges, from which they had successfully repulsed several assaults made by our troops. The approach to the enemy's position was very difficult, owing to deep ravines and depressions partly covered with thick undergrowth. After emerging from this thicket my

regiment moved steadily on under heavy fire from the enemy until gaining the summit of the hill upon which the enemy was posted. When within 15 paces of the enemy, my regiment was halted and poured a deadly fire into his ranks. The enemy gave way before them. I was in the act of making a charge when I received information that they were our friends we were firing upon. My regiment was ordered to cease firing. This mistake gave the enemy time to rally...[202]

According to Maj. French, "an incessant fire was kept up until about sundown, when the enemy ceased firing." Then he explained what happened next when they approached the Union line:

[T]hey proposed to surrender and laid down their arms. When we arrived within about 40 yards of them, they retook their arms and poured a heavy fire into our ranks, which caused us to fall back a short distance to our position on the hill, from which place we continued to fire into them. Our ammunition being now almost exhausted, we supplied ourselves as far as possible from the boxes of the killed and wounded. We again advanced in conjunction with Colonel Trigg's brigade, when we succeeded in capturing 249 prisoners, including several field officers.[203]

Jeffress' Virginia Artillery Battery

According to Maj. Thomas K. Porter, the Chief of Artillery for Buckner's Corps, Preston ordered that the artillery batteries in Leyden's battalion support Preston's infantry brigades. This included the Jeffress' Virginia Battery commanded by Cpt. William C. Jeffress. Porter's report mentioned how Chickamauga's "very thickly wooded" landscape prevented artillerymen from seeing more than 300 yards to the front. About the Virginia artillery battery, he wrote:

Two of the batteries of Leyden's battalion were engaged Saturday and Sunday, but owing to the thickness of the timber and undergrowth, continued but a short time. They were unable to ascertain the damage they inflicted. They suffered a slight loss themselves. One of his batteries (Jeffress') was kept on the extreme left of the original line till the battle ceased.[204]

21. Wisconsin (USA)

1st Wisconsin Infantry
Erected: Unknown
Location: Battleline Road
GPS: 34.93161, -85.25440

10th Wisconsin Infantry
Erected: Unknown
Location: Battle Line Road
GPS: 34.93314, -85.25556

Wisconsin fielded five infantry regiments (1st, 10th, 15th, 21st, and 24th); one cavalry regiment (1st); and three artillery batteries (3rd, 5th, and 8th) at Chickamauga. They suffered heavy casualties, especially among officers and brigade commanders. This section provides a brief overview of the casualty numbers for Wisconsin fighters at Chickamauga.

The highest-ranking U.S. Army officer from Wisconsin to die in the U.S. Civil War was the abolitionist Col. Hans C. Heg (p. 184). Heg's Brigade included the 8th Wisconsin Light Artillery and the 15th Wisconsin Infantry, his original regiment of mostly Norwegian immigrants. The 15th Wisconsin regiment (176 men) reported 13 killed, 53 wounded, 45 missing—a 63 percent casualty rate. The 8th Wisconsin battery, known as "Lyons' Pinery Battery," had no casualties while operating 6 guns in the woodlot northeast of the Viniard house on September 19, according to an NPS cast-iron marker. (The 3rd and 5th Wisconsin artillery batteries—not in Heg's Brigade, but in Van Cleve and Davis' Divisions, respectively—each also had 6 guns, but only the 3rd Wisconsin battery suffered casualties: 2 killed, 13 wounded, 11 missing).[205]

Another senior officer killed at Chickamauga was the poet-lawyer Brig. Gen. William H. Lytle (p. 187), whose brigade included the 24th Wisconsin Infantry. The 24th Wisconsin regiment (487 men), under the command of Lt. Col. Theodore S. West, suffered 3 killed, 73 wounded, 29 missing—a 22 percent casualty rate. Col. West was one of the missing infantrymen.[206]

Lt. Col. George B. Bingham's 1st Wisconsin Infantry regiment (391 men) reported 27 killed, 84 wounded, 77 missing—a 48 percent casualty rate. The 1st Wisconsin Cavalry was under the command of Col. Oscar H. LaGrange. The regiment (384 men) reported 2 wounded, 4 missing—a 1.5 percent casualty rate. See the regiment's monument in the photo, above.[207]

According to Brig. Gen. Benjamin F. Scribner, the opposing army had taken Lt. Col. John H. Ely, commander of the 10th Wisconsin Infantry, prisoner. They also captured Maj. McKercher and most of the regiment's enlisted men. The 10th Wisconsin regiment (240 men) reported 11 killed, 55 wounded, 145 missing—an 88 percent casualty rate. See the regiment's monument in the photo, above.[208]

The Confederates captured Lt. Col. Harrison C. Hobert, commander of the 21st Wisconsin in Starkweather's Brigade, and they sent him to Richmond's Libby Prison. In November 1864, he escaped through a tunnel with more than 100 prisoners. At Chickamauga, the 21st Wisconsin regiment (369 men) reported 2 killed, 43 wounded, 76 missing—a 33 percent casualty rate.[209]

Chapter 11 Listing

	Page
1. Philemon P. Baldwin (USA)	181
2. Peyton H. Colquitt (CSA)	182
3. James Deshler (CSA)	183
4. Hans C. Heg (USA)	184
5. Benjamin H. Helm (CSA)	185
6. Edward A. King (USA)	186
7. William H. Lytle (USA)	187
8. Preston Smith (CSA)	188

Reading Tip: The bicycle cues in Part III include references to this chapter's descriptions of Chickamauga's memorial shell monuments. Therefore, the next eight sections consist of reference material that you can consult during your battlefield tour.

11. Memorial Shell Monuments

> The enemy retreated on Chattanooga last night, leaving his dead and wounded in our hands. His loss is very large in men, artillery, small-arms, and colors. Ours is heavy, but not yet ascertained. ... We have to mourn the loss of many gallant men and officers.[210]
> ~ Gen. Braxton Bragg, CSA

Park engineer Edward E. Betts designed ten-foot-high memorial monuments that honor the eight brigade commanders who died of injuries sustained at the Battle of Chickamauga. Built and installed between 1893 and 1895, the monuments stand at the approximate location of each commander's mortal wounding. Concrete and limestone hold together a stack of eight-inch iron cannonballs to form a pyramid shape. The Union monuments include blue painted metal plaques, whereas the Confederate monuments are red.

Of the brigade commanders who died, four fought for the Union and four for the Confederacy:

Army of the Cumberland (USA):[211]

	Rank	Life	Burial
Philemon P. Baldwin	Col.	1836–63	Unknown
Hans C. Heg	Col.	1829–63	Wisconsin
Edward A. King	Col.	1814–63	Ohio
William H. Lytle	Brig. Gen.	1826–63	Ohio

Army of Tennessee (CSA):

	Rank	Life	Burial
Peyton H. Colquitt	Col.	1831–63	Georgia
James Deshler	Brig. Gen.	1833–63	Alabama
Benjamin H. Helm	Brig. Gen.	1831–63	Kentucky
Preston Smith	Brig. Gen.	1823–63	Tennessee

At age twenty-six, Philemon P. Baldwin was the youngest brigade commander killed at Chickamauga. The oldest was Edward A. King, age forty-nine. Although an equal number of brigade commanders died from both armies, the Army of Tennessee suffered the loss of three brigadier generals, versus one brigadier general from the Army of the Cumberland. The other commanders held the rank of colonel.

Bicycling Chickamauga Battlefield

As you tour the Chickamauga battlefield, refer to this chapter for an overview of the stories of the brigade commanders who died here. The green numbers on the following map mark the location of the memorial shell monuments. The numbers are alphabetical according to the commander's last name.

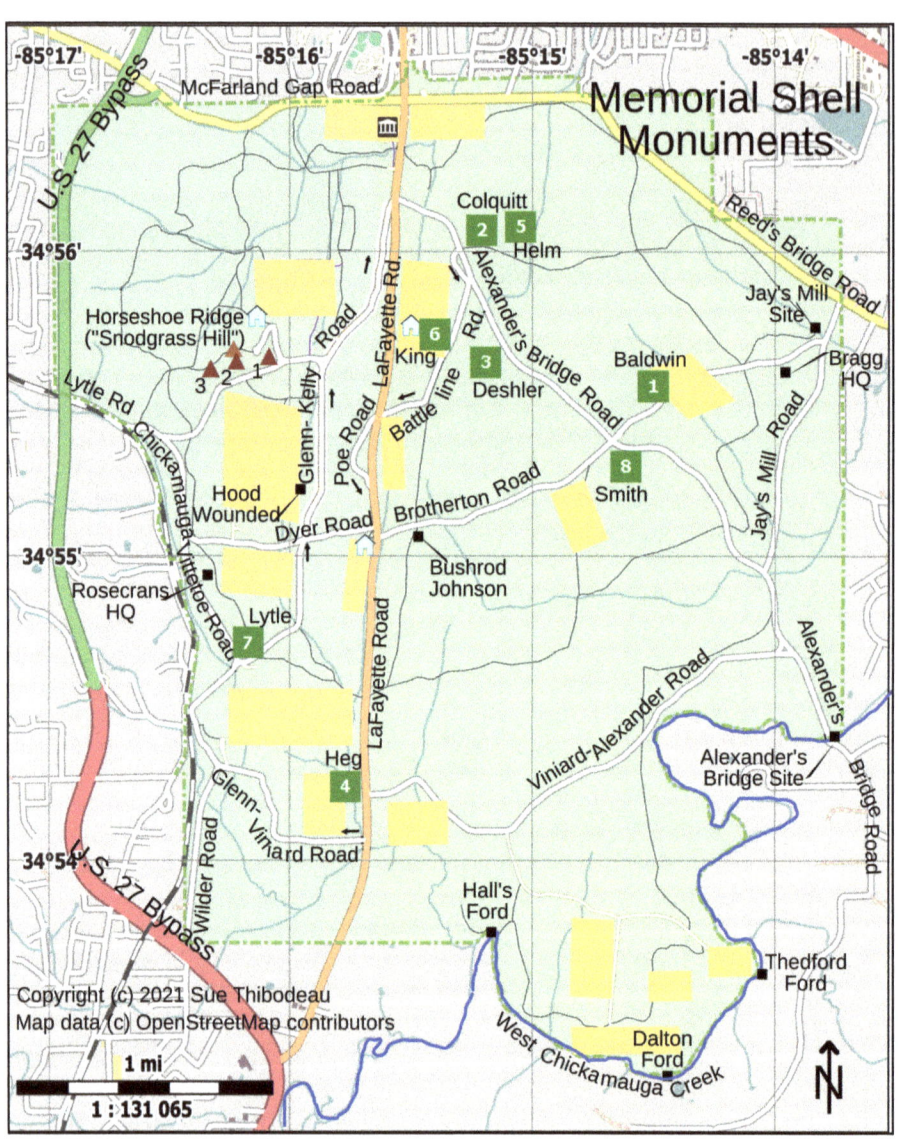

Map 19. Memorial Shell Monuments at Chickamauga

Memorial Shell Monuments

1. Philemon P. Baldwin (USA)

Baldwin Shell Monument[212]
Location: Brotherton Road, north side (Winfrey Field)
GPS (lat, lon): 34.92568, -85.24208
Command: 3rd Brigade, 2nd Division (Richard W. Johnson)
USA Corps: 20th Corps (Thomas L. Crittenden)

Col. Philemon P. Baldwin Shell Monument

Indiana native Col. Philemon P. Baldwin (1836–63) received a mortal bullet wound near this spot in the northwest corner of Winfrey Field on September 19, 1863. (You can spot the marker from Brotherton Road). He was only twenty-six years old. Baldwin's riderless horse signaled to his brigade that their commander had fallen, but they never found his body. A modern gravestone was "erected by the students of Madison Consolidated High School and the Jefferson County Civil War Roundtable" in Springdale Cemetery, Madison, Indiana.[213]

The text on the memorial plaque says that Baldwin died at about 7 p.m., soon after a quiet battlefield erupted with another attack on the Union left flank. Confederate Maj. Gen. Patrick Cleburne attacked Maj. Gen. Thomas' troops as they withdrew westward to regroup for the day's end. Shot, Baldwin fell while riding his horse as he attempted to lead a counterattack. Smoke and early evening darkness contributed to the chaos that also resulted in two Union brigades (under Baird and Baldwin) exchanging friendly fire.

2. Peyton H. Colquitt (CSA)

Colquit (Colquitt) Shell Monument[214]
Location: Woods on east side of Alexander's Bridge Road
GPS (lat, lon): 34.93394, -85.25405
Command: Gist's Brigade in William H.T. Walker's Division
CSA Corps: William H.T. Walker's Reserve Corps

Col. Peyton H. Colquitt Shell Monument

Georgia native Col. Peyton H. Colquitt ("Colquit," 1831–63) fell mortally wounded near this location on September 20, 1863, at about noon, having arrived on the battlefield that morning as part of Gist's brigade. By then, Thomas had built breastworks along modern-day Battleline Road. (Colquitt's monument is a short walk east of the last in a line of Georgia markers). Within the hour, Colquitt fell, and his brigade suffered considerable casualties:

> The enemy now poured forth a most destructive and well-aimed fire upon the entire line... and for some twenty-five minutes the terrific fire was withstood and returned... It was here that the lamented Colquitt fell mortally wounded while cheering on his command...[215]
> ~ Brig. Gen. States Rights Gist, CSA

Colquitt was only thirty-one years old and died two days later. He left behind a wife and was buried in the historic Linwood Cemetery in Columbus, Georgia, the resting place for more than 200 Confederate soldiers.[216]

3. James Deshler (CSA)

Deshler Shell Monument[217]
Location: Battleline Road (see photo on p. 38)
GPS (lat, lon): 34.92707, -85.25510
Command: Deshler's Brigade in Patrick Cleburne's Division
CSA Corps: Daniel H. Hill's Corps

Brig. Gen. James Deshler Shell Monument

Alabama native and 1854 West Point graduate Brig. Gen. James Deshler (1833–63) died near this spot on September 20, 1863, at about noon. An NPS sign along Battleline Road points 555 feet to the Deshler monument, between the Texas and Alabama monuments. Deshler was examining ammunition for his brigade when a shell struck him. Maj. Gen. Patrick R. Cleburne described his death:

> ...General Deshler fell, a shell passing fairly through his chest. It was the first battle in which this gentleman had the honor of commanding as a general officer. He was a brave and efficient one. He brought always to the discharge of his duty a warm zeal and a high conscientiousness. The army and the country will long remember him.[218]
> ~ Maj. Gen. Patrick R. Cleburne, CSA

Deshler was only thirty-years old when he died. Soldiers buried him on the battlefield. Deshler's father, a merchant originally from Pennsylvania, later retrieved his son's body and brought him home for burial in Oakwood Cemetery, Tuscumbia, Alabama.[219]

4. Hans C. Heg (USA)

Heg Shell Monument[220]
Location: LaFayette Road, west side
GPS (lat, lon): 34.90387, -85.26217
Command: 3rd Brigade, 1st Division (Jefferson C. Davis)
USA Corps: 20th Corps (Alexander McDowell McCook)

Col. Hans C. Heg Shell Monument

Norwegian immigrant Col. Hans C. Heg (1829–63), from Wisconsin, received a mortal abdominal wound near this spot in Viniard Field at about 4 p.m. on September 19, 1863. He died at a nearby field hospital on that same day. Col. Heg was only thirty-three years old. His family buried him in Norway Lutheran Church Cemetery, Wind Lake, Wisconsin, on land donated by Heg's father before Wisconsin became a state. An abolitionist, Heg was also the highest-ranking Wisconsin soldier (based on Rosecrans' intent to promote Heg to brigadier general) killed in the U.S. Civil War.[221]

According to historian Steven E. Woodworth, when Heg's men from Illinois, Kansas, and Wisconsin crossed LaFayette Road and into "vines and scrub oak" on September 19, they tripped onto Confederates from Tennessee. One Kansas soldier reflected that "the roar of battle became one steady, deep, and jarring thunder." Heg held the line for a time, but by 4 p.m. Union soldiers had taken refuge in a dry creek bed on the west side of the road, only soon to break to the field farther west. It was in this chaos that Heg fell.[222]

5. Benjamin H. Helm (CSA)

Helm Shell Monument[223]

Location:	Alexander's Bridge Road, east side
GPS (lat, lon):	34.93365, -85.25294
Command:	Orphan Brigade in John Breckinridge's Division
CSA Corps:	Daniel H. Hill's Corps

Brig. Gen. Benjamin H. Helm Shell Monument

Kentucky native and 1851 West Point graduate Brig. Gen. Benjamin H. Helm (1831–63) received a mortal chest wound near this spot at about 10:00 a.m. on September 20, 1863. Not thirty minutes prior, "the battle was opened by Helm's Brigade with great fury," wrote Maj. Gen. Breckinridge in his official report. "Here General Helm, ever ready for action, and endeared to his command by his many virtues, received a mortal wound while in the heroic discharge of his duty." Helm's brigade suffered heavy losses. His men carried his body off the battlefield with no chance of recovery.[224]

Helm was the thirty-two-year-old half-brother-in-law of President Lincoln. (Lincoln's wife, Mary Todd, was the half-sister of Emily Todd, Helm's wife). Helm was also the son of the Kentucky governor. His family buried him in a family cemetery in Elizabethtown, Kentucky.[225]

6. Edward A. King (USA)

King Shell Monument[226]

Location: Battleline Road, Kelly Field (see photo on p. 38)
GPS (lat, lon): 34.92753, -85.25737
Command: 2nd Brigade, 4th Division (Joseph J. Reynolds)
USA Corps: 14th Corps (George H. Thomas)

Col. Edward A. King Shell Monument

Col. Edward A. King (1814–63) died in combat near this spot at about 5:00 p.m. on September 20, 1863. He was forty-nine years old and had a wife and two children.[227] An NPS sign along Battleline Road points 320 feet to the King monument. When he died, artillery and rifle fire on the Kelly Farm had subsided, because the battle was nearly over.

According to Brig. Gen. Wood, King moved forward to scout the Confederate position from the eastern edge of the field (behind the monument in the above photo). Sgt. Henry C. Woods recalled men "begging Colonel King to dismount" but when he finally did, King "was shot in the head and killed instantly." A sharpshooter's ball had struck King above the right eye and passed through his brain.[228]

In 1864, King's burial at Woodland Cemetery and Arboretum in Dayton, Ohio, included full military honors. At the time, the funeral held the claim of being "the largest and most impressive in the city's history."[229]

7. William H. Lytle (USA)

Lytle Shell Monument[230]
Location: Glenn-Kelly Rd. near Vittetoe-Chickamauga Rd.
GPS (lat, lon): 34.91253, -85.26978
Command: 1st Brigade, 3rd Division (Philip H. Sheridan)
USA Corps: 20th Corps (Alexander McDowell McCook)

Brig. Gen. William H. Lytle Shell Monument

Ohio native Brig. Gen. William H. Lytle (1826–63) received a mortal bullet wound and died near this spot about noon on September 20, 1863. Lytle had positioned his brigade between Rosecrans' Union army headquarters and Longstreet's Confederate left wing. On the morning of September 20, Lytle's Brigade advanced under severe fire on both flanks, and during this counterattack, a bullet struck Lytle in the spine. However, it was the next three bullets that felled the thirty-six-year-old brigadier general from his horse.[231] These words from one of Lytle's subordinate officers attest to his hero status:

> During this action he persistently refused to leave the field, but gallantly doing more than his duty to the men he loved, and who worshiped him, he sacrificed himself without reluctance.[232]
> ~ Col. Silas Miller, 36th Illinois Infantry, USA

Before Chickamauga, Lytle suffered two wounding incidents and one imprisonment. He was a lawyer, legislator, soldier, and published poet. Lytle's grave is in Spring Grove Cemetery, Cincinnati, Ohio.[233]

8. Preston Smith (CSA)

Smith Shell Monument[234]

Location:	Near Brock Field, Alexander's Bridge Road
GPS (lat, lon):	34.92134, -85.24383
Command:	Smith's Brigade in Benjamin Cheatham's Division
CSA Corps:	(detached) Leonidas Polk's Right Wing

Brig. Gen. Preston Smith Shell Monument

Tennessee native Brig. Gen. Preston Smith (1823–63) received a mortal chest wound near this spot at about 7:00 p.m. on September 19, 1863. Unaware that Deshler's Confederate brigade had shifted positions away from Smith's front, Smith errantly moved forward into firing range of Union soldiers. It was dark when the 77th Pennsylvania Infantry unleashed a torrential fire upon Smith's scouting party in the and the wooded area around Brock Field. According to Maj. Gen. Benjamin F. Cheatham's official report, Smith died within fifty minutes, and two of his staff officers also died.[235]

Initially buried in Atlanta, in 1868 Smith's body was reburied in Elmwood Cemetery, Memphis, Tennessee.[236]

Did you know ... ?

Several soldiers who fought at Chickamauga are buried in Arlington National Cemetery.[237]

Brig. Gen. Absalom Baird (1824–1905) – 1st Division, 14th Corps, Army of the Cumberland. Section 1, Grave 55 (a polished granite structure west of James Tanner Amphitheater). Baird was born in Pennsylvania and died in Maryland.

John Lincoln Clem (1851–1937) – "The Drummer Boy of Chickamauga," 22nd Michigan, 1st Brigade, Steedman's Division, Reserve Corps, Army of the Cumberland. Section 2, Grave 993 (interred 1937; a simple granite structure to the east of Civil War Unknown). Clem was born in Ohio and died in Texas.

Brig. Gen. William B. Hazen (1830–1887) – 2nd Brigade, Palmer's Division, 21st Corps, Army of the Cumberland. After the Battle of Chickamauga, Hazen played a critical role breaking the Confederate siege of Chattanooga in October 1863. Section 1, Grave 15 (an obelisk to the west of James Tanner Amphitheater). Hazen was born in Vermont and died in Washington, D.C..

Maj. Gen. William S. Rosecrans (1819–1898) – Commander, Army of the Cumberland. At the 1889 veteran reunion, Rosecrans delivered an address on the theme of national reconciliation. Section 3, Grave 1862 (interred 1902; a simple granite structure that is southeast of the Memorial Amphitheater near the Miles Mausoleum). Rosecrans was born in Ohio and died in California.

Maj. Gen. Philip H. Sheridan (1831–1888) – 3rd Division, 20th Corps, Army of the Cumberland. Section 2, Grave S-1 (a polished granite structure with a bronze mounted sculpture that is near the northeast corner of Civil War Unknown). Sheridan was born in New York State and died in Massachusetts.

Maj. Gen. Joseph Wheeler (1836–1906) – CSA Cavalry Corps and USA Spanish-American War. Section 2, Grave 1089 (east of Civil War Unknown). Wheeler was born in Georgia and died in New York City.

PART V: RESOURCES

Bicycling Chickamauga Battlefield

Glossary

Term	Definition
AIC	Art Inventories Catalog. A database of historic art maintained by the Smithsonian Institution as part of the Smithsonian Institution Research Information System (SIRIS). It includes monument descriptions for United States National Parks.
Army	A military organization that is composed of corps. An army contains corps made up of divisions organized by brigade. Two armies fought at Chickamauga, the Army of the Cumberland (USA) and the Army of Tennessee (CSA).
Artillery	Large-caliber, mounted guns often called cannons or ordnance weapons. Or a military unit responsible for the operation, storage, and maintenance of large-caliber arms. Artillery units comprise one of three branches of an army, along with cavalry and infantry units.
Battalion	A battalion is like a regiment but smaller in size. Whereas a fully staffed regiment consists of ten companies, a battalion is four to eight companies. Artillery units are often battalions.
Battery	An artillery unit that consists of four to six cannons and 100+ soldiers, called gunners.
Bicycle Cue	Bicycling directions formatted as text and often abbreviated for quick reading while riding a bicycle.
Border State	A state where slavery existed but the state government did not secede from the Union (Delaware, Kentucky, Maryland, and Missouri). Enslaved people in border states were exempt from President Abraham Lincoln's Emancipation.

Term	Definition
Breastworks	During the Civil War, trenches made of natural material (earth, rocks, and wood) that protect soldiers as they fire at an attacking force. For example, Union Maj. Gen. George H. Thomas's 14th Corps built breastworks on a slight ridge on the east side of Kelly Farm.
Brigade	An infantry brigade consisted of four to six regiments, for a theoretical total of about 4,000 soldiers, although the numbers declined under the cumulative losses of each Civil War battle. Brigades formed divisions. Colonels or brigadier generals led infantry brigades.
Caisson	An open horse-drawn carriage with two wheels that carries an ammunition chest.
Cannon	Also called a "gun," a large, heavy weapon that is mounted on wheels and manned by artillery units. Many types of cannons were used during the Civil War, including "Napoleon," Howitzer, Parrott rifle, and Ordnance rifle cannons.
Casualty	Killed, wounded, missing (or captured). According to American Battlefield Trust, the Battle of Chickamauga produced 34,624 casualties, second only to the Battle of Gettysburg in overall Civil War battle casualties. By the end of the war, there were 642,427 USA and 483,026 CSA casualties, categorized as follows: killed in action (110,100 and 94,000), wounded (275,174 and 194,026), diseased (224,580 and 164,000), and captured (30,192 and 31,000).[238]
Colors	A regimental flag that color bearers carry into battle for the purpose of keeping a unit together during the chaos of battle. Also, a symbol of regimental pride; the loss of colors was considered a disgrace (and the capture of an enemy flag was an honor).

Term	Definition
Commander	A general term for an officer who leads a military unit.
Company	The smallest military unit, no larger than about 100 soldiers. Battlefield losses account for widely varying regimental sizes during the war. The letters A-K (omitting J) identified companies. Usually commanded by captains, companies formed regiments.
Corps	The highest level of military organization in an army, theoretically about 36,000 soldiers. A corps is composed of divisions. At Chickamauga, the Union corps commanders were Maj. Gens. Thomas (14th corps), McCook (20th), Crittenden (21st), and Granger (reserve). The Confederate corps commanders were Lt. Gen. Polk (right wing), Lt. Gen. D.H. Hill, Maj. Gen. Walker (reserve), Lt. Gen. Longstreet (left wing), Maj. Gen. Buckner, Maj. Gen. Hood, and the cavalry corps of Maj. Gen. Wheeler and Brig. Gen. Forrest.
CSA	Confederate States of America, also known as the Confederacy. The confederation of states that seceded from the United States of America. Jefferson Davis was President of the CSA.
Division	The second highest military unit, the building blocks of corps, theoretically about 12,000 soldiers. The size of a division varies widely over time and between armies. Divisions are composed of brigades. Major generals or brigadier generals lead divisions. Numbers identify divisions in the Army of the Cumberland, e.g., 3rd Division (Brannan) 14th Corps (Thomas), and by name in the Army of Tennessee, e.g., Cleburne's Division of Hill's Corps. At Chickamauga, each division had its own artillery, but cavalry had their own corps.

Term	Definition
Federal	Referring to the government, laws, or armies of the United States of America. During the United States Civil War, Federal troops represented the North in the conflict between North and South.
Flank	The end or side of a military line. For example, at Chickamauga, the Confederate right wing under Lt. Gen. Leonidas Polk attacked the Union left flank held by Maj. Gen. George H. Thomas. "Right" and "left" refer to the army's forward-facing orientation, which explains why the Confederate "right" was the Union "left," and vice versa.
GPS	Global Positioning System. A space-based navigation system that identifies locations in terms of longitude and latitude. Cell phones and other GPS devices capture GPS coordinates.
HQ	Headquarters.
LCS	List of Classified Structures. A database of historic structures in United States National Parks. The NPS retired this database in 2019.
Medal of Honor	First awarded in 1863, the highest military decoration granted by the United States government to American military service personnel for distinguished acts of valor.
Minié ball	Named after inventor Claude-Étienne Minié, a grooved bullet that soldiers loaded into a rifle's muzzle. The minié ball was the most common bullet used during the Civil War. Made of lead, the bullet turns white when it rusts.
NPS	National Park Service. An organization within the U.S. government that since 1933 has managed and preserved Chickamauga and Chattanooga National Military Park, established in August 1890.

Term	Definition
Order of Battle	An army's battle roster, including a listing of all military units deployed and their commanders.
OSM	Open Street Map. An openly licensed database of global GPS coordinates maintained by volunteers.
Regiment	A military unit typically commanded by colonels, a regiment consists of about ten companies or about 1,000 soldiers when initially mustered. Regiments formed brigades.
Segment Map	In this book, a detailed map that is part of a bicycle route. Segment names are arbitrarily identified with a capital letter.
Spencer Repeating Rifle	Invented in 1860, a .52-caliber breech-loading small arm that could fire seven shots in thirty seconds. At Chickamauga, Union Col. John T. Wilder's Brigade used this weapon effectively at Alexander's Bridge.
SIRIS	Smithsonian Institution Research Information System (manages the Art Inventories Catalog).
USA	United States of America, or the Union. Abraham Lincoln was President of the USA from 1861–65.
Western Theater	For military operations during the U.S. Civil War, the area of land that is south of Virginia and east of the Mississippi River. The Battle of Chickamauga was fought in the western theater.
Wing Commander	A general in charge of more than one corps. At Chickamauga, James Longstreet commanded the Confederate left wing, and Leonidas Polk, the right.

Bibliography

This bibliography describes additional resources that you may want to consult while planning your tour. The listing includes the following categories: United States Civil War; The Chickamauga Campaign; Chickamauga Battlefield Park; and Tourism.

United States Civil War

Catton, Bruce. *The Civil War*. New York: Houghton Mifflin, 2005.

Davis, William C. *The Civil War: National Park Civil War Series*. Hatboro, PA: Eastern National, 2007.

McPherson, James M., Ed. *The Atlas of the Civil War*. Philadelphia, PA: Running Press Book Publishers, 2010.

———. *Battle Cry of Freedom: The Civil War Era*. New York: Oxford University Press, 2003.

United States War Department. *The War of Rebellion: A Compilation of the Official Records of the Union and Confederate Armies*. Washington, DC: Government Printing Office, 1889.

Varon, Elizabeth R. *Armies of Deliverance: A New History of the Civil War*. New York: Oxford University Press, 2021.

The Chickamauga Campaign

Cozzens, Peter. *This Terrible Sound*. Urbana, IL: University of Illinois Press, 1994.

Linton, Roger C. *Chickamauga: A Battlefield History in Images*. Athens: University of Georgia Press, 2004.

Powell, David A. *The Chickamauga Campaign: Barren Victory; September 21 to October 20, 1863*. 2015. Reprint, El Dorado Hills, CA: Savas Beatie, 2017.

———. *The Chickamauga Campaign: Glory or the Grave; September 20, 1863*. 2015. Reprint, El Dorado Hills, CA: Savas Beatie, 2017.

———. *The Chickamauga Campaign: A Mad Irregular Battle; August 22–September 19, 1863*. El Dorado Hills, CA: Savas Beatie, 2016.

———. *Decisions at Chickamauga: The Twenty-four Critical Decisions That Defined the Battle*. With cartography by David Friedrichs. Knoxville: University of Tennessee Press, 2018.

———. *The Maps of Chickamauga: An Atlas of the Chickamauga Campaign, Including the Tullahoma Operations, June 22–September 23, 1863*. With cartography by David Friedrichs. El Dorado Hills, CA: Savas Beatie, 2009.

Robertson, William Glenn. *The Battle of Chickamauga; Civil War Series*. With cartography by George Skoch. Washington, DC: National Park Service, 1995.

———. *Staff Ride Handbook for the Battle of Chickamauga, 18–20 September 1863*. Fort Leavenworth, KS: U.S. Army Command and General Staff College, 1992.

Sullivan, James R. *Chickamauga and Chattanooga Battlefields*. National Park Service Historical Handbook Series, no. 25. 1956. Reprint, Washington, DC: National Park Service, 1961.

Time-Life Books, eds. *Chickamauga: Voices of the Civil War*. Alexandria, VA: Time-Life Books, 1997.

———. *The Fight for Chattanooga: Chickamauga to Missionary Ridge*. Alexandria, VA: Time-Life Books, 1985.

Tucker, Glenn. *Chickamauga: Bloody Battle in the West*. New York: Smithmark, 1994.

Woodworth, Steven E., ed. *The Chickamauga Campaign*. Carbondale: Southern Illinois University Press, 2010.

———. *A Deep Steady Thunder: The Battle of Chickamauga*. Abilene, TX: McWhiney Foundation Press, 2006.

———. *Six Armies in Tennessee: The Chickamauga and Chattanooga Campaigns*. Lincoln: University of Nebraska Press, 1998.

Chickamauga Battlefield Park

Boynton, H.V., comp. *Dedication of the Chickamauga and Chattanooga National Military Park, September 18–20, 1895*. Washington, DC: Government Printing Office, 1896.

Kerr, Jack. *Monuments and Markers of the Twenty-nine States Engaged at Chickamauga and Chattanooga*. Apison, TN: Jack Kerr, 2003.

Reaves, Stacy W. *A History and Guide to the Monuments of Chickamauga National Military Park*. Charleston, SC: History Press, 2013.

Smith, Timothy B. *A Chickamauga Memorial: The Establishment of America's First Civil War National Military Park*. Knoxville, TN: University of Tennessee Press, 2009.

Tourism

Auto Tours

TravelBrains. *Chickamauga Field Guide*. With text and narration by Peter Cozzens. N.p.: TravelBrains, 2011.

White, William Lee. *Bushwhacking on a Grand Scale: The Battle of Chickamauga, September 18–20, 1863*. El Dorado Hills, CA: Savas Beatie, 2013.

Woodworth, Steven E. *Chickamauga: A Battlefield Guide with a section on Chattanooga*. Lincoln: University of Nebraska Press, 1995.

Hiking & Biking

Carter, Robert L. *The Fight for Snodgrass Hill and the Rock of Chickamauga: A History and Walking Tour*. With cartography by James A. Boyd. Carrollton, GA: Melica Books, 2012.

———. *Longstreet's Breakthrough at Chickamauga: Accidental Victory; A History and Walking Tour*. With cartography by James A. Boyd. Carrollton, GA: Melica Books, 2014.

Manion, Richard L. *Travels with Twister: A Chickamauga Battlefield Horseback and Hiking Tour*. 2nd ed. Lafayette, GA: White Star Battlefield Tours, 2018.

Trailhead Graphics. *Battlefield America: Chickamauga Battlefield*. Civil War Map Series. Revised, Aurora, CO: Trailhead Graphics, 2012.

Notes

ABBREVIATIONS:

ABT	American Battlefield Trust
ADHI	Administrative History of Chickamauga and Chattanooga National Military Park
AIC	Art Inventories Catalog (Smithsonian Institution)
CBCLR	Chickamauga Battlefield Cultural Landscape Report
CHCH	Chickamauga and Chattanooga National Military Park
LCS	List of Classified Structures
NPS	National Park Service
OR	Official Records, Series 1
SIRIS	Smithsonian Institution Research Information System

U.S. Postal Abbreviations

For brevity when referencing a SIRIS AIC record, these notes identify records by Control Number. For web access to a record, substitute the Control Number for the "X" in this template: https://siris-artinventories.si.edu/ipac20/ipac.jsp?term=X&index=.NW.

All web links were accessed September 15, 2021.

1. The term "western theater" of the U.S. Civil War denotes the land area that includes the states of Alabama, Florida, Georgia, Kentucky, Mississippi, North Carolina, South Carolina, and Tennessee. Of all the battles fought in the western theater, the Battle of Chickamauga ranks as the greatest and only Confederate victory. "Chickamauga was a Union disaster," according to historian Bruce Catton. Bruce Catton, *The Civil War* (New York: Houghton Mifflin, 2005), 181.

Strength: Army of Tennessee (CSA), 65,000; Army of the Cumberland (USA), 60,000. American Battlefield Trust, "Catoosa County and Walker County, GA | Sep 18–20, 1863," https://www.battlefields.org/learn/civil-war/battles/chickamauga. Gen. Bragg's army was heavily reinforced to protect Chattanooga and Atlanta. The Confederate fighting strength included about 6,700 soldiers from Lt. Gen. James Longstreet's corps (actual arrivals from Virginia); about 5,000 reinforcements from Maj. Gen. Simon B. Buckner's corps (arriving from Knoxville); about 5,000 men in Maj. Gen. Alexander P. Stewart's division that Buckner was returning to Bragg; and about 9,000 men from Gen. Joseph E. Johnston's Mississippi army (Maj. Gen. W.H.T. Walker's Reserve Corps and Maj. Gen. John C. Breckinridge's division). Reinforcement numbers are from Robert Carter, Facebook post in "The Battle of Chickamauga Discussion Group," September 13, 2021, https://www.facebook.com/groups/1620249201457778/permalink/2002033926612635/.

Casualties: Army of Tennessee, 18,454; Army of the Cumberland, 16,170. ABT, "10 Facts: The Battle of Chickamauga," https://www.battlefields.org/learn/articles/10-facts-battle-chickamauga. The Battle of Chickamauga ranked second only to Gettysburg in terms of casualties (killed, wounded, captured or missing) for all U.S. Civil War battles. The top-ten battles ranked by total casualties are as follows:

1. 51,000 casualties – Gettysburg (July 1–3, 1863)
2. 34,624 casualties – Chickamauga (September 19–20, 1863)
3. 30,000 casualties – Spotsylvania Court House (May 8–21, 1864)
4. 29,800 casualties – The Wilderness (May 5–7, 1864)
5. 24,000 casualties – Chancellorsville (April 30–May 6, 1863)
6. 23,746 casualties – Shiloh (April 6–7, 1862)
7. 23,515 casualties – Stones River (December 31, 1862–January 2, 1863)
8. 22,717 casualties – Antietam (September 17, 1862)
9. 22,180 casualties – Second Manassas (August 28–30, 1862)
10. 19,233 casualties – Siege of Vicksburg (May 18–July 4, 1863)

ABT, "Civil War Facts," https://www.battlefields.org/learn/articles/civil-war-facts.

2. Total protected acreage has increased through time. As of 2004, the NPS reported 5,280 acres. John Milner Associates, *Chickamauga Battlefield Cultural Landscape Report* (Charlottesville, VA: John Milner Associates, 2004), 3–23. Hereafter, *CBCLR*. In 2010, the NPS reported 5,509.51 "permanently protected acres" and 4,371.77 "unprotected, intact acres remaining." NPS, *Update to the Civil War Sites Advisory Commission Report on the Nation's Civil War Battlefields: State of Georgia* (Washington, DC: U.S. Department of the Interior, 2010), 21.

3. At the Battle of Chickamauga, Henry V. Boynton (1835–1905) served as the Lieutenant Colonel for the 35th Ohio Infantry, under Col. Ferdinand Van Derveer (1823–1892). Both men hailed from Ohio. For a short history of veterans' efforts to establish the national military park, see Timothy B. Smith, "A Western Gettysburg: Chickamauga and Chattanooga National Military Park, 1890–1933," chap. 3 in *The Golden Age of Battlefield Preservation* (Knoxville: University of Tennessee Press, 2008). For a longer history, see Smith, *A Chickamauga Memorial: The Establishment of America's First Civil War National Military Park* (Knoxville: University of Tennessee Press, 2009). For a brief overview of the park's commemorative structures, including counts, see *CBCLR*, 3–26. Smith's count of tablets, monuments, and guns differs from *CBCLR*, likely because his numbers are inclusive of the larger battlefield beyond Chickamauga proper. Smith, *A Chickamauga Memorial*, 68–69.

Today, Chickamauga Battlefield is a major historic attraction in Walker County, Georgia, along with the Gordon Lee Mansion (the headquarters for Union Army Maj. Gen. William S. Rosecrans) and McLemore Cove (where Gen. Braxton Bragg failed to trap Rosecrans' army before the Battle of Chickamauga). See Walker County Government, "Chickamauga Battlefield," https://walkercountyga.gov/discover/attractions/chickamauga-battlefield/ and "Historic Sites," https://walkercountyga.gov/discover/attractions/historic-sites/.

4. H.V. Boynton, *The National Military Park: Chickamauga-Chattanooga: An Historical Guide, With Maps and Illustrations* (Cincinnati, OH: Clarke Co., 1895), 226. Boynton described the broad, national significance of CHCH in this way: "It was the pioneer project in giving impartial representation to both sides in preserving the history of the fields and marking the lines of battle. The Gettysburg Memorial Association soon followed and the act establishing a Park at Shiloh, the work preserving the field at Antietam, and the proposed completion of Gettysburg under the Government are proceeding upon the methods inaugurated at Chickamauga and Chattanooga." Boynton, v.

5. Peter Cozzens, *This Terrible Sound: The Battle of Chickamauga* (Chicago: University of Illinois Press, 1994), 140, 434. Also, Charles W. Lusk, *Chattanooga Times*, September, 1923, in James Sartain, *History of Walker County, Georgia*, vol. 1 (Dalton, GA: A.J. Showalter Co., 1932), 108.

6. Cozzens, 418.

7. Sartain, 102. Also, Harry Smeltzer, "The Snodgrass Family at Chickamauga," *HistoryNet*, https://www.historynet.com/snodgrass-family-chickamauga.htm. Chickamauga Battlefield is split into western and eastern sections by the Walker and Catossa County line. Technically in Catoosa County, LaFayette Road roughly bisects the battlefield park.

8. Three distinct hills now known as Horseshoe Ridge dominate the landscape south and west of the Snodgrass cabin (on Snodgrass Hill). According to the topological map by Trailhead Graphics, the peaks of the ridge have an elevation of 940 feet (which is about 185 feet higher than Dyer Field farther south). Trailhead Graphics, *Battlefield America: Chickamauga Battlefield*. Civil War Map Series, rev. (2004; Aurora, CO: Trailhead Graphics, 2012). Public historian Robert L. Carter remarks that the three hills are commonly identified from east to west as Hill 1, Hill 2, and Hill 3. Robert L. Carter, *The Fight for Snodgrass Hill and the Rock of Chickamauga: A History and Walking Tour* (Carrollton, GA: Melica Books, 2012), 18–19, 34.

9. Helm's widow was the twenty-seven-year-old Emilie Todd Helm, a woman who with her half-sister Mary Todd Lincoln had suffered the death of three brothers in Confederate service. When President Lincoln learned of Helm's death, he was grief-stricken and brokenhearted—but careful to hide his family's pain amidst public accusations that Mrs. Lincoln was a Confederate spy. By December, President Lincoln ignored the political vitriol

and invited Emilie and her child to rest at the White House. Daniel Mark Epstein, *The Lincolns: Portrait of a Marriage* (New York: Ballantine Books, 2008), 401–407.

10. Sartain, 101–102. Cozzens, 418. According to William Glenn Robertson, there had been "no appreciable rainfall in the area of operations for approximately six weeks prior to the battle of 18–20 September 1863." William Glenn Robertson, *Staff Ride Handbook for the Battle of Chickamauga, 18–20 September 1863* (Fort Leavenworth, KS: U.S. Army Command and General Staff College, 1992), 173.

11. Sartain, 103–108.

12. U.S. Department of the Interior, *Natural Resource Condition Assessment: Chickamauga and Chattanooga National Military Park* (Fort Collins, CO: National Park Service, 2018), 12–13.

13. Kenneth W. Noe, "Fields of Fire and Frost: The Battle of Chickamauga and Weather in Early American Newspapers," *Readex Report* 13, no. 2 (2018): 1. Concerning Saturday evening, September 19, Col. Nixon reported that the "soldiers suffered considerable from cold, their clothes being wet from wading Chickamauga in the evening." U.S. War Department, *The War of Rebellion: A Compilation of the Official Records of the Union and Confederate Armies* (Washington, D. C.: Government Printing Office, 1889), 30:1, 185. Hereafter, *OR*. Walker County Historian James Sartain reported that beginning September 19 the weather "grew colder," and the Chickamauga families who were camped in a ravine claimed that "on some mornings the children's heads would be white with frost." Sartain, 101. For a list of six meteorological data points relevant to the Chickamauga Campaign, see Robertson, *Staff Ride Handbook for the Battle of Chickamauga, 18–20 September 1863*, 173.

14. *CBCLR*, 3–15. LaFayette Road is a battle era supply route that connects Chattanooga to northwest Georgia. Today, it is a two-lane asphalt roadway. In 2002, commercial traffic was redirected to U.S. Highway 27, thus bypassing the park on its west boundary. According to the Milner study, 13,200 motor vehicles traveled on LaFayette Road each day before the bypass was constructed. After the bypass, traffic dropped to 3,700 motor vehicles per day.

15. On September 20, the left wing of the Confederate army, under the command of Lt. Gen. James Longstreet, crashed through the Union line along LaFayette Road. "Longstreet's Breakthrough" at Chickamauga is often compared to "Longstreet's Assault" (more commonly known as "Pickett's Charge") at Gettysburg. Glenn Tucker makes the comparison well: "When Longstreet had attacked at Gettysburg with the divisions of Pickett, Pettigrew and Trimble consisting of nine brigades, four of them already had been shattered and grievously weakened during the first day of battle. At Chickamauga he formed on a front of half a mile eight brigades, all relatively

fresh and some not yet tried in action. His Chickamauga column was superior and it had the protection of the forest, whereas the Gettysburg advance was across open ground." Glenn Tucker, *Chickamauga: Bloody Battle in the West*, rev. ed. (New York: Bobbs-Merrill, 1961; New York: Smithmark, 1994), 260. Citations refer to the Smithmark edition.

    16. NPS, *Update to the Civil War Sites Advisory Commission Report on the Nation's Civil War Battlefields: State of Georgia*, 5.

    17. Although cellular service is generally good at Chickamauga, Civil War Cycling does not recommend relying exclusively on GPS to navigate the battlefield park. Bicyclists do not want a dropped signal to impact their ride, if only temporarily. Have a backup plan that includes paper maps, or PDFs that one can view on a mobile device during a stop.

    18. Albion W. Tourgée, *The Story of a Thousand* (Buffalo, NY: S. McGerald & Son, 1896), 217–18. In 1895, Boynton implicitly affirmed Tourgée's unofficial assessment when Boyton reported that "most of the forest was thickly obstructed with underbrush" and that "some of the present fields were woods." Boynton, v. For a modern edition with an introduction to Tourgée's work as a champion of African American civil rights during Reconstruction, see Peter Luebke, ed., *The Story of a Thousand* (Kent, OH: Kent State University Press, 2011).

    19. *OR*, 30:1, 136.

    20. *OR*, 30:2, 97.

    21. For more details, see Jill K. Hanson, and Robert W. Blythe, *Chickamauga and Chattanooga National Military Park: Historic Resource Study* (Atlanta, GA: National Park Service, 1999).

    22. *CBCLR*, 2–14. CBCLR counts 65 buildings, not including the church, tanyard, and log schoolhouse.

    23. Steven E. Woodworth, *Six Armies in Tennessee: The Chickamauga and Chattanooga Campaigns* (Lincoln: University of Nebraska Press, 1998), 87.

    24. *CBCLR*, 3–14, 3–22.

    25. James R. Sullivan, *Chickamauga and Chattanooga Battlefields*, National Park Service Historical Handbook Series, 25 (1956; repr., Washington, DC: National Park Service, 1961), 48. On the west side of Battleline Road, USA regimental or artillery battery monuments honor service from the following states: Illinois, Indiana, Kentucky, Ohio, Pennsylvania, Tennessee, Wisconsin, and the U.S. Regulars. On the east side (CSA): Alabama, Georgia, Tennessee, and Texas.

    26. "21st Wisconsin," http://www.secondwi.com/wisconsinregiments/21st_wisconsin_regimental_histor.htm.

27. Scott L. Mingus and Joseph L. Owen, *Unceasing Fury: Texans at the Battle of Chickamauga, September 18–20, 1863* (El Dorado Hills, CA: Savas Beatie, 2021).

28. Sartain, 104–105.

29. These are often referred to as "memorial shell monuments." Each monument includes 323 eight-inch-diameter naval shells that are stacked 10-feet tall in the shape of a pyramid. USA memorial shell monuments: Col. Philemon P. Baldwin (k Sept. 19); Col. Hans Christian Heg (mw Sept. 19); Col. Edward A. King (k Sept. 19); and Brig. Gen. William H. Lytle (k Sept. 19). CSA memorial shell monuments: Col. Peyton H. Colquitt (mw Sept. 20); Brig. Gen. James Deshler (k Sept. 20); Brig. Gen. Benjamin H. Helm (mw Sept. 20); and Brig. Gen. Preston Smith (mw Sept. 19).

30. Maj. Gen. Hood's right arm had already been rendered mostly useless from his July 2, 1863, Gettysburg wound. Now at Chickamauga—and while trying to rally Kershaw's South Carolinians who had crossed from the Glenn–Kelly Road into Dyer field to attack north to the Union line on Snodgrass Hill—a minié ball struck Hood's right leg and brought him down. A surgeon later amputated his leg, and although Hood returned to active duty, he never again fought with his Texas brigade. Cozzens, 411–412.

31. Sartain, 105, 108, 456–57. Lee Dyer built the house in 1875. Then ca. 1891 the Park Commission purchased the house. Today, the reconstructed building is a rangers' quarters. Hanson and Blythe, 41. The nearby large cedar trees date to the commemorative period of the late nineteenth and early twentieth centuries. *CBCLR*, 3–18.

32. NPS, "Mark Thrash," https://www.nps.gov/people/mark-thrash.htm.

33. For John P. Alexander, see William Lee White, *Bushwhacking on a Grand Scale: The Battle of Chickamauga, September 18–20, 1863* (El Dorado Hills, CA: Savas Beatie, 2013), 13. For Tabler C. Viniard, see NPS, "Tour Stop # 5: Viniard Field," https://www.nps.gov/places/tourstop5viniardfield.htm, and White, 157. For an interesting NPS park ranger video about the fighting at Viniard Farm, see NPS, "For They Were Falling in Heaps: Eli Lilly and the Ditch of Death," September 19, 2020, https://www.nps.gov/media/video/view.htm?id=B9F3B325-E53E-82D1-88D7B175C061292E.

34. Unless otherwise noted, all site elevation data is derived from this topographical map: Trailhead Graphics, *Battlefield America: Chickamauga Battlefield*. Civil War Map Series, rev. (2004; Aurora, CO: Trailhead Graphics, 2012).

35. White, 19–21.

36. Woodworth, *A Deep Steady Thunder*, 44.

37. White, 153–154.

38. From the cast iron marker (with slight punctuation and capitalization changes for easier reading): "The division was formed on this line at 7 a.m..

At 11:10 a.m. it advanced. Wood's Union division was now moving to the left from the front of Johnson. The latter division advanced into the opening under a heavy fire from adjacent lines soon broke the Union center and gained the Dyer fields. Upon entering these fields the division bore slightly to the right capturing fifteen guns on the high ground west and northwest of the Dyer house and separating the Union divisions of David and Sheridan from the rest of the army. With the assistance of Hood's and McLaws' Divisions which had first followed in the track of Johnson and then turned more to the right the Union center was thrown into disorder. At 2 o'clock Johnson's line faced Snodgrass Hill at Vittetoe's ready to assault."

39. For background on the Fuller Gun Collection, see Sullivan, 48. Also NPS, "The Fuller Gun Collection, https://www.nps.gov/chch/learn/history culture/fuller-gun-collection.htm.

40. Pvt. Van R. Willard, 3rd Wisconsin Volunteer Infantry, quoted in Steven S. Rabb, ed., *With the 3rd Wisconsin Badgers: The Living Experience of the Civil War Through the Diaries of Van R. Willard* (Mechanicsburg, PA: Stackpole Books, 1999), 249.

41. William Glenn Robertson, *River of Death: The Chickamauga Campaign* (Chapel Hill: University of North Carolina, 2018), 404. According to Bruce Catton, "Chickamauga was an old Cherokee word ... meaning 'river of death,' and there was an awful literalness to its meaning" now that the Battle of Chickamauga had cut down the size of each army by nearly one-third. Catton, 181. See also, Steven E. Woodworth, *A Deep Steady Thunder: The Battle of Chickamauga* (Abilene, TX: McWhiney Foundation, 2006), 13. For the 1878 Yellow Fever epidemic, see the gravestone of Hattie Ackerman, Forest Hills Cemetery, Chattanooga, which identifies the number of Chattanooga citizens that died. Cozzens describes Chickamauga Creek as being "neither clear nor swift nor especially deep," and mentions that "its banks were steep and rocky or low and swampy." Cozzens, 92. Woodward poetically begins his book, *A Deep Steady Thunder*, with this sentence: "The Chickamauga is a quiet brown stream that meanders between steep muddy banks and its unhurried way through a long Georgia valley to the Tennessee River." Woodworth, *A Deep Steady Thunder*, 13.

42. John B. Turchin, *Chickamauga* (Chicago: Fergus Printing, 1888), 56.

43. "Anonymous Plantation Boy," quoted in Time-Life Books, eds., *Chickamauga: Voices of the Civil War* (Alexandria, VA: Time-Life Books, 1997), 91.

44. Woodworth, *A Deep Steady Thunder*, 13. For a short history, see City of Chickamauga, "History of Chickamauga, Georgia," http://cityof chickamauga.org/about-history.asp.

45. *CBCLR*, 3–23.

46. Jill K. Hanson and Robert W. Blythe, *Chickamauga and Chattanooga National Military Park Historic Resource Study* (Atlanta: NPS, 1999), 11. For a web version, *see* http://www.nps.gov/chch/hrs/hrs.htm.

47. *OR*, 30:1, 286–287.

48. Sartain, 108. The Winfreys escaped to the "Snodgrass refugee camp."

49. Tucker, 185. Confederate Maj. Gen. Patrick R. Cleburne (D.H. Hill's Corps) initiated the nighttime attack.

50. *OR*, 30:2, 361–363.

51. David A. Powell, *The Chickamauga Campaign: A Mad Irregular Battle* (El Dorado Hills, CA: Savas Beatie, 2016), 368. According to Sartain, John Brock was sixty-five years old at the time of the battle, and although he farmed the land, he lived "a short distance west of the McDonald house, on the road to McFarland's gap." Sartain, 105.

52. For William and John Brock, see Sartain, 105. For information pertaining to which Chickamauga families camped without shelter in a ravine for eight days, see Sartain, 98–110.

53. For a description of the ravine deep in the Snodgrass woods, see Cozzens, 418. For a brief description of the fighting in Brook Field, see Woodworth, *A Deep Steady Thunder*, 39–41.

54. Woodworth, *A Deep Steady Thunder*, 41.

55. Sartain, 108. According to Sartain, it was believed that Mr. Viniard was the brother of a Chattanooga man who fought for the Confederacy, and who was captured, imprisoned, and died shortly thereafter.

56. As an aside, according to the NPS, "hundreds and possibly thousands, of African Americans" worked for the Union armies during the U.S. Civil War. One such man was the formerly enslaved man, Peter Dabney, whom the 15th Wisconsin Infantry emancipated in 1862. Mr. Dabney was an officer's attendant in Col. Heg's regiment at the Battle of Chickamauga. NPS, "African American Participation in the Civil War Campaign for Chattanooga," https://www.nps.gov/articles/chickamauga africanamericans.htm.

57. Sartain, 103.

58. Sartain, 102–103. The quote about Chickamauga's "pig trails" is from NPS, "War Comes to the Brothertons," Wayside Exhibit, Chickamauga Battlefield. The sign also says that Tom told his brother Jim, "It's a sorry lad that won't fight for his own home." Cozzens describes Tom's role this way: "To explain the topography, Longstreet had at his side young Tom Brotherton, who had left his father's farm to enlist in the Confederate Army." Cozzens, 316. The Brotherton cabin description is from *CBCLR*, 3–24.

59. Woodworth, *A Deep Steady Thunder*, 44.

60. NPS, "Confederate Breakthrough" wayside exhibit. When Longstreet's 8 brigades (about 11,000 soldiers) "swept across the La Fayette Road," they "surprised the Federal divisions of Wood, Davis, and Sheridan who were in motion and unprepared to fight."

61. Robert L. Carter, *Longstreet's Breakthrough at Chickamauga: Accidental Victory; A History and Walking Tour*, with cartography by James A. Boyd (Carrollton, GA: Melica Books, 2014).

62. Sartain, 99.

63. Sartain, 99–100.

64. *OR* 30:2, 358. Sartain, 100.

65. Sullivan, 48.

66. Like seven other mortally wounded or killed brigade commanders, Lytle's memorial monument is a pyramid structure composed of black cannon shells. Local author Jack Kerr published a monument booklet that includes a full-page spread on the eight brigade commanders killed at the Battle of Chickamauga. Jack Kerr, *Monuments and Markets of the 29 States Engaged at Chickamauga and Chattanooga* (Apison, TN: Jack Kerr, 2003), 8.

67. NPS Marker Number MT-423L identifies the location of the Glenn house. The 1890 marker has this inscription: "Site of Widow Glenn's House / Burned during the battle / September 20, 1863." You will find the marker in the field on which the Wilder Brigade Monument stands (Glenn-Viniard Road).

68. *OR*, 30:1, 261.

69. Ibid.

70. Sartain, 156–157. According to Clement A. Evans (1833–1911), a former Confederate brigadier-general who edited a 12-volume Confederate military history, Mr. Dyer helped Maj. Gen. Preston understand "the nature of the topography in the front," which would be Dyer Field north to Horseshoe Ridge. Clement A. Evans, ed., *Confederate Military History: A Library of Confederate States History* (Atlanta, GA: Confederate Publishing Company, 1899), 9:180.

71. Sartain, 107–108.

72. *OR*, 30:2, 289.

73. The Snodgrass cabin description is from *CBCLR*, 3–25.

74. Sartain, 101. Much of Sartain's account of the Snodgrass family is from an interview by local judge Charles W. Lusk (published in the *Chattanooga Times*, September 1923). Lusk interviewed George Snodgrass' daughter, Julia Kittie (Snodgrass) Green, who was six years old at the time of the battle.

75. Carter, *The Fight for Snodgrass Hill and the Rock of Chickamauga*, 19.

76. Ibid.

77. *OR*, 30:2, 186. For a set of maps that include the movement of the 48th Tennessee Infantry (CSA) from 4:30–6:00 p.m. in their attack through Kelly Field, see David A. Powell, *The Maps of Chickamauga: An Atlas of the Chickamauga Campaign, Including the Tullahoma Operations, June 22–September 23, 1863*, with cartography by David Friedrichs (El Dorado Hills, CA: Savas Beatie, 2009), 240–49.

78. *CBCLR*, 3–25. Hanson and Blythe, 51.

79. *OR*, 30:2, 185.

80. Sartain, 105.

81. Turchin, 95.

82. Powell, *The Maps of Chickamauga*, 244.

83. *OR*, 30:2, 253.

84. In the 1923 newspaper interview by Judge Charles W. Lusk, William McDonald said that his father, John, having been picked up and sent to Gen. Rosecrans, was ordered to serve as Rosecrans' guide during the Battle of Chickamauga. After the battle, Rosecrans took John McDonald to Chattanooga and did not release him until after the Battle of Missionary Ridge, some ten weeks later. The McDonald house burned down sometime after the battle. John McDonald died in 1864. Sartain, 103–104.

85. Sullivan, 17. Cozzens, 548–50. Powell, *The Chickamauga Campaign: A Mad Irregular Battle*, 644–645.

86. Sullivan, 17. Cozzens, 548–50. Powell, *The Chickamauga Campaign: A Mad Irregular Battle*, 648–652.

87. Cozzens, 536.

88. See Note 1.

89. For an excellent introduction to the Siege of Chattanooga and the Chattanooga Campaign, see Gary W. Gallagher, "American Civil War: Grant Dismantles Bragg's Siege of Chattanooga," *The Great Courses Daily* (website), December 31, 2021, https://www.thegreatcoursesdaily.com/american-civil-war-grant-dismantles-braggs-siege-of-chattanooga/.

90. Tucker, 8.

91. In his official report, Union Maj. Gen. William S. Rosecrans described the rationale for a nighttime march to extend his army's left flank—and thus anchor the 14th Corps in Kelly Field—as follows: "The roar of battle hushed in the darkness of night, and our troops, weary with a night of marching and a day of fighting, rested on their arms, having everywhere maintained their positions, developed the enemy, and gained through command of the Rossville and Dry Valley roads to Chattanooga, the great

object of the battle of the 19th of September. ... [T]he battle the next day must be for the safety of the army and the possession of Chattanooga." *OR*, 30:1, 57.

92. *OR*, 30:1, 467. Notably, Capt. Eli Lilly, 18th Indiana Battery, was a pharmacist before the U.S. Civil War, and afterward founded the Eli Lilly pharmaceutical company.

93. Woodworth, *A Deep Steady Thunder*, 43.

94. Sartain, 101.

95. Cpl. James Fenton, 19th Illinois Infantry, quoted in Time-Life Books, eds., *Chickamauga: Voices of the Civil War*, 72–73.

96. Sam Watkins, *Company Aytch*, ed. by M. Thomas Inge (New York: Penguin Putnam, 1999), 85.

97. *OR*, 30:2, 486. More broadly, Col. Keeble wrote: "Here commenced the most desperate conflict of the day. For three hours and forty minutes it raged most furiously. With our small band, whose ranks were becoming every moment thinner, we charged the full columns of the enemy and drove them before us. Four desperate assaults and charges were made upon us, hurling upon us their immense columns, line after line, but as stubbornly were resisted. The battle-field here baffled description. ... Both sides felt that this was the turning tide of the battle."

98. Catton, 181. For a summary of the Siege of Chattanooga and its lifting through the generalship of Grant, Sherman, Thomas, and Hooker, see Catton, 181–185.

99. According to the NPS, the U.S. Civil War produced 1,125,453 casualties (642,427 Union and 483,026 Confederate), categorized as follows: 204,100 killed in action (110,100 and 94,000); 469,200 wounded (275,174 and 194,026); 388,580 diseased (224,580 and 164,000); and 61,192 captured (30,192 and 31,000). NPS, "Facts," https://www.nps.gov/civilwar/facts.htm. But different categories are required to estimate "total deaths" that would include mortal combat wounds and fatal battlefield illness. William F. Fox (who fought at Antietam) and Thomas L. Livermore used muster lists, military reports, and pension records, in their landmark 1889 study to conclude that the U.S. Civil War produced 618,222 total deaths (360,222 Union and 258,000 Confederate). In 2012, J. David Hacker consulted 1850–1880 census records and recalculated the death toll as being 750,000 (and perhaps up to 850,000). J. David Hacker, "A Census-Based Count of the Civil War Dead," *Civil War History* 57, no. 4 (December 2011): 307–348. The matter is by no means settled.

For context, the NPS estimates U.S. Civil War enlistment strength as follows: 2,672,341 (Union) and 750,000–1,227,890 (Confederate). On the Union side, 2,489,836 were "white;" 178,975 African American; and 3,530

Native American. Confederate records are incomplete or were destroyed. NPS, https://www.nps.gov/civilwar/facts.htm.

100. Dates of secession: South Carolina (December 20, 1860); Mississippi (January 9, 1861); Florida (January 10, 1861); Alabama (January 11, 1861); Georgia (January 19, 1861); Louisiana (January 26, 1861); Texas (February 1, 1861); Virginia (April 17, 1861); Arkansas (May 6, 1861); North Carolina (May 20, 1861); and Tennessee (June 8, 1861).

101. NPS, "The Cost of Chickamauga." Wayside Exhibit, Chickamauga Battlefield.

102. White, 153–154.

103. The Brock family moved to Alabama, for example. Sartain, 105. Historian Timothy B. Smith describes the challenges faced by the federally appointed land agent (former Georgia Congressman, Judson C. Clements) whose job it was to buy or condemn land for the Chickamauga and Chattanooga National Military Park. See Smith, *A Chickamauga Memorial*, 41–43. See also John C. Paige and Jerome A. Greene, *Administrative History of Chickamauga and Chattanooga National Military Park* (Denver, CO: National Park Service, 1983), 24–8. Hereafter, *ADHI*.

104. Robert P. Broadwater, *Civil War Medal of Honor Recipients: A Complete Illustrated Record* (Jefferson, NC: McFarland, 2007), 43, 45–6, 145, 160, 166, 168, 198, 217. See also Robertson, *Staff Ride Handbook for the Battle of Chickamauga, 18–20 September 1863*, 169–171. The Historical Marker Database describes the Medal of Honor Heritage Trail Marker at Chickamauga, https://www.hmdb.org/m.asp?m=142972.

105. Robertson cites June 12, 1895. Ibid., 170. Broadwater cites June 15. Ibid., 46.

106. Robertson cites December 4, 1893. Ibid., 170. Broadwater cites November 2, 1896. Ibid., 198.

107. Thibodeau, "Gathering Your Gear," 87–91.

108. Georgia State law requires that all persons under sixteen years old shall wear an approved helmet while operating or riding a bicycle on public property (O.C.G.A. Sec. 40-6-296(d)).

109. NPS, "Chickamauga and Chattanooga Administrative History," June 1, 2002, https://www.nps.gov/parkhistory/online_books/chch/adhi7.htm.

110. William C. Oates, "Address of Governor W.C. Oates," in *Dedication of the Chickamauga and Chattanooga National Military Park, September 18–20, 1895*, comp. H.V. Boynton (Washington, DC: Government Printing Office, 1896), 175.

111. The consideration of state monuments installed beyond Chickamauga are out of scope for this guidebook—for example, Connecticut (1904, Orchard Knob); Illinois (1899, Bragg Reservation and Orchard Knob); Maryland (1903, Orchard Knob); Massachusetts (1895, Orchard Knob); New

Jersey (1896, Orchard Knob); New York (1896, Lookout Mountain); and Ohio (1903, Ohio Reservation and 1917, Cravens Terrace). For dedication dates, see Reaves 42 (CT), 91 (IL), 114 (MD), 40 (MA), 45 (NJ), 81 (NY), 54 and 58 (OH). Stacey W. Reaves, *A History and Guide to the Monuments of Chickamauga National Military Park* (Charleston, SC: History Press, 2013).

112. Chickamauga and Chattanooga National Military Park was established for the purpose of "preserving and suitably marking for historical and professional military study the fields of some of the most remarkable maneuvers and most brilliant fighting in the war of the rebellion..." U.S. Code Title 16, Section 424, Chickamauga and Chattanooga National Military Park, in Cornell Law School Legal Information Institute, https://www.law.cornell.edu/uscode/text/16/424. The listing of state commissions draws from two sources: Hanson and Blythe, 31; and Reaves, 42, 94, 114. From Reaves, we add three states that formed commissions in the 20th century: Connecticut (1903–4), Iowa (1902), and Maryland (1903).

Although Chickamauga was not the first battlefield for which state and local commissions had been established to preserve fields of study and commemoration, it was the first battlefield to secure federal approval and oversight. Congress approved Shiloh in 1894, Gettysburg in 1895, and Vicksburg in 1899. Antietam was an exception: On August 30, 1890, the U.S. Congress passed an appropriations bill that funded the establishment of Antietam National Battlefield, but no Congressional act ever designated Antietam as a "national military park."

113. Hanson and Blythe, 33.

114. Ibid., 38.

115. H.V. Boynton, "Preliminary Report" in *Dedication of the Chickamauga and Chattanooga National Military Park*, 11–12. Paige and Greene, 18. In his dedication address on September 20, 1895, Congressman Grosvenor struck the theme of "brothers, not enemies." Charles H. Grosvenor, "Address of Gen. Charles H. Grosvenor," Ibid., 69–70. For a different but not overtly incompatible statement, see the speech of Peter Turney, who said, "I was on the losing side. I believed I was right." Peter Turney, "Address of Governor Peter Turney of Tennessee," Ibid., 83. Governor William C. Oates of Alabama was even more direct in his use of Lost Cause rhetoric. For a twenty-first century perspective on the full breadth of feelings and opinions amongst Civil War veterans during reunions and dedications, see Caroline E. Janney, "I Yield to No Man an Iota of My Convictions: Chickamauga and Chattanooga National Military Park and the Limits of Reconciliation," *Journal of the Civil War Era*, 2, no. 3 (2012): 394-420.

116. Joseph S. Fullerton, Call to Order at the "Dedication of the Chickamauga Field," September 19, 1895, in *Dedication of the Chickamauga and Chattanooga National Military Park*, 25.

117. "Our dedication today is but a ceremony. In the words of the immortal Lincoln, at Gettysburg—'But in a larger sense, we cannot consecrate, we cannot hallow this ground. The brave men living and dead who struggled here have consecrated it far above our power to add or detract.'" Adlai E. Stevenson, "Address of Vice-President Stevenson," September 19, 1895 in *Dedication of the Chickamauga and Chattanooga National Military Park*, 27–28. Confederate Lt. Gen. Longstreet began his address as follows: "Lades and Gentlemen: On a similar occasion, at Gettysburg, President Abraham Lincoln said: 'It is for us, the living, rather to be dedicated here to the unfinished work.'" James Longstreet, "Address of Gen. James Longstreet," Ibid., 40. Union Maj. Gen. Oliver O. Howard also quoted President Lincoln's words about Gettysburg, where "there laid down their lives that the country might live." Oliver O. Howard, "Address of Gen. O. O. Howard," Ibid., 117. Finally, the explanation given for the absence of Maj. Gens. Rosecrans and Thomas was provided by Union Maj. Gen. Gen. John M. Palmer, Thomas' 14th Corps. John M. Palmer, "Address of Gen. John M. Palmer," Ibid., 29.

118. Reaves, 134.

119. Reaves, 136. The NPS List of Classified Structures was retired in 2019, http://www.hscl.cr.nps.gov/insidenps/summary.asp?PARK=CHCH&STATE=GA&STRUCTURE=&SORT=1. According to Waymarking, the LCS record identifies "Cozant, Tocoa & Betts, E. E." as the monument's designer. Waymarking.com, "Alabama State Monument—Chickamauga National Battlefield," LCS MT-1239. See also The Historical Marker Database, "Alabama State Monument," https://www.hmdb.org/m.asp?m=96893.

120. In this chapter, brigade listings are ordered alphabetically by the commander's last name, grouped by infantry then artillery and cavalry. See Woodworth for an easy-to-read Order of Battle. Woodworth, *A Deep Steady Thunder*, 100–121. Since Woodworth's listing inexplicably omits the provisional division command of Brig. Gen. Bushrod Johnson (and the brigades of Gregg, McNair, and Fulton), see also Powell, *The Maps of Chickamauga*, 268–280.

121. AIC GA000415. Reaves, 136. Waymarking.com, "Florida State Monument—Chickamauga National Battlefield," LCS MT-1253. The Historical Marker Database erroneously identifies the sculptor as "L. Mihlimm." See The Historical Marker Database, "Florida Monument," https://www.hmdb.org/m.asp?m=103192.

122. AIC GA000413. *ADHI*, 306. Contrary to these sources, Reaves identifies the dedication date as May 10 (not May 4), 1899, and mentions that the governor of Georgia joined veterans from Georgia, Tennessee, and Kentucky for the dedication ceremonies. Reaves, 123. See also Waymarking.com, "State of Georgia Troop Memorial at Chickamauga;" The Historical Marker Database, "Georgia State Monument," https://www.hmdb.org/m.asp?m=121201; and Civil War Battlefield

Monuments, "Georgia State Monument: Battle of Chickamauga," LCS MT-1320, https://www.cwbfm.org/Monument/MonumentDetails/4850.

123. For the contractor and dedication date, see AIC GA000416 and Reaves, 106. The LCS identifies the monument's architect. The Historical Marker Database, "Kentucky State Memorial," https://www.hmdb.org/m.asp?m=87302. See also Waymarking.com, "Kentucky Soldiers Monument: Chickamauga, Georgia;" and Civil War Battlefield Monuments, "Kentucky State Monument: Battle of Chickamauga," LCS MT-860A, http://cwbfm.org/Monument/MonumentDetails/3479.

124. The 1903 Maryland State Monument on Orchard Knob, Chattanooga likewise honored soldiers who fought on both sides of the conflict. The monument has a bronze statue of a Confederate artilleryman and a Union infantryman.

125. AIC GA000694. Reaves, 126.

126. From the monument inscription. The Smithsonian American Art Museum identifies the foundry as "Ames Manufacturing Company." AIC GA000694. Reaves does not provide the foundry name but concurs with the AIC record that the Stewart Stone Company was awarded a contract. Reaves, 126. Only AIC lists the Winsboro Granite Corporation as a second contractor. The LCS record for MT-1342 has been retired is not accessible. For photos, including one with the palmetto tree installed, see The Historical Marker Database, "South Carolina State Monument," https://www.hmdb.org/m.asp?m=88988.

127. AIC GA000694.

128. From the monument inscription. Reaves identifies April, 1963 as the month that the Texas state commission erected the Texas State Monument. Reaves, 138. The LCS record for MT-1415A has been retired and is not accessible.

129. Reaves, 138.

130. Excerpt from "The Battle-Field," a poem by American romantic writer William Cullen Bryant (1794–1878). For the full poem, see https://quod.lib.umich.edu/a/amverse/BAD0508.0001.001/1:111?rgn=div1;view=fulltext.

131. Tabulated by the author using an Excel copy of Wikipedia, "Chickamauga Union order of battle," https://en.wikipedia.org/wiki/Chickamauga_Union_order_of_battle. The determination of which states have what kind of monuments is derived in part from Hanson and Blythe, "Appendix C," 1–16.

132. Tabulated by the author using an Excel copy of Wikipedia, "Chickamauga Confederate order of battle: Army of Tennessee (September 20, 1863)," https://en.wikipedia.org/wiki/Chickamauga_Confederate_

order of battle. The determination of which states have what kind of monuments is derived in part from Hanson and Blythe, "Appendix C," 1–16.

133. *OR* 30:1, 402.

134. Longstreet's original plan was for Maj. Gen. Hood to form the main column of attack, but before Longstreet was able to adjust his line (currently from left (south) to right (north), the divisions of Preston, Hindman, Johnson, Stewart), the attack was underway. See *OR* 30:2, 287–291.

135. For an excellent summary and tactical map of this battle action, see Powell, *The Maps of Chickamauga*, 170–171.

136. *OR* 30:2, 302–306.

137. Ezra J. Warner, *Generals in Gray: Lives of the Confederate Commanders* (Baton Rouge: Louisiana State University Press, 1987), 205–206.

138. *OR* 30:2, 457. For two maps that show McNair's starting position and then attacking movement, see Powell, *The Maps of Chickamauga*, 167, 169.

139. *OR* 30:2, 288–289.

140. Powell, *The Maps of Chickamauga*, 278.

141. Tucker, 367. For a nice map, see Carter, in *The Fight for Snodgrass Hill and the Rock of Chickamauga,* 70.

142. From the monument inscription. NPS MT-1224.

143. General Assembly of the State of Georgia, "Appropriation for Monuments on Chickamauga Battlefield, No. 223," in *Acts and Resolutions of the General Assembly of the State of Georgia, 1895* (Atlanta, GA: Geo W. Harrison State Printer, 1896), 11–12.

144. General Assembly of the State of Illinois, Appropriation for "Dedication of Battlefield Monuments," in *Laws of the State of Illinois Enacted by the Forty-First General Assembly, 1899* (Springfield, IL: Phillips Bros. State Printers, 1899), 7–8.

145. David, Graham, "A Fight for a Principle: The 24th Illinois Volunteer Infantry Regiment." *Journal of the Illinois State Historical Society (1998-)* 104, no. 1/2 (2011): 38-55. The fate of Pvt. Dressel is described in Graham, 52. Casualty numbers for the 24th Illinois are from William Wagner, *History of the 24th Illinois Volunteer Infantry Regiment* (Chicago: Illinois Staats-Zeitung, 1864, translated in 1911), 8. Wagner fought as a soldier in the 24th Illinois.

146. Sullivan, 50–51. Wilder's Brigade was part of the 4th Division (Reynolds), 14th Corps (Thomas), Army of the Cumberland (Rosecrans).

147. Division of Military History and Diplomacy, National Museum of American History, "Spencer Carbine," https://amhistory.si.edu/militaryhistory/collection/object.asp?ID=117. This catalog record includes an interesting story about President Lincoln testing the Spencer repeating rifle "on a weedy

plain extending from the White House to the unfinished Washington Monument" on August 18, 1863.

148. Benjamin E. Sawyer, "Chickamauga," chap. 32 in Peter Cozzens, ed., *Battles and Leaders of the Civil War* (Urbana: University of Illinois Press, 2002), 5:422–428. Originally published as "Chickamauga," Philadelphia *Weekly Times*, March 13, 1886.

149. Smith D. Atkins, "Wilder's Brigade Monument Dedication," *Journal of the Illinois State Historical Society (1908-1984)* 13, no. 1 (1920): 51. Originally published by the *Chattanooga Daily News*, September 20, 1899.

150. Ibid., 55, 62.

151. Ibid., 53.

152. Ibid., 54.

153. Abbreviated Inscription from the east (back) side of the 8th Kansas Infantry Monument, LaFayette Road. For NPS structure data for the Kansas monument, see Waymarking.com, "8th Kansas Volunteer Infantry Regiment Monument: Chickamauga National Battlefield," LCS MT-858. Waymarking reproduces the text of the retired LCS record. See also The Historical Marker Database, "8th Kansas Volunteer Infantry," https://www.hmdb.org/m.asp?m=102224.

154. *Report of the Adjutant General of the State of Kansas, 1861-1865*, (Topeka, KS: 1896 reprint) in Alan Russ, Dale Vaughn, and Erma Payne, eds., "Civil War: The 8th Kansas Volunteer Infantry," *Museum of the Kansas National Guard* website, https://www.kansasguardmuseum.com/civil-war-the-8th-kansas-volunteer-infantry/. For a broad description of the back-and-forth actions in Viniard Field on September 19, 1863, that includes the 8th Kansas Infantry, see Powell, *The Maps of Chickamauga*, 88–89.

155. Kentucky USA military units: 1st, 2nd, 3rd, 4th, 5th, 6th, 8th, 9th, 10th, 15th, 17th, 18th, 23rd infantry regiments; and 2nd, 4th, 5th, 6th cavalry regiments. Kentucky CSA military units: 2nd, 4th, 5th, 6th, and 9th infantry regiments; 2nd and 3rd cavalry regiments; and Cobb's and Graves' Batteries. Not included is the fact that Company I, 2nd Kentucky Cavalry served as Maj. Gen. McCook's escort.

156. Charles W. Bennett, *Historical Sketches of the Ninth Michigan Infantry* (Coldwater, MI: Daily Courier Print, 1913), 34. For an interesting discussion of the interaction of the 9th Michigan with the 5th Kentucky, see Andrew Miller, "Saving General Thomas' Rations," Emerging Civil War website, December 14, 2017, https://emergingcivilwar.com/2017/12/14/saving-general-thomas-rations/.

157. *OR*, 30:1, 916. Maj. Gen. Rosecrans' overarching strategy for September 20 was to move his army north to reinforce the army's left flank at Kelly Field, where Maj. Gen. Thomas positioned his 14th Corps. The army's supply wagons and field hospitals were considerably south of the army's

fighting units. That is where we meet Col. Watkins in the story of the Battle of Chickamauga. For strategic context (and brief mention of Watkins' Kentucky brigade), see Dave Powell, *Decisions at Chickamauga: The Twenty-four Critical Decisions That Defined the Battle* (Knoxville: University of Tennessee, 2018), 80–84.

    158. *OR*, 30:1, 914–916. Casualty numbers are from Powell, *The Maps of Chickamauga*, 273.

    159. Powell, *The Maps of Chickamauga*, 154–155. For context, around 11:00 a.m. on September 20, 1863, Brig. Gen. Daniel W. Adams' brigade (from Louisiana, but also Alabama) and Brig. Gen. Marcellus A. Stovall's brigade (from Florida, Georgia, and North Carolina) played a critical role in "Breckinridge's Assault" as they attacked south along both sides of LaFayette Road.

    160. From the monument inscription. NPS MT-1088.

    161. Lowell H. Harrison, "Kentucky-born Generals in the Civil War," *The Register of the Kentucky Historical Society* 64, no. 2 (1966): 129-60.

    162. Capt. Borden M. Hicks, quoted in Time-Life Books, eds., *Chickamauga: Voices of the Civil War*, 106.

    163. Casualty statistics are from Powell, *The Maps of Chickamauga*, 273.

    164. According to the monument inscription (back side).

    165. *OR*, 30:1, 430, 433. According to Col. Van Derveer, "from this time until dark we were hotly engaged."

    166. *OR*, 30:1, 433.

    167. Judson W. Bishop, *The Story of a Regiment, Being a Narrative of the Service of the Second Regiment, Minnesota Veteran Volunteer Infantry, In the Civil War of 1861–1865* (St. Paul, MN: n.p., 1890), 108–109. A brief biography of J.W. Bishop is available at Minnesota Historical Society, Manuscripts Collection, "J.W. (Judson Wade) Bishop and Family," http://www2.mnhs.org/library/findaids/00875.xml.

    168. *OR*, 30:1, 430.

    169. *OR*, 30:1, 432–434.

    170. Powell, *The Maps of Chickamauga*, 269.

    171. Ibid., 38–39.

    172. Ibid., 60–61.

    173. Ibid., 216–217. Quotations are from *OR*, 30:2, 462–463.

    174. Tucker, 269–270. David A. Powell, *The Chickamauga Campaign: Glory or the Grave* (El Dorado Hills, CA: Savas Beatie, 2017), 178 n. 47. *OR*, 30:1, 593–594.

175. *OR*, 30:1, 593–594. Rounds of ammunition expended for the 12-pounder gun: 94 case-shot, 9 canister, 86 shell, 26 solid shot. Rounds of ammunition expended for the 10-pounder Parrott gun: 5 case-shot, 57 shell.

176. *OR*, 30:2, 460–461, 467.

177. Calculated by the author. At Chickamauga, only Virginia and Missouri fielded a lower number of regiments, battalions, and batteries. Tennessee, Alabama, Georgia, and Mississippi had the greatest number (in descending order).

178. Powell, *The Maps of Chickamauga*, 279.

179. *OR*, 30:2, 445.

180. Ibid.

181. Ibid.

182. Ibid., 445–446.

183. Casualty statistics are from Powell, *The Maps of Chickamauga*, 276. Inscription from the 58th North Carolina Monument: "Erected by the state of North Carolina to mark the extreme point attained in a charge by the right of the 58th N.C. Regiment about 6 P.M., September 20th 1863."

184. Calculated by the author. Count of Ohio regiments or batteries by division, Army of the Cumberland: Baird 3, Brannan 7, Crook 3, Davis 1, Johnson 6, Negley 5, D. McCook 2, E. McCook 1, Palmer 7, Reynolds 4, Sheridan 0, Steedman 6, Van Cleve 5, and Wood 6. Not included is the fact that Company L, 1st Ohio Cavalry served as Maj. Gen. Thomas' escort. The following Chickamauga generals were from Ohio: George Crook, James A. Garfield, Alexander M. McCook, William S. Rosecrans, and Philip H. Sheridan.

185. Typically, each battery would have six to eight guns.

186. *OR*, 30:1, 354. According to the official report of Col. James Barnett, Chief of Artillery for Negley's Division, Battery M lost four James rifles and two 3-inch rifled guns at the Battle of Chickamauga. *OR*, 30:1, 234.

187. David B. Floyd, *History of the 75th Regiment of Indiana Infantry Volunteers: Its Organization, Campaigns, and Battles, 1862-1865* (Philadelphia, PA: Lutheran Publication Society, 1893), 57.

188. Powell, *The Chickamauga Campaign: A Mad Irregular Battle*, 376–377. For a military biography of Higgins, see Pasadena Museum of History, "The Reverend Colonel Higgins," May 12, 2015, https://pasadenahistory.org/civil-war-soldiers/reverend-colonel-higgins/. Casualty counts are from the monument inscription. For Higgins official report, see *OR*, 30:1, 798–799.

189. *OR*, 30:1, 757.

190. *OR*, 30:1, 298.

191. Statistics calculated by the author. 1st Lt. Anthony Taylor, Co. A, 15th Pennsylvania Cavalry, won the Medal of Honor for his actions on

September 20, 1863. His citation says: "Held out to the last with a small force against the advance of superior numbers of the enemy." Pennsylvania natives William J. Carson and Horace Porter received Medals of Honor for their service in the U.S. Regular Army. The NPS mentions Jack Hines at https://www.nps.gov/articles/chickamaugaafricanamericans.htm. For a short biography, including Hines' role as an army "under cook" in Co. K, 15th Pennsylvania Cavalry, see Faces of War blog, "Jack Hines Faces Capture at Chickamauga," November 25, 2013, http://facesofthecivilwar.blogspot.com/2013/11/jack-hines-faces-capture-at-chickamauga.html

192. From the monument inscription, quoted by The Historical Marker Database, "7th Pennsylvania Cavalry," https://www.hmdb.org/m.asp?m=99312.

193. John M. Johnston, "At Chickamauga: A Soldier's Story of the Battle," Lancaster *New Era,* September 10, 1892, quoted in Powell, *The Chickamauga Campaign: Glory or the Grave,* 554–556.

194. Casualty statistics are from Powell, *The Maps of Chickamauga,* 278.

195. Sons of Confederate Veterans Website, "Elbert Bland," https://scv.org/2020/01/07/elbert-bland/.

196. Calculated by the author.

197. The commanders of the five Texas infantry brigades are: Deshler, Ector, Gregg, Harrison, and Robertson. The one artillery unit is Douglas' Texas Battery in Cleburne's Division. The two Texas cavalry regiments in Wheeler's Cavalry Corps are the 8th and 11th Texas. Casualty statistics for the Texas Brigade are from Powell, *Maps of Chickamauga,* 278.

198. *OR*, 30:2, 513.

199. *OR*, 30:2, 514–515.

200. *OR*, 30:2, 516–517.

201. Clement A. Evans, ed., *Confederate Military History: A Library of Confederate States History* (Atlanta, GA: Confederate Publishing Company, 1899), 9:179.

202. *OR*, 30:2, 447.

203. *OR*, 30:2, 448.

204. *OR*, 30:2, 359–360.

205. Statistics are from Powell, *Maps of Chickamauga,* 270.

206. *OR*, 30:1, 587. Powell, Ibid., 270.

207. Powell, Ibid., 268, 272.

208. Ibid.

209. *OR*, 30:1, 288–289. For Hobart, see Wisconsin Historical Society, "Hobart, Col. Harrison C. (1815–1902): Wisconsin Civil War Officer,

Politician, University of Wisconsin Regent," https://www.wisconsinhistory.org/Records/Article/CS2553. Casualty statistics are from Powell, *Maps of Chickamauga*, 269.

210. *OR*, 30:2, 22.

211. The Union often named its armies and battles after rivers, mountains, and other natural landmarks; and the Confederacy often selected towns or physical landmarks (like a Shiloh church) for names. That would explain, for example, why Gen. Bragg's Army of *Tennessee* is a Confederate army (named for a state), whereas the Maj. Gen. William T. Sherman's Army of *the Tennessee* is a Union army (named for a river). At Chickamauga, Maj. Gen. William S. Rosecrans commanded the Union army, the Army of *the Cumberland* (named for a river). For a helpful list of paired battle names, see Wikipedia, "Names of the American Civil War," https://en.wikipedia.org/wiki/Names_of_the_American_Civil_War.

212. For NPS structure data for the Baldwin memorial, see Waymarking.com, "Philemon P. Baldwin Memorial Shell Monument: Chickamauga National Battlefield," LCS MT-452A. Waymarking reproduces the text of the retired LCS record. See also The Historical Marker Database, "Philemon P. Baldwin Memorial Shell Monument," https://www.hmdb.org/m.asp?m=137905.

213. Find a Grave Photo of "Col. Philemon Baldwin" gravestone, added by Eric Lowman, January 20, 2008, https://www.findagrave.com/memorial/24060910/philemon-prindle-baldwin. Col. Baldwin was born on October 29, 1836, in Clark County, Indiana. He died on September 19, 1863, on the Chickamauga battlefield.

214. The spelling on the 1895 memorial plaque is "Colquit," but this book adopts the more common spelling, "Colquitt." See *OR*, 30:2, 246; Cozzens, 352–353; Powell, *The Chickamauga Campaign: Glory or the Grave*, 205–6; Tucker, 247. For NPS structure data for the Colquitt memorial, see Waymarking.com, "Peyton H. Colquit Memorial Shell Monument: Chickamauga National Battlefield," LCS MT-487. Waymarking reproduces the text of the retired LCS record.

215. *OR*, 30:2, 246.

216. Col. Colquitt was born on ca. October 8, 1831, and died on September 22, 1863 from his wounds at the Battle of Chickamauga. See also Find a Grave, "Col Peyton H. Colquitt," https://www.findagrave.com/memorial/8092571/peyton-h.-colquitt.

217. The NPS assigns LCS MT-467 as the memorial structure number.

218. *OR*, 30:2, 156.

219. Warner, *Generals in Gray*, 71–72. Brig. Gen. Deshler was born on February 18, 1833, and died on September 20, 1863, at the Battle of Chickamauga. See also NPS, "James Deshler,"

https://www.nps.gov/chch/learn/historyculture/james-deshler.htm and https://www.nps.gov/people/james-deshler.htm. Also Find a Grave, "James Deshler," https://www.findagrave.com/memorial/8967/james-deshler.

220. The NPS assigns LCS MT-424 as the memorial structure number. The Historical Mark Database, "Hans C. Heg Memorial Shell Monument," https://www.hmdb.org/m.asp?m=102047. Col. Heg was born on December 21, 1829, and died on September 20, 1863, at the Battle of Chickamauga. See also Find a Grave, "Col Hans Christian Heg," https://www.findagrave.com/memorial/7489797/hans-christian-heg.

221. NPS, "Hans Heg," https://www.nps.gov/people/hans-heg.htm. For his wounding and death, see Waymarking.com, "Hans C Heg," https://www.waymarking.com/waymarks/WM2BK9.

222. Woodworth, *A Deep Steady Thunder*, 47–51.

223. For NPS structure data for Helm's memorial, see Waymarking.com, "Benjamin H. Helm Memorial Shell Monument: Chickamauga National Military Park," LCS MT-486. Waymarking reproduces the text of the retired LCS record. See also The Historical Marker Database, "Benjamin H. Helm Memorial Shell Monument," https://www.hmdb.org/m.asp?m=100848.

224. *OR*, 30:2, 199.

225. Warner, *Generals in Gray*, 132–133. Brig. Gen. Helm was born on June 2, 1831, and died on September 21, 1863, at the Battle of Chickamauga. See also Find a Grave, "Benjamin Hardin Helm," https://www.findagrave.com/memorial/8925/benjamin-hardin-helm. For his wounding, see Waymarking.com, "Benjamin H. Helm Memorial Shell Monument."

226. The NPS assigns LCS MT-466 as the memorial structure number. The Historical Mark Database, "Edward A. King Memorial Shell Monument," https://www.hmdb.org/m.asp?m=68409. Col. King was born on April 3, 1814, and died on September 20, 1863, at the Battle of Chickamauga. See also Find a Grave, "Edward Augustine King," https://www.findagrave.com/memorial/10543321/edward-augustine-king.

227. Find a Grave, "Sarah McNaughton King," https://www.findagrave.com/memorial/107524651/sarah-king.

228. For Sgt. Henry C. Woods, see Edwin W. High, *History of the Sixty-eighth Regiment: Indiana Volunteer Infantry, 1862–1865* (United States: n.p., 1902), 96, quoted in Tucker, 360. For a description of King's wounding, see Indiana Commission for the Chickamauga and Chattanooga National Park, *Indiana at Chickamauga, 1863–1900: Report of Indiana Commissioners* (Indianapolis, IN: Wm. B. Burford, 1901), 199–200. According to the commission's report, Col. King's body was removed from the battlefield on a caisson of the 19th Indiana Battery.

229. Ibid., 95–96, 280, quoted in Tucker, 360–362, 419 n31.2.

230. For NPS structure data for the Lytle memorial, see Waymarking.com, "William H. Lytle Memorial Shell Monument: Chickamauga National Battlefield," LCS MT-452. Waymarking reproduces the text of the retired LCS record. See also The Historical Marker Database, "William H. Lytle Memorial Shell Monument," https://www.hmdb.org/m.asp?m=120503.

231. Maj. Gen. Philip H. Sheridan reported that "among the killed early in the engagement of the 20th was Brig. Gen. W.H. Lytle, who was three times wounded, but refused to leave the field." *OR* 30:1, 581. For a captivating story, see Tucker, 291–298.

232. *OR* 30:1, 583.

233. Brig. Gen. Lytle was born on November 2, 1826, and died on September 20, 1863, at the Battle of Chickamauga. See Ezra J. Warner, *Generals in Blue: Lives of the Union Commanders* (Baton Rouge: Louisiana State University Press, 1992), 287–8; and Find a Grave, "William Haines Lytle," https://www.findagrave.com/memorial/5843271/william-haines-lytle.

234. The NPS assigns LCS MT-463 as the memorial structure number. The Historical Mark Database, "Preston Smith Memorial Shell Monument," https://www.hmdb.org/m.asp?m=96958. Brig. Gen. Smith was born on December 25, 1823, and died on September 19, 1863, at the Battle of Chickamauga. See also Find a Grave, "Preston Smith," https://www.findagrave.com/memorial/20741/preston-smith.

235. *OR* 30:2, 79.

236. Warner, *Generals in Gray*, 283–284.

237. Arlington National Cemetery (ANC) is in Virginia. On June 15, 1864, the U.S. government established the national cemetery on 200 acres of the property of Mary Anna Custis Lee (great-granddaughter of Martha Washington) and her husband, Robert E. Lee. Today, 70 sections divide its 639 acres. In Section 16, which was established by President William McKinley in 1898, more than 400 Confederate graves surround the 1914 Confederate Memorial on Jackson Circle. See ANC, "Confederate Memorial: Section 16," https://www.arlingtoncemetery.mil/Explore/Monuments-and-Memorials/Confederate-Memorial. Sections 1–3 and 26–27 contain Union Civil War graves. Section 26 has the remnants of unknown Union and Confederate soldiers. See ANC, "Tomb of the Civil War Unknowns," https://www.arlingtoncemetery.mil/Explore/Monuments-and-Memorials/Civil-War-Unknowns. From May–June 1864, interments in Section 27 were racially integrated, but that changed after June 15 when the section was reserved for African American burials—notably, more than 3,800 "freedpeople" and about 1,500 U.S. Colored Troops. See ANC, "Section 27," https://www.arlingtoncemetery.mil/Explore/History-of-Arlington-National-Cemetery/Section-27. Also, ANC Explorer, https://ancexplorer.army.mil/publicwmv/#/arlington-national/.

238. NPS, "Facts," https://www.nps.gov/civilwar/facts.htm.

Index

In this index, USA military command structures appear as "(corps-division-brigade);" e.g., "(14-1-2)" identifies the 14th corps, 1st division, 2nd brigade. CSA command structures appear as lists of names; e.g., "(Polk-Cheatham-Maney)." See the Orders of Battle on pp. 68–69 for details.

Abney, Rob, remarks about McDonald's Field, 65
Adams, Daniel W., 69 (Polk-Hill-Breckinridge), 153–155; capture, 154–155
African American ancestry, 41–42, 159, 168, 208n56, 223n236
Alabama, 142; Breckinridge's Assault, 74, 153; brigade commander captured, 155; Deshler state affiliation, 183; encounter with Wilder's Brigade, 147–148; fighting in Brock Field, 55; fighting in McDonald Field, 65–66; Longstreet's Breakthrough, 142; monuments and markers, 63; state monument, 128, 132
Alabama units, strength, 141
Artillery, *Dent's Battery*, 142; *Fowler's Battery*, 65–66; *Garrity's Battery*, 142; *Water's Battery*, 142
Infantry, *15th*, Oates, 127; *24th*, 147; *32nd*, 155; *41st*, 153
Alexander, E. Porter, 69 (Longstreet-Porter)
Alexander, John P., 42
Alexander's Bridge, 21, 42–43, 72, 102; location on map, 24–25, 76, 104; visit, 15, 17, 33; Wilder and Walthall's Brigades, 159
Anderson, Patton, 69 (Longstreet-Hindman-Anderson), 132; fighting on Horseshoe Ridge, 159
Andersonville Prison, Georgia, 146

Antietam, 16, 17, 38, 56, 87, 89, 103, 118; casualties, 202n1; military park, 213n111
Arkansas, 143; attempt to cross Chickamauga Creek, 42; Cleburne's Assault, 74; fighting in McDonald Field, 65; markers near Brotherton Cabin, 48
Arkansas units, strength, 141
Artillery, *Calvert's Battery*, 143; *Humphreys' Battery*, 143; *Wiggins' Battery*, 143
Cavalry, *1st and 2nd Mounted Rifles*, 143
Infantry, *3rd*, 172; *25th, 4th and 31st, 4th Battalion*, 143
Arlington National Cemetery, Chickamauga burials, 189; sections, 223n236
Armstrong, Frank C., 69 (Longstreet-Forrest-Armstrong), 135, 143
Army of the Cumberland, 71, 74–75, 80; casualties, 80, 202n1; Ohio, 163; order of battle, 69; retreat, 158; strength, 12, 140, 201n1; memorial shell monuments, 179; *see* William S. Rosecrans
Army of East Tennessee, 74
Army of Northern Virginia, 74, 170
Army of Tennessee, 12, 14, 24, 31, 51, 71; casualties, 80, 202n1; order of battle, 69; strength, 12, 141, 201n1; memorial shell monuments, 179; *see* Braxton Bragg

Atkins, Smith D., 148
Atlanta Campaign, 11, 24
Baird, Absalom, 54, 68 (14-1); Arlington Nat'l Cemetery, 189; attacked by Breckinridge, 154; division hospital on Dyer property, 61; fighting Forrest, 72; fighting in Winfrey Field, 72, 159; friendly fire with Baldwin, 181; main battle line, 146, 169; Sept. 18–19 maps, 76–77
Baldwin, Philemon P., 54, 68 (20-2-3), 73, 135, 179; friendly fire with Baird, 181; memorial shell monument, 179, 181
Bane, John P., 173
Barnes, Sidney M., 68 (21-3-3), 135
Barnett, James, 219n185
Bassett, R.H., 173
Bate, William B., 69 (Longstreet-Buckner-Stewart), 132, 134
Battle of Chickamauga, casualties, 80; overview, 71–75; maps, 76–79; results, 80–82
Beatty, John, 68 (14-2-1), 135, 154
Beatty, Maxwell Major, 165
Beatty, Samuel, 68 (21-3-1), 135
Benning, Henry L., 69 (Longstreet-Hood-Law), 73, 134
Betts, Edward E., 179
Bicycle routes, selecting, 100; Route 1, 101–115; Route 2, 117–119; Route 3, 121–123
Bingham, George B., 177
Bishop, Judson Wade, 157
Blackburn, J.C.S., 144
Bland, Elbert, 170
Boynton, Henry Van Ness, 12, 128–129, 148; H.R. 6454, 128, 202n3, 202n4
Bradley, Luther P., 68 (20-3-3), 160
Bragg, Braxton, 12, 21, 24, 31, 36, 37, 41, 54, 61, 69, 75, 141; comments about the Union retreat, 179; death, 130;

headquarters, 77, 78; orders to Polk, 74; orders to Stewart, 55; strategy, 72, 156; siege, 80
Brannan, John M., 68 (14-3); fighting Forrest, 72; fighting in Winfrey Field, 72; report describing Longstreet's Breakthrough, 142; Sept. 18–20 maps, 76–77, 79
Breastworks, 36, 73, 142–143, 148, 169, 173, 182
Breckinridge, John C., 69 (Polk-Hill-Breckinridge), 135, 144; assault, 74, 153–154, 155, 157, 161, 185; Sept. 20 maps, 78–79
Brock, John, 14, 55, 208n51; house site, 53
Brock Field, fighting in, 45, 55, 72; Smith memorial shell monument, 188; Sept. 19 map, 77
Brotherton, George and Mary, 14, 45; cabin, 41, 57; daughter, Adaline, 45; daughter, Sarah, 57; photos, 57–58; sons, James L. and Thomas, 57, 208n58
Brotherton Field, 45; fighting in, 57; Longstreet's Breakthrough, 45, 142; Sept. 19 map, 77
Brown, John C., 69 (Longstreet-Buckner-Stewart)
Buckner, Simon B., 59, 69 (Longstreet-Buckner), 74, 133, 159, 174–175; Sept. 20 map, 79
Buell, George P., 68 (21-1-1), 156
Butterfield, Daniel, 165
Campbell, Archibald P., 68 (Cavalry Corps-1-1), 156, 168
Carlin, William P., 68 (20-1-2), 73, 142
Carlton, Caleb H., 75
Carson, William J., 83
Casualties, Chickamauga, 80; U.S. Civil War, 202n1, 211n98

Index

Cavalry Corps, CSA. *See* Nathan B. Forrest and Joseph Wheeler
Cavalry Corps, USA. *See* Robert B. Mitchell
Cavalry, dismounted, 143, 144, 172
Cedar glades, 33, 45
Chamberlain, Orville T., 83
Chandler household, 159
Chattanooga, 11–12, 24, 31, 33, 36, 51, 65, 71, 75, 93–95, 128–130, 152, 156, 158, 170; area map, 23; Confederate Cemetery, 22; National Cemetery, 22, 43, 82; Robert Dyer, 61; siege, 21, 24, 80
Chattanooga Road, 66, 72, 77, 103, 173. *See* LaFayette Road
Cheatham, Benjamin F., 55, 69 (Polk-Cheatham); fighting in Brock and Winfrey Fields, 72–73; Sept. 19 map, 77; Sept. 20 map, 79
Chickamauga and Chattanooga National Military Park, 11–12, 20, 22–24, 42; Chickamauga Memorial Commission, 129; dedication ceremonies, 130; established purpose, 213n111; maps, 23, 26, 35, 49; monuments beyond the Chickamauga battlefield, 212n110; Visitor Center, 19, 25, 50, 63, 89, 93, 95, 100
Chickamauga Creek, soldiers' description, 51; name, 52
Cilley, Clinton A., 83
Clay, T.T., 173
Clayton, Henry D., 69 (Longstreet-Buckner-Stewart), 132
Cleburne, Patrick R., 69 (Polk-Hill-Cleburne); Cleburne's Assault, 74, 163; report of Deshler's death, 183; Sept. 19 map, 77; Sept. 20 map, 79

Clem, John Lincoln, Arlington Nat'l Cemetery, 189
Cleveland, J.S., 173
Coleman, David, 161
Colquitt, Peyton H., memorial shell monument, 179, 182
Connell, John M., 68 (14-3-1); fighting in Winfrey Field, 72
Cooper's Gap, 152
Creasman, William B., 161
Crews, C.C., 69 (Longstreet-Wheeler-Wharton)
Crittenden, Thomas L., 63, 68 (21st Corps), 73, 75, 80, 181
Crook, George, 68 (Cavalry Corps-2), 168
Croxton, John T., 68 (14-3-2); fighting in Winfrey Field, 72
Cruft, Charles, 68 (21-2-1), 135, 167
CSA Regulars units, strength, 141 Infantry, *1st*, 146
Dalton, 66
Dalton Ford, 23–25
Davidson, H.B., 69 (Longstreet-Forrest-Pegram)
Davis, Jefferson C., 55, 68 (20-1); Brannan's report, 142; Sept. 20 map, 78
Deas, Zachariah C., 69 (Longstreet-Hindman-Deas), Longstreet's Breakthrough, 142
Deshler, James, 69 (Polk-Hill-Cleburne), 73, 137, 143, 188; memorial shell monument, 179, 183; death described by Cleburne, 183; Sept. 20 map, 78
Dibrell, George G., 69 (Longstreet-Forrest-Armstrong)
Dick, George F., 68 (21-3-2)
Ditch of Death. *See* Viniard Field
Dodge, Joseph B., 68 (20-2-2), 154, 168
Dressel, Christian, 146

Drummer Boy of Chickamauga. *See* Clem, John Lincoln
Dyer, Ellen, 61
Dyer, Robert and Carrie, 14
Dyer, Spill B. and John, 61, 209n70; house site, 53, 206n32
Dyer Field, fighting in, 61, 164, 206n38; Sept. 20 map, 78
Ector, Matthew D., 69 (Polk-Walker-Gist), 72, 132, 137, 161; fighting in Winfrey Field, 72
Farms at Chickamauga, 52–66; destruction, 82; map, 53
Fenton, James, comment about the road to Chattanooga, 77
Florida, 144; state monument, 128, 133
Florida units, strength, 141
    Artillery, Buckner's Reserve, 133; *McCants' Battery*, 144
    Infantry, Stovall's and Trigg's Brigades, 133
Folk, George N., 161
Fords, Chickamauga Creek, 23, 25
Forrest, Nathan B., 69 (Longstreet-Forrest), 72, 156; Sept. 19 map, 77
Fort Oglethorpe, 50, 93, 95
Fowler, William, 65
French, James M., 174; advance with Trigg's Brigade, 175; description of friendly-fire incident, 174–175
French ancestry, 13
Fuller Gun Collection, 50
Fullerton, Joseph F., 129–130
Fulton, John S., 69 (Longstreet-Buckner-Johnson); Longstreet's Breakthrough, 142
Garfield, James A., 68
George, James, 157–158
Georgia, 145; monument symbols, 106; state monument, 128, 134

Georgia units, strength, 141
    Cavalry, *1st*, 44, 72; *4th*, 59
    Infantry, *1st*, 14, 40, 43, 65–66, 81; *2nd Battalion Sharpshooters*, 146; *4th Battalion Sharpshooters*, 107; *5th*, 146
German ancestry, 146, 164
Gettysburg, 17, 34, 38, 56, 71, 87, 89, 93, 103, 118, 170, 172; casualties, 202n1; Hood's arm, 206n30; Lincoln's address, 130; Pickett's Charge, 204n15
Gist, S.R., 54, 69 (Polk-Walker-Gist); report mentioning Colquitt, 182; Sept. 20 map, 79
Glenn, Eliza Camp, 39; house site, 53, 209n67; husband John, 39; Sept. 19 map, 77
Glenn Field, fighting in, 60
Govan, Daniel C., 65, 69 (Polk-Walker-Liddell), 143, 155
Gracie, Archibald, Jr., 69 (Longstreet-Buckner-Preston), 132
Granger, Gordon, 68 (Reserve Corps); arrival at Snodgrass Hill, 63, 75, 170; report of Van Derveer, 158
Grant, Ulysses S., 11, 24, 31, 42, 71, 75, 80
Gray, Horace, 156
Gregg, John, 69 (Longstreet-Buckner-Johnson); 160
Grose, William, 68 (21-2-3), 135, 154
Gross, Ferdinand H., report of, 61
Grosvenor, Charles H., 128, 130, 213n114
Halleck, Henry, 31
Hambright, Henry A., 169
Hard, John S., 170
Harding, R.J., 172
Harker, Charles G., 68 (21-1-3), 75, 135,
Harrison, Benjamin, 128

Harrison, Thomas, 69 (Longstreet-Wheeler-Wharton), 135, 137
Hazen, William B., 68 (21-2-2), 135; Arlington Nat'l Cemetery, 189
Heg, Hans C., 68 (20-1-3), 73, 142, 151, 176; memorial shell monument, 56, 179, 184
Helm , Benjamin H., 69 (Polk-Hill-Breckinridge); connection to Lincoln, 14, 185, 203n9; memorial shell monument, 179, 185; part of Breckinridge's Assault, 153
Hescock, Henry, 160
Hicks, Borden M., report on the capture of Brig. Gen. Adams, 155–156
Higgins, David J., 166
Hill, Daniel H., 69 (Polk-Hill), 73, 74, 155, 183, 185; comment about the Southern soldier, 71
Hills One, Two, and Three, 102, 203n8. See Horseshoe Ridge
Hindman, Thomas C., 69 (Longstreet-Hindman), 74, 142, 159, 170; Sept. 20 map, 79
Hobart, Harrison C., 38, 177
Hood, John B., 40, 56, 69 (Longstreet-Hood), 73–75, 143, 160, 169, 172; Longstreet's Breakthrough, 143; leg injury, 75, 143, 172, 206n30; marker, 17
Hooker, Joseph, with Grant, 71
Horseshoe Ridge, 34, 58, 61–62, 74–75, 102, 113, 118, 142, 157–159, 161, 170, 174; Sept. 20 map, 78, 203n8
Howard, Oliver O., speech, 214n116
Humphreys, Benjamin G., 69 (Longstreet-Hood-Humphreys), 143; Sept. 20 map, 79
Hunt Cemetery, 52
Hunter, James T., 173
Hutchins, R.P., 167
Illinois, 146–148
Illinois units, strength, 140
    Artillery, *Bridges' Battery Light*, 164
    Infantry, *19th*, 77; *24th*, 146; *36th*, 187; *74th*, 83; *92nd*, 148
Indiana, 149; ; Medal of Honor recipient, 83; monuments, 149–150; photo, 11, 36, 150
Indiana units, strength, 140
    Artillery, *4th Battery*, 123, 149; *5th Battery*, 149
    Cavalry, *3rd*, 156
    Infantry, *6th*, 150; *24th*, 146; *31st*, 150; *35th*, 150; *38th*, 36, 150
Ingraham, John, 14, 65, 81–82
Irish ancestry, 150
Jackson, John K., 69 (Polk-Cheatham-Jackson), 81, 134, 145, 146
Jay, William, 44; Jay's Mill Site, 44–47, 102, 156, 168; Sept. 18 map, 76
Jeffress, William C., 174–175
Johnson, Bushrod R., 69 (Longstreet-Buckner-Johnson); action at Reed's Bridge, 72, 156; Longstreet's Breakthrough, 72–73, 142; monument, 45; Sept. 18 map, 76; Sept. 20 maps, 78–79
Johnson, Richard W., 68 (20-2); fighting in Winfrey Field, 72; Sept. 19 map, 77
Johnston, Albert Sidney, 14
Johnston, John, 169
Kansas, 58, 128, 184, *8th Infantry*, 151; strength, 140
Keeble, R.H., report on fighting on Snodgrass Hill, 79
Kellogg, Sanford C., 129
Kelly, Elisha and Elijah, 14, 40, 64

Kelly, George, 65
Kelly, John H., 69 (Longstreet-Buckner-Preston), 134, 135, 161, 174
  Kentucky, 152; Breckinridge's Assault, 74, 153; Helm, 185; monuments, 63; native sons, Abraham Lincoln and Jefferson Davis, 154; state monument, 128, 135
Kelly Field, fighting in, 64; King memorial shell monument, 186
Kentucky units, CSA, strength, 141
  Infantry, *2nd, 4th, 6th, and 9th*, 153; *5th*, 174
Kentucky units, USA, strength, 140
  Cavalry, Mitchell's Brigade, *4th, 5th, and 6th*, 152
Kershaw, Joseph P., 69 (Longstreet-Hood-Kershaw), 75, 136, 170; Sept. 20 map, 79. See *South Carolina*
King, Edward A., 68 (14-2), 180; memorial shell monument, 179, 186; Sept. 19 map, 77
King, John H., 68 (14-1-3)
LaFayette Road, 41, 42, 47, 50, 77, 203n7, 204n14; Brotherton Cabin, 14, 45; Florida State Monument, 133; Georgia State Monument, 134; Heg Memorial Shell Monument, 184; Kentucky State Monument, 135; Longstreet's Breakthrough, 57–61, 72–74; maps, 77–78; near the Ditch of Death, 56; Poe Site, 15; traffic, 17, 25, 39, 41, 46
LaGrange, Oscar H., 177
Laiboldt, Bernard, 68 (20-3-2), 160
Lamont, Daniel S., 129
Lancaster Rifles, 169
Landmarks at Chickamauga, 48–66
Law, Evander M., 42–43, 69 (Longstreet-Hood-Law), 73–74, 132, 143; Sept. 20 map, 79
Le Favour, Herber, 75

Lee, Robert E., 14, 42, 223n236
Lee and Gordon's Mill, 33, 93
Leyden's Battalion, 175
Libby Prison, Richmond, 177
Liddell, St. John R., 54, 69 (Polk-Walker-Liddell); crossing Chickamauga Creek, 72; fighting at Alexander's Bridge, 159; fighting in McDonald Field, 65; fighting in Winfrey Field, 72; Sept. 18 map, 76; Sept. 20 map, 79
Lightning Brigade, 43, 56, 73, 147; *see* Wilder, John T.
Lilly, Eli, 73, 211n92; Sept. 18 map, 76
Lincoln, Abraham, 130, 135, 154, 185
Long, Eli, 68 (Cavalry Corps-2-2), 135
Longstreet, James, 69 (Left Wing), 73–74; comments about Snodgrass property, 62; at park dedication ceremonies, 130; speech, 214n116
Longstreet's Breakthrough, 17–18, 58, 74, 142 (Deas), 143 (McNair), 160, 171 (Johnson), 172 (Texas), 174–175 (Virginia), 204n15, 208n60, 215n133; Sept. 20 maps, 78–79
Lookout Mountain, 24, 31, 51, 152
Lost Regiments, 144, 174. *See* 21st Ohio, 89th Ohio, and 22nd Michigan
Louisiana, 65, 74, 128, 155; Breckinridge's Assault, 74; fighting in McDonald Field, 65
Louisiana units, strength, 141
  Artillery, *Le Gardeur's Battery*, 155; *Robinson's Battery*, 155; *Slocomb's Battery*, 155
  Infantry, *Adams' Brigade (13th and 20th, 16th and 25th,*

19th, and 14th Battalion), 155; *1st, 1st Regulars, and 4th Battalion*, 155
Lytle, William H., 68 (20-3-1), 142, 156, 177, 223n232; memorial shell monument, 179, 180, 187
Lytle Hill, 60; *see* Lytle
Maney, George, 31, 69 (Polk-Cheatham-Maney)
Manigault, Arthur M., 69 (Longstreet-Hindman- Manigault), 132, 136, 142
Martin, John A., 142, 151
Martin, William T., 69 (Longstreet-Wheeler-Martin)
Marshall, Alexander, 164
Maxwell, Obadiah C., 165
McClure, Thomas, 166
McCook, Alexander McDowell, 68 (20th Corps), 73, 75, 80, 160, 184, 187
McCook, Daniel, 44, 68 (Reserve Corps-2), 72
McCook, Edward M., 68 (Cavalry Corps-1), 168
McDonald, John and Priscilla, 14, 19, 55, 66, 82; son William, 65, 66, 210n84
McDonald Field, capture of Adams, 155; fighting in, 50, 65–66, 155, 159; Fowler battery tablet, 66; Liddell's description, 66
McFarland's Gap, 63, 151; *8th Kansas*, 151
McKinley, William, 223n236
McLaws' Division, 69, 170. See Kershaw
McLemore's Cove, 51
McNair, Evander, 69 (Longstreet-Buckner-Johnson), 136, 161; Longstreet's Breakthrough, 143
Medal of Honor, recipients, 83
Memorial shell monuments, 20, 40, 46, 95, 127, 153, 178–188, 206n29; Baldwin, 181; Colquitt, 182; Deshler, 183; Heg, 184;

Helm, 185; King, 186; Lytle, 187; map, 180; Smith, 188
Michigan, 128, 130, 156; Clem's burial in Arlington Nat'l Cemetery, 189; capture of Adams, 155; cavalry, 156; fighting in Winfrey Field, 54; Lost Regiment, 144, 174; Medal of Honor recipient, 83; monuments in Viniard Field, 56; on Brotherton property, 58; on Snodgrass Hill, 63, 144; Sept. 20 map, 79; with Granger, 75
Michigan units, strength, 140
  Cavalry, *4th*, 156
  Infantry, *1st*, 54; *11th*, 83; *22nd*, 75, 144, 174
Mihalotzy, Geza, 146
Miller, Silas, report on Lytle's death, 187
Minnesota, Medal of Honor recipients, 83
Minnesota units, strength, 140
  Artillery, *2nd Battery Light*, 157
  Infantry, *2nd*, 83, 157–158
Minty, Robert H.G., 68 (Cavalry Corps-2-1), 156, 168; action at Reed's Bridge, 72, 76, 169
Missionary Ridge, 31, 146, 160, 174
Mississippi, 159; fighting at Alexander's Bridge, 42; fighting in Brock Field, 55; at Horseshoe Ridge, 159; in McDonald Field, 65; in Winfrey Field, 54
Mississippi units, strength, 141
  Infantry, *44th*, 159; Anderson at Horseshoe Ridge, 159; Walthall at Alexander's Bridge and Winfrey Field, 159
Missouri, 60, 128–129, 130, 160
Missouri units, USA, strength, 140
  Artillery, *Hescock's Battery G 1st*, 160, photo, 60;

230   Index

Bledsoe's Battery 1st, 160
Mitchell, John G., 68 (Reserve Corps-1-2)
Mitchell, Robert B., 68 (Cavalry Corps), 72, 152
Moccasin Bend, 24; map, 23
Morgan, John T., 69 (Longstreet-Wheeler-Martin), 132
Myers, George S., 83
Negley, James S., 63, 68 (14-2), 73, 75, 154, 164; Sept. 19–20 maps, 77–78
Niehaus, Charles H., 165
Nixon, George H., 15; fighting in Kelly Field, 64
North Carolina, 128, 143, 161–162; *58th*, 174; monuments 63
North Carolina units, strength, 141
  Cavalry, *6th*, 161
  Infantry, *29th*, 161–162; *39th*, 143, 161; *58th*, 161–162, 174; *60th*, 161–162
Norwegian ancestry, 176, 184
Oates, William C., speech, 127, 213n114
Ohio, 65, 75, 83; attacked by Wright's Tennessee Brigade, 166; contribution in strength, 163; Grosvenor, 128; Lost Regiments, 144, 174; Lytle, 187; main line, 149, 167; Medal of Honor recipients, 83; monuments, 130, 163–167; fighting on Horseshoe Ridge, 157–159, 174; Sept. 20 map, 79
Ohio units, strength, 140
  Artillery, *Battery F, 1st Ohio Light*, 163; *Schultz's Battery M, 1st Ohio Light*, 164
  Infantry, *1st*, 163; *2nd*, 165–166; *15th*, 83; *21st*, 75, 144, 157, 159, 174; *24th*, 166; *33rd*, 166; *36th*, 65; *49th*, 166; *89th*, 75, 144, 174; *90th*, 167; *94th*, 167; *101st*, 83
Orchard Knob, 22, 24, 31, 146

Order of Battle, Army of the Cumberland, 68; Army of Tennessee, 69; *see* 201n1
Orphan Brigade. *See* Helm
Palmer, John B., 161
Palmer, John M., 68 (21-2); fighting in Brock and Winfrey Fields, 72–73; Sept. 19 map, 77
Peavine Ridge, 31, 156
Pegram, John, 69 (Longstreet-Forrest), 155, 161
Pennsylvania, Medal of Honor recipients, 83; monuments, 168–169
Pennsylvania units, strength, 140
  Artillery, *Battery B Light*, 168
  Cavalry, *7th*, 156, 168–169; *9th*, 168; *15th*, 83, 168
  Infantry, *77th*, 168–169, 188; *79th*, v, 168–169
Poe, Larkin H., description of the battle's aftermath, 59; house site, 53; wife Sarah, 59
Poe Field, fighting in, photo, 59
Point Park, 24
Polk, Leonidas, 21, 54, 69 (Right Wing), 73–74, 143; death, 149, 188; fighting at Kelly Field, 65; Sept. 20 map, 79
Polk, Lucius E., 64–65, 69 (Polk-Hill-Cleburne)
Porter, Horace, 83
Porter, Thomas K., 175
Post, Sidney, 68 (20-1-1)
Presidential visits, 100
Preston, William, 69 (Longstreet-Buckner-Preston), 175; Sept. 19 map, 77; Sept. 20 map, 79
Proctor, Redfield, 129
Ray, Daniel M., 68 (Cavalry Corps-1-2)
Ray, James M., 161
Reed, Alex H., 83
Reed's Bridge, 76, 171
Reynolds, Joseph J., 68 (14-4), 186; Sept. 18 map, 76

Richey, William E., 83
Ringgold, 66, 95
Rippey, Charles H., 167
River of Death, 51, 207n41. *See* Chickamauga Creek
Roads at Chickamauga, 34–47
Robertson, Felix H., 69 (Longstreet-Robertson)
Robertson, Jerome B., 69 (Longstreet-Hood-Law), 73, 173
Rock of Chickamauga. *See* Thomas, George H.
Rogers, J.C., 173
Rosecrans, William S., 12, 24, 31, 36, 44, 54, 58, 68, 71–75, 80, 140, 187; Arlington Nat'l Cemetery, 189; description of Chickamauga, 31; headquarters, 13, 39–40, 60, 77, 78, 147; and Heg, 184; ill health, 130; on the fighting in Viniard Field, 151; order to Wood, 21, 58; use of Dyer as a guide, 61
Rossville, 63
Rossville Gap, 158
Russell, A.A., 69 (Longstreet-Wheeler-Martin)
Russian ancestry, 51
Sawyer, Benjamin, description of Wilder's Spencer rifles, 147–148
Secession, dates of, 211n99
Schueler, Gustavus, 160
Schultz, Frederick, 164
Scott, John S., 69 (Longstreet-Forrest-Pegram)
Scribner, Benjamin F., 68 (14-1-1); report of, 54; fighting in Winfrey Field, 159
September 18, 1863, 72; map highlights, 27; map, crossing Chickamauga Creek, 76
September 19, 1863, 72–73; letter from Rosecrans to Halleck, 31; map highlights, 27; map, fight east of LaFayette Road, 77; weather, 15
September 20, 1863, 74–75; map highlights, 27; maps, Longstreet's Breakthrough, 77, and Stand-Off at Snodgrass Hill, 79
Sheffield, James L., 69 (Longstreet-Hood-Law)
Shell monuments. *See* memorial shell monuments
Sheridan, Philip H., 68 (20-3); Arlington Nat'l Cemetery, 189; Sept. 19–20 maps, 77–78
Sherman, William T., with Grant, 71; *see* Atlanta Campaign
Shiloh, 155, 221n210; casualties, 202n1 ; military park, 213n111
Sirwell, William, 68 (14-2-3)
Smith, Preston, 54, 69 (Polk-Cheatham-Smith), 73, 180; memorial shell monument, 179, 188, 223n233
Snodgrass, Charles, 62
Snodgrass, George and Elizabeth, 13–15, 19, 209n74; cabin 13, 32–33, 52–53, 62–63, 102, 144, 157, 170; woods, 55, 59, 61, 65
Snodgrass Hill, 13–15, 17, 31, 39, 45–46, 58, 62–63, 65, 75, 80, 157, 161, 170; ascent, 87; gate, 100; hiking, 90, 95, 102; Sept. 20 map, 79; Segment B, 102, map 109; South Carolina State Monument, 41, 95; *see* Horseshoe Ridge
Snodgrass ravine, 13–14, 55, 59, 62, 204n13
South Carolina, 170; fighting on Horseshoe Ridge, 170; monuments, 40–41, 63; state monument, 128, 136, 164
South Carolina units, strength, 141 Infantry, *2nd, 3rd, 7th, 8th, and 15th*, 170; 3rd Battalion, 170

Spencer Repeating Rifles, 72, 147–148; cavalry tactics, 148
Stanley, Timothy R., 68 (14-2-2)
Starkweather, John C., 68 (14-1-2), 146; fighting in Winfrey Field, 159
States at Chickamauga, 67, 139–141; map, 131; state monuments, 127–137, *Alabama*, 132, *Florida*, 133, *Georgia*, 134, *Kentucky*, 135, *South Carolina*, 136, *Texas*, 137; regimental monuments, 139–177
Steedman, James B., 68 (Reserve Corps-1); arrival at Snodgrass Hill, 63, 75; Sept. 20 map, 79
Stevenson, Adlai E., 130, 213n116
Stewart, Alexander P., 69 (Longstreet-Buckner-Stewart), 129; fighting in Brock Field, 73; report of, 55; Sept. 19–20 maps, 77–79
Stones River, 155, 202n1
Stoughton, Dwella M., 75; fighting on Horseshoe Ridge, 159
Stovall, Marcellus A., 69 (Polk-Hill-Breckinridge), 133, 134, 144, 153–154, 161
Strahl, Otho F., 69 (Polk-Cheatham-Strahl)
Sugg, Cyrus A., 160
Taylor, Anthony, 83, 219n190
Template, Morris D., description of artillery fire in Dyer Field, 164
Tennessee, 171; Cleburne's Assault, 74; fighting in Brock Field, 55; Johnson monument, 171
Tennessee River, 24, 33, 51
Tennessee units, CSA, strength, 141
  Infantry, *1st*, 78; *2nd, 3rd and 5th, and 35th*, 107; *26th*, 66; *48th*, 64
Tennessee units, USA, strength, 140
  Cavalry, *1st and 2nd*, 171
Texas, 172; state monument, 128, 137; photo, 38
Texas Brigade, 75, 172
Texas units, strength, 141
  Infantry, *1st*, 172; *4th*, 173; *5th*, 173
Thedford Ford, 25, 43
Thomas, George H., 68 (14th Corps), 72–75; corps symbol, 165; all-night march to Kelly Farm, 72, 210n90; assumes field command, 80; fighting on Horseshoe Ridge, 136, 157, 170; at Winfrey Field, 181; main line, 149, 169, 182; not at park dedication, 130; provost guard, 156; retreat, 144; Rock of Chickamauga, 13; Sept. 18–20 map, 76–79; with Grant, 71
Thrash, Mark, 41–42
Tourgée, Albion W., description of Chickamauga area, 31
Trigg, Robert C., 69 (Longstreet-Buckner-Preston), 133, 174; capture of the Lost Regiments, 144; with the *63rd Virginia* on Horseshoe Ridge, 175
Turchin, John B., 51, 68 (14-3); fighting in McDonald Field, 65; Sept. 19 map, 77
Turney, Peter, 130, 213n114
U.S. Regulars, Medal of Honor recipients, 83
U.S. Regulars units, strength, 140
  Cavalry, *4th*, 56; *5th*, 129
  Infantry, *5th Kentucky*, 149; *15th*, 83, 107
U.S. War Department, 153
Van Cleve, Horatio P., 55, 68 (21-3); fighting in Brock Field, 73; Sept. 19 map, 77
Van Derveer, Ferdinand, 68 (14-3-3), 157–158; H.R. 6454, 128, fighting on Kelly Farm, 144, 154; in Winfrey Field, 72; report on Granger, 158
Van Pelt, George, 54

Vidito. *See* Vittetoe
Viniard, Tabler and Anna, 42–43; 208n51; son James, 43
Viniard Field, Ditch of Death, 43, 56, 73; fighting in, 54, 56, 73, 151, 184; house site, 53; Sept. 18–19 maps, 76, 77
Virginia, 174–175; Civil War generals from Virginia, 154; families that moved from Virginia, 57, 62; Thomas' family in Virginia, 13–14
Virginia units, strength, 141
  Artillery, *Jeffress' Battery*, 175
  Infantry, *54th*, 144, 174; *63rd*, 174
Vittetoe, Hiram, 13; house site, 53, 62, 160; monuments on Chickamauga-Vittetoe Road, 60, 147, 187
Wagner, George D., 68 (21-1-2)
Walker, William H.T., 69 (Polk-Walker), 72, 134, 145, 154–155, 159, 161, 170; Sept. 19 map, 77; Sept. 20 map, 79
Walthall, Edward C., 69 (Polk-Walker-Liddell), 159; fighting at Alexander's Bridge, 159; fighting in McDonald Field, 65; in Winfrey Field, 159
Watkins, Louis D., 68 (Cavalry Corps-1-3), 135, 152, 217n156
Watkins, Sam, description of Chickamauga, 78
West, Theodore S., 177
Western theater, 12, 24, 80, 170, 201n1
Wharton, John A., 69 (Longstreet-Wheeler-Wharton)
Wheeler, James T., 69 (Longstreet-Forrest-Armstrong), 135
Wheeler, Joseph, 69 (Longstreet-Wheeler), 143, 172; Arlington Nat'l Cemetery, 189; cavalry encounter with Watkins' Brigade, 152
Whitaker, Walter C., 68 (Reserve Corps-1-1), 144, 156
Whitney, William G., 83
Widow Glenn House. *See* Glenn, Eliza Camp
Wilder, John T., 68 (14-1), 147–148; fighting at Alexander's Bridge, 42, 72; 76, 159; bicycling amenities, 25, 89, 95; monument, 147–148; Sept. 18–20 maps, 76–78; speech, 148; fighting at Viniard Farm against Hood, 42–43, 56, 73, 147, 169. *See* Spencer Repeating Rifles
Willard, Van R., description of Chickamauga Creek, 51
Willich, August, 68 (20-2-1), 154
Wilson, Claudius C., 69 (Polk-Walker-Gist), 72, 134, 145, 155; fighting in Winfrey Field, 72–73
Winfrey, George, 54
Winfrey Field, 17; Baldwin memorial shell monument, 181; fighting in, 54, 72, 159, 163; house site, 53; Sept. 19 map, 77
Wisconsin, 176; Heg, 184; monuments, 37
Wisconsin units, strength, 140
  Artillery, *3rd and 5th batteries*, 176–177; *8th Light*, 176
  Cavalry, *1st*, 176
  Infantry, *1st*, 176; *3rd*, Willard quote, 51; *10th*, 176–177; *15th*, 56, 176; *21st*, 37–38; *24th*, 177
Wood, R.L., 160
Wood, Sterling A.M., 69 (Polk-Hill-Cleburne), 132
Wood, Thomas J., 68 (21-1), 74, 186; Brannan's report, 142; Sept. 19–20 maps, 77–79
Woods, Henry C., 186
Wright, Marcus J., 69 (Polk-Cheatham-Wright), 166

Other Guidebooks by Sue Thibodeau:

ISBN 9781732603806

286 pages, color maps and photos
6" x 9" perfect bound paperback

Published March 2019
Civil War Cycling
www.civilwarcycling.com

Available for order at your favorite book seller.

ISBN 9781732603813

208 pages, color maps and photos
6" x 9" perfect bound paperback

Published November 2020
Civil War Cycling
www.civilwarcycling.com

Available for order at your favorite book seller.

"*Bicycling Gettysburg* is comprehensible to readers and riders of all ages and expertise... concise and readable for both aficionados and novices." *~ Civil War Monitor*

"Sue Thibodeau's *Bicycling Gettysburg National Military Park: The Cyclist's Civil War Travel Guide* is a must-have for your next visit to Gettysburg. ... it should be in the daypack of anybody touring the park and/or town of Gettysburg." *~ Civil War Times*

Digital (PDF) companion maps are available for separate purchase from Civil War Cycling, https://civilwarcycling.com/shop/.

www.ingramcontent.com/pod-product-compliance
Lightning Source LLC
Chambersburg PA
CBHW042318090526
44583CB00024BA/3029